Professional Lives, Personal Struggles

Professional Lives, Personal Struggles

Ethics and Advocacy in Research on Homelessness

Edited by

Trenna Valado, PhD
and
Randall Amster, JD, PhD

LEXINGTON BOOKS
Lanham • Boulder • New York • Toronto • Plymouth, UK

Published by Lexington Books
A wholly owned subsidiary of The Rowman & Littlefield Publishing Group, Inc.
4501 Forbes Boulevard, Suite 200, Lanham, Maryland 20706
www.rowman.com

10 Thornbury Road, Plymouth PL6 7PP, United Kingdom

British Library Cataloguing in Publication Information Available

Library of Congress Cataloging-in-Publication Data

Professional lives, personal struggles : ethics and advocacy in research on homelessness /
edited by Trenna Valado and Randall Amster.
    p. cm.
  Includes bibliographical references and index.
  ISBN 978-0-7391-7428-9 (cloth : alk. paper)—ISBN 978-0-7391-7429-6 (electronic)
1. Homelessness. 2. Homeless persons . 3. Research—Moral and ethical aspects. I.
Valado, Trenna, 1972– II. Amster, Randall.
  HV4480.P76 2012
  174'.9362592—dc23

                                                                        2012015274

⊖™ The paper used in this publication meets the minimum requirements of American
National Standard for Information Sciences—Permanence of Paper for Printed Library
Materials, ANSI/NISO Z39.48-1992.

Printed in the United States of America

Dedication

To all the homeless people we have encountered, and to those who work with
and for them . . .

Contents

Foreword
Jeff Ferrell

Allow me if you will to start not with the usual introductory niceties, but with a straightforward proposition: In research on the homeless and other groups made marginal by the cancer of contemporary inequality, "ethics" and "advocacy" aren't optional. To engage in such research is to submerse oneself in fundamental ethical issues of shelter, decency, and survival, and so to become a part of them in one way or another. To engage in this research is also to confront the nature of power, the shame of its misuse, and the life-or-death calculus of its consequences—and so, it seems to me, to forfeit the right to hide such research behind protestations of "neutrality" or "objectivity." They say in Harlan County, there are no neutrals there—at least that's what Florence Reese said and wrote into song during the bloody Harlan County, Kentucky, coal strike back in the 1930s, with lives and livelihoods on the line. I'd say that there are no neutrals today, either—and certainly not as regards the homeless and those who inquire into their lives. Ignoring the ethics of homelessness and homelessness research leaves us with little but the false comfort of moral default; imagining that our research into homelessness can avoid advocacy allows our silence to stand as a quiet endorsement of injustice and inequality.

In the current political and economic climate these issues of ethics and advocacy matter all the more. It is not only that homelessness continues to accelerate as a social problem under the ongoing crisis of late capitalism; it is that the official response to this problem is today most often one of enforced invisibility. As a number of contemporary researchers have documented— including some of those gathered in this volume—political and economic authorities regularly "address" the problem of urban homelessness by herding homeless populations away from high-end commercial areas and excluding them from the city's high-profile public events. Meanwhile, legal and political authorities design campaigns to criminalize the everyday necessities of life on the streets—hanging out in public, sitting on the sidewalk, sleeping rough, finding food, walking the city's grid of streets and alleys—in an effort to hide the homeless from legitimate public visibility and public sympathy. Faced with these contemporary campaigns of perceptual erasure, we can hardly afford research strategies that contribute to this orchestrated invisibility by relying only on official accounts, or by shying away from advocacy on behalf of those who are made to disappear. Social research always goes forward in particular cultural and political contexts—and in the present context I would argue that research into homelessness should function, at a minimum, as a visible counter-discourse on the homeless, and as advocacy for the honest acknowledgment of homelessness itself.

As the contributors to this volume argue, this contemporary context also suggests that to study homelessness is also to study the structural conditions under which homelessness is made to appear and disappear. To put it bluntly, a holistic analysis of homelessness must surely include in its purview not just people on the streets, but the political economy of the housing market, the global degradation of work, the seductive betrayals of consumer society, and the machinations of public policy. In this sense research into homelessness necessitates a critical inquiry into the very structure of contemporary society, and as much so a willingness and ability to make ethical judgments about this structure. Finley Peter Dunne—or maybe Mother Jones or H. L. Mencken, depending on which historical account you consult—once suggested that we do our jobs best when we comfort the afflicted and afflict the comfortable. Social life is probably not quite that neatly dichotomous, but the point remains: research into homelessness inevitably invokes issues of ethics and advocacy precisely because such research must address both the afflicted and the comfortable, and must critically examine the social distance that separates and connects them.

Of course taking the stance that ethics and advocacy are essential components of homelessness research is one thing; carefully exploring the tensions and contradictions inherent in this stance, as this volume does, is quite another. As the following essays elegantly show, such tensions can't be fully resolved—but they can be addressed humanely and thoughtfully, and in ways that can promote both better research and more ethical forms of advocacy. In preface to *Let Us Now Praise Famous Men*, his impassioned ethnography of Depression-era Southern tenant farmers—folks who were housed, it is true, but just barely—James Agee (2001) wrote that it was "curious, not to say obscene and thoroughly terrifying," that an accomplished writer like himself could be sent to document the lives of people denied even the possibility of accomplishment. Put differently, Agee was deeply troubled by the fact that it was his own privileged status that allowed him the luxury of investigating, even passionately siding with, those afforded no such privilege or status—and so in his writing Agee carefully explored not only the lives of those he researched, but his own contradictory role as a researcher. The same sort of tension holds for those of us who engage in research with, or advocate for, the homeless—and indeed it is a curious, obscene, and terrifying sort of tension. Because of this it is incumbent on us, as it was on Agee, to confront this tension, to think it through individually and collectively, and to consider ways in which it can be turned toward progressive ends. As exemplified by the essays collected in this volume, this sort of scholarly self-reflection is not a matter of inward-looking intellectual narcissism. Quite the opposite: it is an essential component of scholarly praxis, of the process by which we attune our scholarship to the needs of the social world.

In all of this I'm reminded of the great sociologist Max Weber's notion of *verstehen*. For Weber, no sociology of a group or situation was complete until the sociological researcher was able to achieve some degree of *verstehen*—sympathetic understanding and appreciation—of those under study. If we are to understand the meaning and consequences of social life for those we study, Weber argued, we must take those people on their own terms, and so move beyond mere description and on to a degree of empathic understanding. More recently, I and other researchers have pushed the notion of *verstehen* further still, arguing that researchers' deep emotional immersion in risky research situations, even deep emotional affinity with those under duress, is necessary if researchers are to capture the lived experience of marginality and social impoverishment. With *Professional Lives, Personal Struggles: Ethics and Advocacy in Research on Homelessness*, it seems to me the notion of *verstehen* expands yet again. Here, the shared understanding that connects homelessness researchers to those they study transcends situations of emotional affinity, and incorporates a larger, ongoing process of human engagement, intellectual insight, and political advocacy. Dangerous business, this struggle for shared understanding across the boundaries of privilege and profession; dangerous, and absolutely essential.

Introduction
Rediscovering Homelessness . . . and Ourselves
Randall Amster

Across the academic disciplines, scholars examining social, economic, and political marginalization are confronted with inevitable issues of ethics and advocacy throughout the course of their work. How these challenges are viewed, and whether they can be turned into opportunities for enhancing research and/or alleviating marginalization, are central yet oftentimes unaddressed questions in social science scholarship. This edited volume seeks to illuminate these critical issues through the particular lens of homelessness, bringing together some of the leading scholars in the field from an array of disciplines and perspectives to explore this condition of marginalization and the ethical dilemmas that it often manifests. In so doing, the authors provide insights into the realities and challenges of social research that will be of guidance to students, activists, practitioners, and service providers, as well as to both novice and seasoned researchers in fields of inquiry ranging from anthropology and sociology to geography and cultural studies.

Although many texts have explored the subject of homelessness in general, few have attempted to encapsulate and examine the complex process of *researching* this issue as a phenomenon unto itself. The matter of homelessness raises myriad questions about ethics and advocacy in the minds of researchers. When investigating social phenomena such as experiences of marginalization, what duty of care is owed to the individuals and groups one is studying? Should the researcher of marginalized populations also be an advocate on some level? If so, what are the ethical implications of involving oneself in the work to this extent, both in terms of research bias and the ways in which one's "results" are presented? If not, what are the ethical implications of drawing upon the margin-

1

alized for one's professional gain or personal satisfaction yet not seeking to likewise promote the affected group's interests as well? And if we do choose to become advocates in the process of conducting research, how do we manage concerns about "representation" of others and seek to foster conditions in which people can find their own voices? In short, can an ethical researcher also be an advocate—or perhaps more to the point, can an ethical researcher of marginalized populations *not* be an advocate?

This volume seeks to address these fundamental research questions by exploring the issue of homelessness through the experiences of some of the field's leading scholars. By examining the central queries from a broad range of perspectives—from the intensely personal to the meta-theoretical—the authors presented here draw upon years of rich investigations to generate an operational framework that will be instructive for researchers and activists across a wide spectrum of areas of inquiry. In giving these scholars the opportunity to self-consciously consider the ethical aspects of their work, it is likewise the case that the lessons culled from this endeavor will have resonance not only for fellow researchers, scholars, and interested readers, but for these very authors themselves—and for the marginalized populations they seek to highlight and understand. In the end, the task of reconciling the necessities of professional life with personal commitments is a rich and complex subject that merits our thoughtful attention.

Rediscovering Ethics

Homelessness is an ethical issue as much as it is a material one. Considerations of distributive justice, equal opportunity, and access to resources all have profound moral implications. From the laissez-faire libertarian model of Robert Nozick to the more redistributive perspectives of John Rawls and Michael Walzer, the question of how a society manages its collective resources is among the most fundamental and pressing sociopolitical issues. Basic theories of capitalism tracing at least to Adam Smith similarly confront these matters through an ethical lens, further suggesting that such concerns ought to be at the forefront of any analysis of an important "social problem."

The issue of homelessness in particular squarely (and perhaps even quintessentially) raises these issues and concerns. By shining a light on processes of deprivation and marginalization, as well as matters of wealth distribution and equality of treatment, homelessness calls into question some of the most basic principles of a democratic society. And yet, as with many discussions of social issues, the focus on ethics is often muted by the tendency to report research findings or develop policy recommendations. While these are important aims, they can also serve to mask the fact that there are human beings with all of their complexities at the root of the matter, sometimes leading to a distancing phenomenon that has the trappings of "good research" but that can inadvertently exacerbate the issue at hand by relegating the human aspects of the equation. As an illustration, this tendency to gloss over the human dimensions of issues such as poverty and homelessness was evidenced on the presidential campaign trail in early 2012, when Republican contender Mitt Romney was quoted (in Landler 2012) as saying, "I'm not concerned about the very poor. We have a safety net there. If it needs repair, I'll fix it."

To be sure, there is a great deal of research on pressing social matters that fosters greater empathy and humanization. What we strive for in this volume is a straightforward investigation into these parts of the research paradigm, using the rubric of "ethics and advocacy" as a touchstone. Whereas ethics is in the realm of theory that is sometimes (but not always) applied, advocacy oftentimes devolves upon applications that may (or may not) be informed by theory. In this volume we seek to combine the best of both perspectives, calling upon some of the leading scholars in the field of homelessness research and asking them to engage directly with the ethical and advocacy-based issues that are most pertinent to their work. In so doing, we hope not only to provide an outlet for these authors and scholars to explore new dimensions in their research, but also to encourage the rediscovery of critical human aspects that are thoroughly interwoven with the larger issue of homelessness itself.

Rediscovering Homelessness

Recent years have seen the hastening of a global economic crisis that has left multitudes at risk of being homeless. A 2005 United Nations Special Report found that worldwide approximately 1.6 billion people were "inadequately housed," including at least 100 million who were "completely homeless"; these numbers have risen in the intervening years (see Szep 2008), including most recently a spike in displaced peoples as a result of warfare, environmental degradation, and natural disasters. The United Nations report cited contributing factors to this crisis including lack of affordable housing, gentrification and privatization, and a growing inequality of wealth referred to as an "urban apartheid" taking place around the globe. Also specifically noted in this report was a growing tendency to criminalize the homeless and landless rather than expend resources to help address the roots of the problem.

A 2008 survey by the U.S. Conference of Mayors showed that nineteen of twenty-five cities in their sample (83 percent) saw an increase in homelessness in that year, and on average the cities in the survey experienced a 12 percent rise in homelessness. "Homeless advocates say families are flooding homeless shelters across the United States in numbers not seen for years, camping out in motels or staying with friends and relatives following foreclosures on tens of thousands of homes during the worst financial crisis since the Great Depression," noted a December 2008 Reuters article ("Homelessness Rising as Economy Slides"), and "demand for emergency food assistance rose in 20 of the 25 cities surveyed" (Szep 2008). The Mayors' report itself concluded that among sectors of the homeless population showing a marked increase—namely women, children, and whole family units—the leading causes noted included strong economic correlations. Indeed, the Occupy Wall Street movements that emerged in the fall of 2011 rose to the fore of the political discourse in rapid fashion largely as a vehicle for considering similar (and ongoing) concerns about gross economic inequalities, the vulnerability of working people, and a deepening global financial crisis.

Homelessness, of course, is nothing new in industrialized societies. Periodic economic upheavals will often generate marked spikes in the number of homeless individuals, but the everyday operations of the economy likewise create large numbers of dispossessed and marginalized people as well. Perhaps due to its status as a regular and ongoing phenomenon, homelessness generally receives little attention in political arenas and the media. One of the many instructive effects of the recent economic crises experienced starkly in the West and around the globe is that they have raised public consciousness about homelessness in a meaningful way. Whether that awareness will hold is another matter, since waves of crisis and homelessness have occurred before without necessarily producing that result. In fact, well before the current cycle of financial downturn there were stories in the news about surging rates of homelessness due to economic circumstances, such as in this *USA Today* article from August 2003 (Armour):

> As Americans file for bankruptcy in record numbers and credit card debt explodes, more workers are a paycheck away from losing their homes. Now the frail economy is pushing them over the edge. With 9 million unemployed workers in July, the face of homelessness is changing to include more families shaken by joblessness. . . . "There is still a mind-set that the homeless are substance abusers who have made bad life decisions," says Ralph Plumb, CEO of the Union Rescue Mission in Los Angeles. "But more and more, they are individuals responding to a catastrophic financial event. The homeless are us. They're regular folk."

This spike in homelessness was something of a harbinger of the more recent crises, and news items over the ensuing span of years have been eerily similar in tone to those from 2003. In December 2008, for instance, Reuters reported that "homelessness and [the] demand for emergency food are rising in the United States as the economy founders" (Szep), and two months later *The Nation* ran an article titled "Homelessness is at Record Highs" (Markee and Ratner 2009) which cogently observed that this is all, unfortunately, quite familiar:

> While the recession has swollen the ranks of the homeless population, modern homelessness has been with us for more than a quarter-century. Long before subprime mortgages, credit default swaps and the most recent stock market crash, the United States was in the grip of the longest period of sustained mass homelessness since the Great Depression. Indeed, even before the current eco-

nomic downturn some 3.5 million Americans (including 1.4 million children) experienced homelessness during the course of a year. For this we can thank not a periodic dip in the business cycle but an affordable-housing crunch spawned by nearly three decades of slash-and-burn housing policy.

There is a basic tautology emerging, namely that homelessness is largely and ultimately a product of "people being displaced from homes" (Huus 2009), as the widespread spike in home foreclosures has dramatically demonstrated. Homelessness, in this sense, is an affectation of political economy—which the Occupy movement steadily has come to grasp (see Amster 2011)—and it is an expanding condition of human existence that exists just beneath the veneer of our sacrosanct ideals and common perceptions about what constitutes the "good life" in modern society.

Rediscovering Research

The term "economy" derives from the Greek word for "household management." As anyone engaged in such a task will attest, being a good manager involves elements of both ethics and advocacy. Decisions about where to apply resources involve choices that are informed by ethical considerations, and one must oftentimes become an advocate for their "household" in order to further its interests and secure its future. In that sense, the "ethics and advocacy" framework that we explore here has salience not only economically, but politically and socially as well. And it is also essential to any scholarly endeavor, since research is a fundamental component of the myriad ways we understand and manage the world in which we live. Research on issues involving basic questions of democracy and humanity in particular require deeper explorations of ethics and biases.

It is well understood and broadly accepted by now that research is constitutive, and not merely descriptive. That is, in describing the world, research also helps to create it at the same time, comprising a reflexive relationship that has become part of the standard parlance in many fields of inquiry. And yet, it remains the case that there is little scholarship squarely entertaining the full implications of reflexivity in a systematic manner, despite the fact that this is an endemic quality of all research. Indeed, reflexivity is particularly germane to scholarship that engages marginalized populations, in which the subject of study often raises inherent questions of power, status, and contestation. Homelessness represents an area of inquiry that directly frames these issues, illuminating important concepts for social scientists across a broad range of academic disciplines and research paradigms.

This volume addresses these concerns, but it is not intended as an exhaustive compendium on subjects such as bias, research ethics, or advocacy work. There are a plethora of texts on research methodologies that amply consider these themes in depth. What we do intend here is to collect in one space for the first time reflections and analyses around issues of bias, ethics, and advocacy focused on the particular social issue of homelessness. We believe that this issue—given its inherent contemplation of power relations, socio-economic forces, criminal justice processes, and patterns of social control—is fertile ground for a detailed consideration of questions of ethics and advocacy. Beyond this, we believe that scholars in the field have been grappling with such issues, yet have rarely been asked to reflect specifically along these lines.

To that end, a brief word about our own methodologies is in order. This project grew out of a panel discussion in April 2005 at the annual meeting of the Society for Applied Anthropology. Following the session, an informal discussion among the participants (many of whom are contributors to this volume) extended the inquiry into the realm of research ethics and positions of advocacy. While we did not all agree on the precise roles these forces ought to play in our research, we did concur that these sorts of questions were indeed important, even to the extent of being fundamental. Over the following year these queries were sharpened and a call for proposals was issued. Receiving many enthusiastic responses, the project was well underway, and the concept was met with great appreciation from scholars in the field who had been grappling with such concerns largely in isolation. The resulting volume before you accordingly reflects multiple levels of scholarly collaboration and mutually supportive reflection.

Rediscovering Ourselves

The analysis presented here focuses on three distinct yet related spheres of inquiry. First, we look specifically at the relationship between *advocacy and identity*, exploring the inherent nexus between what we stand for and who we are. Next we consider the challenges and virtues of immersion in compelling social issues such as homelessness, focusing in particular on the *relationships and experiences* that inhere among researchers and those ostensibly being researched. Finally, we explore the *transformative potential* of academic research, as well as the ethical implications of engaging in the sort of praxis-oriented inquiry undertaken by the authors in this volume. The individual chapters presented in these sections are each illustrative of many of these issues in their own right, and also stand together as a whole to present a more complete picture of the essential interconnection between ethics and advocacy in academic work.

In Chapter 1, Talmadge Wright provides a compelling personal narrative that, among other things, suggests the virtues and limitations of "studying down" as a form of advocacy that enables one to assist others while still maintaining both ethics and employability. Rob Rosenthal extends these themes in Chapter 2, reminding us of the potential pitfalls of advocacy as well as the inherent limitations of neutrality, and asking why researchers often spend less time studying elite decision-makers rather than marginalized populations like the homeless. In Chapter 3, Kathleen Arnold provides a partial response to Rosenthal's query, observing that homeless people ought to be seen as political agents capable of advocating on their own behalf, even as they remain imbricated within an overarching system defined by patterns of racism, sexism, and class bias. In the final chapter of this section on "Advocacy and Identity," Trenna Valado investigates the inherent dilemmas in any attempt to depict, characterize, or deploy the conditions and identities of others, and looks at critical ethical concerns for ongoing and future research on homelessness such as representation, mischaracterization, and the potential policy-oriented impacts of our work as scholars and advocates.

The next section focuses squarely on "Relationships and Ethics," beginning with Michael Rowe's investigation in Chapter 5 of research as a mechanism for creating implied (yet often difficult to fulfill) promises to participants and the ethical dilemmas that arise out this aspect. In Chapter 6, Jürgen von Mahs considers the role of the "buddy researcher," grappling with the ways in which we evaluate and disseminate the information we obtain doing research, and reminding us of the responsibilities inherent in that posture. Kurt Borchard amplifies these themes in Chapter 7, weaving together "tales from the field" in a manner that highlights the many challenges researchers face, yet ultimately concluding that it would be far worse *not* to write about issues like homelessness. Concluding this experientially focused section, Julie Adkins explores the all-important issues of power, roles, and goals, with a specific emphasis on how volunteerism and research present overlapping but sometimes oppositional obligations.

The final section on "Research and Transformation" opens with Vin Lyon-Callo's pointed analysis in Chapter 9 of the limitations of prior research on homelessness, arguing for a reinvigorated ethic of connecting the issue more straightforwardly to broader questions of political economy and relying less upon emotional appeals as a tool of transformation. In Chapter 10, I take up these structural and political concerns, exploring the import of "internal displacement" as an increasing motif of homelessness that is demonstrated in particular by the grim experience of post-Katrina New Orleans, struggling with the personal dimensions of generating scholarship and functioning as an advocate in circumstances that remain an open wound for myself and myriad others. David Cook extends this sense of personal struggle and transformation in Chapter 11, weaving a compelling narrative of homeless existence and resistance together with the self-reflective journey of an ethical researcher. Chapter 12, jointly authored by Don Mitchell and Lynn A. Staeheli, brings the issue of "using the homeless" into sharper focus, problematizing this concern by indicating the ways in which it is potentially constructive and destructive all at once. The conclusion by Valado synthesizes the lessons derived from this volume, presenting a systematic overview of points for researchers to consider and posing critical questions for future work in any field of social inquiry.

Taken as a whole, these chapters speak to both the dedication of the individual researchers as well as to the utility of capturing the researcher's voice for promoting productive scholarship and positive outcomes. In this sense, researchers are always already advocates, and must confront ethical dilemmas as a matter of course. By placing these conditions and concerns front and center, we hope to suggest that they are not hindrances but in fact are fruitful avenues of inquiry in themselves. In the end, the chapters collected in this volume indicate that researchers working with marginalized populations need not attempt to overcompensate for their sympathies by adopting an ill-fitting cloak of neutrality, but actually can begin to resolve the ethical challenges of working in the margins by deepening their spirit of advocacy. This, we believe, will only inure to the benefit of the research itself and, perhaps more importantly, to the people existing in the margins whose experiences we draw upon in our scholarly pursuits. Indeed, it might even be said that this is, in fact, simply the ethical thing to do.

Part One
Advocacy and Identity

Who are "the homeless" and what does it mean to be an advocate for them? How can we reconcile the oftentimes competing roles of researcher, scholar, activist, and educator in the context of working with marginalized populations and confronting issues as profound as the operative principles of social justice and the workings of the prevailing political economy? Is it possible simultaneously to address both the personal and structural causes of homelessness, while negotiating the ethics of representing others and the real-world consequences of one's research? Perhaps more to the point, how do we strive to ethically discharge our duties as researchers while reconciling them with the basic duty of care we owe toward one another simply by virtue of our common humanity? In short, can we maintain a stance of advocacy in the context of our multifarious identities, while respecting the identities and capacities of others?

These questions strike at the core of advocacy research, and in this section we hear from a range of leading figures in the field as to how they have struggled to navigate this terrain. The accounts presented here are self-revealing, soul-searching, and poignant in their depictions and analyses alike. Talmadge Wright deftly weaves together the threads of a personal journey through the vicissitudes of academia while maintaining an unswerving stance of advocacy for the homeless in the process. Rob Rosenthal explores an apparent (and perhaps systemically inherent) irony in which more effective advocacy may actually come at the expense of more grounded and nuanced research, thus calling upon us to reinvestigate many of the assumptions that we take into the field. Kathleen Arnold picks up this call and reexamines years of work in different cities through a compelling lens of race, gender, and the spectrum of identity constructions; she challenges our perceptions of what it is to be "normal" and concludes that whatever we do ought to include empowering others to become advocates on their own behalf. Trenna Valado expands the analysis to include not only the homeless in our ethical calculus, but others including policymakers, service providers, law enforcement officials, and the general public, in an attempt to find common ground and effectively address the baseline injustices that produce and perpetuate homelessness.

The terrain covered here is familiar yet exotic, equal parts perspiration and inspiration. To be an advocate for marginalized people while bearing the indicia of relative privilege—and doing it all within the confines of academic and policymaking venues—takes dedication, fortitude, and an overarching commitment to the intrinsic value of one's work. And it is *work*, not something for the faint of heart or academic tourists seeking a quick thrill or an easy path to publication. As the revelatory accounts presented in this opening section suggest, to be an effective advocate researcher is in fact to embark on a "life's work" toward the pursuit of justice—in the full recognition that the root causes of homelessness implicate nothing less than the very foundations of our social structures and, in the process, of our identities as they have come to be realized in the context of those structures. Advocacy meets identity, and in that union we discover that each is emboldened and enriched by the experience of the other.

Chapter 1
Social Justice, Ethics, and Advocacy in Street Research: A Personal Accounting
Talmadge Wright

Abstract. Having worked in the area of homeless research since 1987, I recount the experiences and conflicts that have emerged from my engagement with diverse homeless populations, policymakers, and academics in various parts of the United States. The struggle for social justice with the dispossessed demands an ethical position of advocacy-based research. Sociological research can be a vehicle for both moving from personal troubles to social issues, and also in confronting those issues with concrete action that works to make life better for those who are the objects of such research. Woven throughout this personal account of engagement, research, and activism is commentary on the literature which has surrounded the field of homeless research, the ethical problems such research raises, and the responsibility that all of us as academic researchers must shoulder for the work we do. Such "studying down" has received its share of legitimate criticism from those who understand that working with powerless people involves a basic ethical conundrum. It is for this reason that I believe studying down can only be ethically responsible insofar as there is a determined effort to apply such knowledge for the betterment of those involved. Therefore social activism is an essential element of research, a combination of knowledge and praxis. It is clear that opportunities for studying the poor are much greater than studying the wealthy simply because they have fewer resources to block a researcher's access and are publicly more visible, especially in the case of homeless families and individuals. It is the researcher's responsibility to do what they can to advocate for those who cannot advocate for themselves, but more importantly, to listen and act in a way which respects the poor without romanticizing their marginality. Such respect demands a confrontation with those larger structural and political forces that work to produce and reproduce homelessness in the broader society. Throughout this commentary I also discuss my own position as an academic/advocate and the conflicts emerging from this work.

Year after year academic reports, books, articles, speeches, and the like are published, read, and spoken about the poor and the dispossessed. Unnecessary human suffering is so widespread that it appears normal, tainted by assumptions of culpability, individual dysfunctions, and self-loathing, often blinding ourselves to the possibilities for real structural change. In the early 1980s media reports focused on homeless women, so called "bag-ladies," and only gradually expanded the types of homeless people into categories of homeless adolescents, car campers, homeless single men, etc. In other words, homelessness became the new term within which to isolate unhoused from housed poor people. Homelessness as a term allowed the policymaking community to medicalize the condition of being without a place to live as well as to deflect from the overall structural study of poverty. This rhetorical deflection also worked within the category of homelessness, by separating out deserving homeless families and children from undeserving single homeless men—a policy strategy which has its roots in the early Elizabethan Poor Laws.

What are the ethics, then, of our research, the moral implications of working with versus studying the poor and dispossessed in the context of these historical deflections? (see Cloke et al. 2000; Gounis 1996). When you talk back to social workers, police, and "experts" on behalf of those who have no voice you also discover your own voice, but you also discover how power operates to keep the poor in their place. How does this change the accounts we write and discuss of the poor? The questions of closeness to one's research, the ethical conundrums you find working on the street, and the messiness of field work, all come into play when you take seriously the suffering of others. For me this chapter is a small account of what I have learned working with various homeless populations since 1987 and what they have taught me, and to a large degree offers a chance to reflect on the pain I witnessed and experienced.

There are many ways to talk about this. But perhaps the best way is to start from the beginning, how I got involved and what that involvement has meant on a personal, political, social and cultural level. This is my way of telling a story which has remained hidden in plain sight for over twenty years. Maybe my story will help other young researchers struggling with these issues. And struggle they will—because if you are being real, this work will tear at your heart and soul demanding that your critical intellect grasp the larger picture while you come to grips with how to take care of yourself in the midst of suffering others.

As C. Wright Mills understood, our biographical histories are deeply embedded in the larger social structural issues that we have to negotiate. For me, this was making the transition between graduate school and finding employment in the academic world. Like many new PhD recipients, I could only find a series of part-time jobs and teaching positions. This lasted for six years. This status as an academic "freeway flyer" was accompanied by a three-year position, thirty hours a week as a housing analyst for a nonprofit group that specialized in housing discrimination. Living in rental housing, never sure if I had steady employment from semester to semester, at wages which guaranteed marginal housing, driving a car that broke down frequently, and yet applying to so many academic positions that I was left with rejection notices in folders three inches thick—it was all too easy to fall into despair. At least the work I was now doing provided some emotional compensation by assisting others in their struggle for adequate housing. The late 1980s was not a good time to be looking for academic work. This social and economic marginalization, after spending years in a university context where having an advanced degree was considered a ticket to quick academic success, was quite unsettling and prepared the way for what was to happen next. With a stoic attitude I moved from teaching in a university into a short six-month stint as a canvasser with a political advocacy group in Los Angeles, then with the failure of my seven-year personal relationship, moved back to Orange County, California, to accept a new part-time position from the Orange County Fair Housing Council as their housing analyst.

Applying what I learned in graduate school, I plunged into analyzing housing trends in Orange County and Los Angeles as well as attending meetings of housing advocates and speaking out at city council meetings on the need for affordable low-income housing. On the one hand I had been trained academically to look at issues of mass media, ideology, and consumer culture, mostly trained in qualitative research methods. And yet on the other hand, I found myself dealing with the practical everyday realities of families without housing, housing discrimination, and the institutions set up to manage poverty in the United States. The political world had grown quite a bit colder with the re-election of a President (Reagan) dedicated to eliminating welfare as we knew it and generally reducing social spending across the board in relationship to need. Increasingly, I felt my academic interests in media and urban spaces were less significant than grappling with the concrete needs of those who came into our offices. This changed later when I began to reflect on working with the homeless communities I had assisted. Indeed, in part, my selection as housing analyst was influenced by my previous involvement in community activism centered on Central American solidarity issues as well as working with parts of the local immigrant community.

It was within that context that in the spring of 1987, the plight of four homeless families came to my attention through a call placed by a local shelter provider and activist. The families had been rousted out of a nearby parking lot at 4:00 a.m. and told by the police to move along. Even though the owner of the lot had given them permission to camp there, the police said they had to move and that car camping was considered a "health hazard." Prior to this, I had attended monthly meetings of local shelter providers, meeting those entrusted with assisting the dispossessed, one of whom made the call to us in our office. These "institutional" meetings reflected the fact that all of us were receiving a salary for attending, with little in the way of showing how our attendance was improving the lives of those we were expected to serve. This social work approach to poverty focused on managing institutional resources and balancing staffing needs more than actually solving homelessness or poverty issues. The phone call concerning the plight of these homeless families threw this convenient arrangement into question and called for an ethical or moral response to their plight.

Far too often, I had to tell people who called our offices requesting shelter that there was no housing for them, and that they needed to call the County housing agency to get on a three-year waiting list for Section 8 housing certificates. The systemic, county-wide lack of low-income housing was bolstered by city policies which discouraged low-income housing and blocked the construction of local shelters. This felt like a continuous uphill battle, which made me sad, frustrated, and angry at the lack of consideration (and even blatant contempt) for our less fortunate brothers and sisters. What I saw was a privileged, well-fed, and housed population preoccupied with closing the latest real estate deal or making money in the market while neglecting the poor around them, and justifying that neglect with age-old historical rationalizations from the culture of poor people to laziness and "bad" morals. In fairness, however, many were merely concerned with their property values given that a home was maybe all that they had between them and the street. But without a collective response or leadership from political leaders, such fear created the conditions for many cases of NIMBY (Not-In-My-Backyard). More immediately, the practical question, the ethical question, became: what should I do, and what should my organization do about the plight of these four families?

Since I had allied with several members of the shelter task force, myself and a colleague suggested that we should go and investigate, talk to the people living in their cars and trucks, and get some understanding of what their needs were and how we could help. My employer at the time agreed, and the shelter activist accompanied us to the park introducing us to a diverse array of characters. And for the next few months between May and November, my colleague and I met weekly with the four families, plus seventeen single men and women who made their daytime lives the roads and bushes of Garden Grove Park. I was given time away from the office to go to the parks and work with my colleagues in other agencies to assess the situation. With my colleague who worked as the Mental Health Outreach worker for the county, and who knew some of these people from her own field work, we started visiting Garden Grove Park, talking with the campers about what happened, and attempted to document their trials and tribulations. The results of these encounters are told in our published account of the formation of the Homeless Action Project (HAP) and the various strategies of authority and resistance we encountered (see Wright and Vermund 1996).

With the support of my agency, we were able to provide the initial meeting place for the gathering of a large group of homeless car campers, single homeless individuals, and their supporters, who elected Paul (who was homeless at the time) and a housed person as co-chairs for the group. The name "Homeless Action Project" was given to the group by the homeless families we had been supporting. Given that the group now had a name and eventually secured its own location at a nearby food pantry, advocacy for people's needs accelerated. Some were involved in welfare advocacy, others in securing funding. Still others became involved in monitoring police activity while other people examined what housing options were available if any throughout Orange County. My involvement with the group went through several phases from simply collecting information, to direct advocacy on the part of several members with a local welfare office and attempts to integrate their struggles with the general lack of affordable housing throughout the county. While I was teaching only one class at a local community college, my main employer, a nonprofit agency, was better placed than a university to push an advocacy agenda. What I brought to this work was my training as a social scientist with research skills and academic connections. Hence, it was imperative for me to move the analysis of the plight of these families beyond simply understanding their situation as one of an individual lack of resources to a systematic analysis of homelessness in general in American society and indeed the world. And it was this developing analysis that I shared with the families themselves over the months we interacted.

It should also be remembered that this was a time of intense homeless activism across the country, from Mitch Snyder's protest in Washington, D.C. to Ted Hayes and the establishment of the Justiceville encampments in Los Angeles. My colleague and I visited Justiceville as well as took in the work of John Malpede and the Los Angeles Poverty Department, who conducted theater performances utilizing homeless actors. We came to understand that homelessness was not simply about being without resources or a product of individual dysfunction, but rather a systematic byproduct of elite decision makers who had rejected the welfare-state solutions of earlier years for the cutthroat slash-and-burn policies of a "post-Fordist" economy best represented by President Reagan's busting of labor unions, slashing of social funds, and the shrinkage of the federal government's role in providing housing for the poor.

My ethical response could have ended with an assumption that homeless people were to blame for their own situation—and therefore all they needed was more help for their individual problems, proper attitudes, proper training, etc. However, such a simplistic analysis flew in the face of my experiences living in Mexico, my graduate school understandings of social inequality and power, and a class analysis which linked the issues of poverty with the development of privilege and power. Theories of individual dysfunction simply could not explain the widespread impoverishment of working people.

While my job required me to analyze various efforts on the part of local cities to develop low-income housing, mostly by looking at their city and housing documents, to make larger sense of what these plans meant required a framework of analysis developed by housing researchers, planners, geographers and urban sociologists like Peter Marcuse, Mike Davis, Jennifer Wolch, Michael Dear, Chester Hartman, John Gilderbloom, Neil Smith, and others. Through my position, I was in contact with low-income housing advocate groups nationally and statewide. However, working with HAP meant integrating the housing issue with the homeless question. It was also clear to me that, at the time, activists working on housing issues were not necessarily interested in working on homeless issues. Housing activism appeared better established, better funded, and more institutionalized than homeless activism, which was often confined to street demonstrations by the Union of the Homeless, local activists protesting police abuse, and the attempt to set up a nationwide Coalition on Homelessness in the nation's capital. Homeless activism remained local, but the implications extended into a much broader critique of privilege and power. And it is that fact that drew me into the movement, beyond helping individuals secure resources.

Homeless people were the "canaries in the mineshaft" indicating a deeper disturbance in the operation of corporate capitalism with implications for all citizens. I did not see my role as a social worker, as one who facilitates the acquisition of resources by the dispossessed (although I did engage in such activity), but rather as understanding how poverty and homelessness were a direct result of political, economic, and social policies produced by the powerful for the benefit of the privileged.[1] This meant working with homeless people where I could, students and researchers at times, and policymakers and nonprofits at other points. Homelessness is a form of "social death," a violence imposed upon the less powerful segments of society by the powerful—the dispassionate brutality of a capitalist housing market without regulations, a market where winners take all and losers are cast into the street. Needless to say such an understanding does not make for comfortable feelings or polite cocktail party conversations. And the reports and research I began to read merely confirmed what I had suspected from my experience.

While there are many intellectual influences I could quote, the two which had a direct impact on my early understanding of homeless activism was a small essay by the urban researcher, Peter Marcuse (1988), "Neutralizing Homelessness," and the work of Piven and Cloward (1997). Marcuse clearly connected the issues of urban redevelopment, capitalism, and the exclusion of homeless people by demonstrating how the changes in urban economics had a direct impact on who gets to be accepted and who gets rejected in the new downtowns. However, as I stated in my ensuing book (Wright 1997), he neglects to discuss the understanding of these developments by homeless people and their ability to mobilize around these issues as reflected in the work of Susan Ruddick, David Wagner, Rob Rosenthal, and others. Still, Marcuse's arguments did provide an excellent structural analysis within which to locate homeless movements. Piven and Cloward's earlier work on welfare and civil rights movements demonstrated that maintaining constant political pressure through disruption is essential if marginalized groups are going to win concessions from authorities. This seemed to be clearly the case with homeless activism. Without the marches, building occupations, and protests there would be little reason for city authorities to take the plight of homeless people seriously. Both Susan Ruddick and Roger Keil (who were at the University of California, Los Angeles) befriended me during this time, and through our discussions and friendship we were able to explore the issue of homelessness beyond the simple individual dysfunction typical of the literature. Their connections with the Los Angles community of activists and academics inspired me to move forward in my analysis. Similarly Michael Dear and Jennifer Wolch, geographers at University of Southern California, were also very supportive and encouraged me to combine both the academic and activist components of this research. They invited me to present my observations at an annual meeting of urban planners in Southern California.

Therefore, the work I was doing with HAP, while directed at securing resources for the homeless car campers, had implications far beyond providing social services. In fact, one form of disruption we engaged in was to secure the names and phone numbers of the supervisors of social service caseworkers handling the geographic areas where local homeless people gathered. In our work, many homeless men and women stated frankly that they were often denied benefits they deserved by caseworkers who had little interest in their plight. According to them, they were never informed that they could appeal these rejections. We encouraged them to always ask for the worker's supervisor if benefits were not forthcoming. The result was a flood of calls to the local agencies, eventually with the agencies contacting my place of employment at the Fair Housing Council and my colleagues asking us to "back off." The result at the county level and at my own place of employment was to ask us to reduce the time we spent with HAP. Part of this political pressure came no doubt from the fact that our agency was funded with Community Development Block Grant (CDBG) money, as well as funding from local cities as part of a legal arrangement in dealing with housing discrimination.

The ethical implications of this should seem obvious. Who do I answer to: my employer, the populations I was working with, the county? As long as my employer was supportive there were few problems. The assumption that this research/activism was objective was simply nonsense. What was objective was the concrete suffering that was obvious to anyone who did not have an ulterior agenda. The question was not how to conduct "objective" research, but rather what responsibility the researcher has to reduce human suffering. It was not at all clear that the so-called mission statements of institutions reflected their real practices. Calling these practices into question is risky. When pressure from city and county agencies increased I was faced with an ethical dilemma: how to maintain support for the population I was working with while still keeping my job. I attempted to surf the middle. While still doing the necessary work for my nonprofit agency I also took breaks and lunch hours to meet with the homeless families as well as go after work to their new offices at a local food pantry.

My involvement with the group came to an end in June of 1988 when my position as housing analyst was eliminated due to budget cutbacks in the CDBG program, a favorite target of political conservatives at the time. This meant scrambling for more part-time teaching positions to support myself. Eventually, I was able to secure a position teaching three classes a semester as a part-time instructor at San Jose State University in Northern California, leading to my departure from Southern California.

Looking back at this time period between 1986 and 1989, I realized that my involvement in homeless advocacy, solidarity movements, and social justice in general had a deeper moral and ethical component which can be traced back to my religious roots growing up, understanding that how we treat those perceived as less worthy than ourselves is a reflection of our own humanity; it is a position embraced by all social justice movements and especially the civil rights movement, which deeply affected my understanding of the ethics of homeless research. It is not enough to study a subordinated population as if they are animals in a zoo, but rather, as Dorothy Smith (1987) understood and feminist theory in general supports, to make alliances with those who are less fortunate, to adopt "standpoint theory" as a foundation of knowledge accompanied by an action-oriented methodology which ethnographic research can provide.

While a structural analysis of the causes of homelessness and poverty was essential, it was not sufficient. It was also important to work to give a voice to those who could not be heard—to allow those who are oppressed to talk back effectively to power. It is for that reason that I look back at my work during that period as a formative stage in developing an integration of theory, research, and action with the desire to blend theory and praxis in the best critical sociology tradition. Some people choose to study homelessness as a topic of research, a cultural interest, or for some other academic reason. For me it was different. Homelessness as a topic came to my doorstep, and I had a choice to either let it in or close the door. This was an ethical decision on my part which I made consciously without regard to the cost it might carry. Did I/we do the right thing? Indeed, at the time, I really did not understand what cost it might have on my well-being. Doing this work has not been easy, either for my personal life or my career—but it has felt like the right thing to do. Perhaps this work was made easier because my own feelings of academic marginality, of feeling outside of established patterns of academic success, allowed me to identify with those who had been themselves marginalized and impoverished through years of neglect.

During the following three years I spent in Northern California, I was fortunate to have the opportunity to teach Community Concepts in the Social Work Department at San Jose State University, as well as Urban Sociology at the University of California at Berkeley. Even though much of my teaching revolved around issues of mass media, urban sociology, social theory, and social inequality, these two opportunities allowed me to put into practice what I had learned in Southern California working with both housing and homeless groups. The

Community Concepts class, which applied service learning with social theory, involved direct work between students and homeless street persons living in San Jose. Students visited homeless encampments, set up a soup kitchen, researched legal defenses for homeless persons, and did what they could to humanize those living on the streets. And, in turn, homeless individuals visited the campus, talked with students about their experiences and developed strategies in discussions with students about what to do about homelessness and the abuses they experienced daily from the local police. Beyond this form of exposure, a deeper alliance between the community and the university was established by using ethnographic techniques and advocate strategies, covered in my book *Out of Place*. This new alliance of students, community activists, and homeless people created a new organization, the Student Homeless Alliance (SHA).

The catalyst for the formation of the group, aside from the work students performed in these street communities, was the reaction against police sweeps of homeless camps and the consideration of a city housing budget which grossly undercounted the need for affordable low-income housing. My students in Urban Sociology at UC Berkeley had completed a study of San Jose's redevelopment policies based on earlier work I had done comparing housing, jobs, and transportation data in Orange County, as well as drawing upon regional housing data in the Bay Area. Their study could have remained a simple group class project but for the fact that our group in San Jose found the research useful for their own advocacy. Was it right to share this study and use it in an advocacy context? I think it was morally imperative insofar as the study, using data from respectable sources, highlighted the need for more housing in San Jose and better facilities for homeless persons. Whether or not I was worried about how the city might find this study remained less significant than the truth which the study revealed about the neglect of low-income housing construction. And it was this truth which was spoken by the student team at a meeting between city officials and shelter providers before an important city council vote on their upcoming budget for the year. Hence, the actual work done by the students increased in relevancy because it was concerned with real-life changes, and the students could witness the impact of their own research. In this fashion, the study worked as a tool to teach students in urban sociology about how city governments, planning agencies, and housing budgets actually worked. But it also had the effect of giving hope to the SHA, in that they now had a study which supported their claims for more housing for the poor.

What followed were a series of protests at San Jose's City Hall, covered by local media. Presentations were made at city council meetings and protests held in the Mayor's office. During these events students would record how media reporters covered and then "framed" the protests, taking their recordings of the event back to local shelters to play them alongside recorded TV broadcasts. The contrast in coverage was then analyzed for what it had to say about how poverty and homelessness were treated by the mainstream media. One particular effect noted was the marginalization of any homeless person's comments in favor of a perceived "expert." In one instance I noted that a reporter singled me out for an interview and not someone from our group. One way we attempted to alter this process was to have all spokespersons for the group wear a white shirt and black pants at the next event and crowd around any reporter attempting to gather a story to ensure that the framing of the story was both fair and accurate. This was not an intimidation tactic but rather a witnessing by group participants to explore how their stories were reported. Initially, media coverage was poor, with the use of stereotypical rhetoric deployed about the poor and a greater weight given to the Mayor's responses than to the homeless group's explanations. In fact, most of the information reported in our study was never used in any media reports, only the Mayor's comments about the report. This awareness on the part of the group produced another protest, this time in front of the *San Jose Mercury News*, where the issue of media framing of the poor was made the central feature. After this, news coverage took a more balanced perspective.

While much of the political activism of the SHA started in the late spring of 1991, the building of the group's solidarity had occurred over the previous three years I was teaching in the Bay Area. That same spring I was hired at Loyola University in Chicago for a full-time tenure track position, leaving the Bay Area for the Midwest in August of 1991. SHA continued with its activism and research in the fall, setting up several building occupations and protests over city budget priorities. After I left, SHA moved off campus, eventually renaming itself the Community Homeless Alliance (CHA), and then later the Community Homeless Alliance Ministry (CHAM). The main organizer of the group, Scott Wagers, my former student, had moved on to divinity school, receiving his theology degree, and then returned as Pastor of the local First Christian Church close to San Jose State University. He continues to this day, as do other members of the group, embracing a much broader community coalition of Latino groups, poor and homeless people, and community activists of all kinds throughout the Bay Area.

When I arrived in Chicago to take up my new position as Assistant Professor at Loyola, I sought out the local Coalition on Homelessness, led at the time by Les Brown, to see what the situation was like in Chicago. I also met several members of HOME (Homeless on the Move for Equality), a group of homeless men and women who were working with people living in cardboard boxes on Lower Wacker Drive. They had also started a campaign with a housing advocacy group, the Mad Housers of Atlanta, to put together a series of plywood shacks throughout the city to highlight the issue of homelessness in Chicago. My involvement with the new shantytowns was accelerated by an invitation to be part of a panel at the Randolph Street Art Gallery, a local art museum that was hosting the Mad Housers. It was really the combination of local artists with the gallery, the Mad Housers, and the Coalition that worked to establish more than twenty-one encampments throughout the city over the next six months.

While not directly involved in the new encampments, I did meet some of the participants and, indeed, had many of my students attend the various sites and discuss what they learned in class. During this period the work of researchers such as David Wagner, Rob Rosenthal, David Snow, Henri Lefebvre, Margit Mayer, Neil Smith, Mark Gottdiener, and others was critical in helping me formulate an approach of how to integrate theory and practice around these experiences.

After the shacks were removed by the city, and those homeless individuals involved given new places in the Chicago Housing Authority buildings, I switched focus and began to research homeless individuals living on Lower Wacker Drive, which runs under the main streets of downtown Chicago going around the Loop. Many homeless men made their sleeping arrangements on elevated concrete docks, under heating vents from the hotels located above. This was a decision I made partly because many of those staying in the original shacks had discussed Lower Wacker as the main sleeping area for most of them before acquiring a shack. City shelters were always perceived as the least desirable option, often overcrowded and with attitudes on the part of staff that often served to confirm the status of homeless people as having what Erving Goffman called "spoiled identities." For the next several years between 1992 and 1995, I would "hang out" weekly on Lower Wacker, often in the evening, talking with various people who were living in cardboard boxes or sleeping in the open next to heating grates. In 1994, I conducted a series of interviews with those I had come to know on Lower Wacker, attempting to learn in more detail the specifics of street life and the survival game. Interviews were conducted in both the dead of winter as well as during fall balminess. Cold concrete, a particularly brutal hardness of street life, often contrasted with the alternating suspicion and warmth plus compassion of those sleeping on Lower Wacker, punctuated by a high degree of solidarity, community knowledge, and fear.

I began to realize that the more time I spent on the streets, the angrier I was getting and the more despondent I felt about ever changing the conditions of poverty with ameliorative solutions that ignored a socially just alternative. Witnessing an eight-month pregnant woman living in a cardboard box in the dead of winter, followed by the death from exposure of one of the people I had spent time with, was extremely difficult knowing that solutions would not be forthcoming (although the homeless men on the street did band together to help the pregnant woman into a church shelter). This discouragement was perhaps, in reflection, partly a result of the death of my mother and relocating my father, plus the particular homeless population I was working with—even the previous homeless activists I had interviewed in the Mad Houser huts looked down upon those living on Lower Wacker as the lowest of the low. While I refused to accept that distinction, it was true that the depth of despair, defiance, anger and indeed, rage, was much more on the surface with those I hung out with on Lower Wacker than I saw in earlier populations. I found myself also learning that same anger, especially when I heard constant stories of police abuse or civilian harassment of those I was talking with on a regular basis.

What to do? I was unwilling to simply settle for social work "solutions," to advocate for more shelters or services. Emotionally the pain, despair, and deep rage I witnessed was tearing me apart, even while I attempted to deny it. Something about their situation sparked a resonance within my soul, something that could not be concealed with alcohol or flippant expressions of liberal support. I would wager to say few middle-class people witness the shock of the absolute poor, and when they do the natural reaction always seems to be to look away.[2] It was even difficult for me to remain "objective," for example, to interview public officials and believe their comments, especially given what I had learned about reading city documents in my prior work as a housing analyst. Interviewing officials seemed like a simple recitation of public relations, when in actuality city plans were always revealed in their published documents. In fact, what I was experiencing was an understanding that "solving" the problem of homelessness was not on the agenda of any official—only "managing" homelessness. And if this was true, what was my role in simply helping to facilitate this management? Sure, it was a good idea to attempt to generate conditions in which those who have no power are allowed to speak—but for what purpose? It is one thing to give those who are marginal a voice, but quite another to get those who have the power to change such conditions to listen. In other words, my deeply felt concern for social injustice and the manifestation of such injustice in the crime of poverty came up smack against the social-structural reality of established power and wealth.

As I pulled away from doing direct street research I began to think of other ways that I as a sociologist could intervene in a situation which I realized was both individual and structural. One of the projects I established in 1994, after meeting with a group of homeless community activists in Berlin, Germany, was to develop an international news service with a focus on homelessness and poverty. This entailed setting up an FTP site, through a group in Boulder, Colorado, for the Homeless News Service. Through this site I was able to assist the local Chicago street newspaper, *Streetwise*, in publishing articles about international homeless issues from Berlin to Rome and other countries. I was supported in this by Loyola's Policy Research and Action Group (PRAG) through 1997. The project was then handed off to *Real Change*, the homeless street paper in Seattle, Washington.

In 1996 I made contact with a colleague at San Francisco State University, Roma Guy, who had established the Bay Area Homelessness Project (BAHP) with the task of informing the public and developing educational programs that would expand understanding and action around homeless issues. Through our collaboration I was able to develop a project which examined the differences in approaches in various homeless activist groups throughout the Bay Area.[3] In other words, I realized that unless normative public understandings of homeless people as simply victims who need charity or conversely as "bums" who needed discipline were challenged at the intellectual level, nothing much would change in seeking solutions to end homelessness, only more of the same policies designed to manage poverty. Spending a sabbatical at San Francisco State both teaching about homelessness to students and working on the research aspects of BAHP, we began to develop a plan which required more extensive funding. We applied for grant money through several funding agencies, including the Open Society Foundation. However, the final result was the drying up of any funds which could be used to expand both research and advocacy on the topic, unless it was directed towards direct aid. In other words, "think tank" funding which would seriously challenge the dominant understandings of poverty and homelessness was thought of as unimportant by progressive funders at the time. Of course, rightwing political movements have spent millions of dollars over the past thirty years on think tanks to promote their agenda. This did not seem to change until Democrats failed in both capturing the Presidency and in advancing within Congress. The power of conservative think tanks, demonstrated in the reframing of language used to sell conservative social policies, was highly visible in the early promotion of Dinesh D'Souza's diatribe on "Illiberal Education" designed to demonize political correctness in 1991. He had spent extensive time at a conservative think tank—and there were many more cases. The progressive forces who wished to seriously contest the dominant understandings of poverty had nothing comparable at the time.

The failure of BAHP to secure funding for our research agenda prompted us to rethink how we should proceed. One idea we came up with was to attempt to establish a social indicators program, which would give grades to various cities depending upon how they treated their poor. We held meetings with San Francisco's Department of Public Health as well as some nonprofit groups to organize an approach to examine what such an indicator might look like. However, again, we could not secure funding, and with the loss of funding for BAHP our project came to a close.

Conclusion

The problem of homelessness has not gone away; it has not been even reasonably managed, much less solved. Instead, criminalization of homeless people has accelerated, and the criminal justice system has now taken up the task of absorbing those who are too tired, too poor, or too sick to fit into mainstream society. In addition, many homeless people have suffered from having their services removed from downtown areas, relocated to marginal industrial areas away from the gaze of middle-income shoppers and store owners. I concluded my own work with publishing an article in *Contemporary Sociology* with what I thought were reasonable steps that could be taken to solve homelessness at both a local, state, and national level (Wright 2000). Perhaps my own romantic and naive nature kept me optimistic. However, over time I have come to realize that this issue of radical inequality and social violence will not be solved through the current measures employed by city, state, and the federal government.

Privilege and power are too well ingrained at the expense of the American people, and only a large mass political and cultural movement dedicated to true equality and set against a mindless and ruthless individualism will have any chance of combating the roots of homelessness. Change must occur in Washington as well as change at the bottom. And given the state of both Democratic and Republican thinking on poverty, this is not about to happen any time soon. So given this, what would it have meant for me to keep researching the topic of homelessness, in particular the behaviors of homeless street populations, after writing what I thought were practical solutions? For me to continue researching the ethnographic accounts of street people therefore implicated me in the reproduction of homelessness by simply continuing to use the poor as objects for my own advancement. Ethically, I just could not bring myself to continue this illusion that somehow my work could make a difference in the lives of those whose stories I had listened to. Does this mean that research on homelessness should not be done? No. But we need to focus on the kind of research that makes a difference.

What should be examined is not simply the micro-survival and resistant strategies of people without homes, as interesting as it might be, but rather the process by which public attitudes are shaped around poverty. For this reason, expanding think tanks, developing new social media outlets to address poverty, interconnecting activist, labor, and academic groups, and other aspects of what we would define as a social movement are essential to move beyond the politics of amelioration. As Dorothy Smith (1987) points out, the dominant "relations of ruling" must be called into question and serious alternatives proposed and fought for. Topics such as the media framing of poverty, nonprofits and the State, the role of the police and business in furthering homelessness, city and private developers' actions, and many more themes could prove fruitful. Rather than take homeless populations as problematic, we must understand how their plight is a result of larger social and political forces at work and engage those forces to end the rapidly developing social inequality that threatens our democracy. The point is that, as William Domhoff once asserted, we must "study up" to look at how power is exercised by those with the ability to change and challenge public agendas. As Emily Paradis (2000) states: "Feminist and community research ethics must go beyond the avoidance of harm to an active investment in the well-being of marginalized individuals and communities." And I would add that well-being must be understood in the context of how political power works in direct opposition to the powerless. One person's privilege is bought at another's expense. To become an "activist researcher" (Pain 2003) therefore is not simply about privileging collective empowerment of the poor over the preferred policy of individual empowerment. It also means seriously contesting political power, confronting conservative agendas that work to marginalize the poor and working class, and to push seriously for a social agenda in which democracy and freedom can truly rule, not oligarchy and plutocracy.

As a final note, since I wrote the first draft of this reflection a serious movement to contest entrenched multinational corporate power and widespread, expanding social, political, and economic inequality has emerged with the Occupy movement. It is this global confrontation between the 99 percent and the top 1 percent, the recognition that the suffering of each of us in light of the corporate crimes committed in our name, would finally be taken to task and the mantle of justice brought to bear on the necks of the powerful. As our homeless populations make common cause with our working-class and middle-class brethren, what we may be witnessing is an emerging earthquake which will shake the walls of privilege and power that lock out so many in the name of free markets and business as usual. But as was once stated during the revolt of the 1960s, "No Business as Usual." The time for change is now.

Notes

1. This is not to imply that all social work is merely attending to changing the individual. The radical social work movements of the 1960s, as a case in point, made great strides in integrating political struggles with individual social issues. However, the institutionalization of social work in established agencies risks the de-politicizing of social work, reducing the assistance of the poor to clinical interventions.

2. The exception being members of church communities who make it their moral position to always assist the poor and members of radical Left organizations. While one group may wish to convert and witness, the other wants to make revolutionaries. Both types tend to be treated with great skepticism by street populations, unless they can prove themselves by staying for the long haul.

3. The different approaches various organizations had to dealing with homelessness and poverty often prevented them from effectively working together in a united front because of widely different mission statements, staffing and financial considerations. This made for discouraging splits between housing and homeless activists, between those who worked for shelters and those who worked directly with street populations. Our research attempted to pinpoint some of these differences (see Wright and Roschelle 2003).

Chapter 2
The Advocate Researcher
Rob Rosenthal

Abstract. Relations between homeless *activists* and housed *advocates* involved in anti-homelessness work are framed by a series of issues which must be navigated. These come into play for researchers who are participant observers (i.e., advocate researchers) as do a number of practical and ethical questions tied to the research enterprise itself. Advocacy carries with it dangers of even greater subjectivity than that found in the usual social science investigation, through both conscious and unconscious motives. This not only may weaken the research itself; even the *appearance* of subjectivity weakens the impact research may have on public policy. And ironically, research subjectively distorted out of identification with and concern for homeless contact may not always end up being beneficial to the homeless people being studied. A more "neutral" stance, on the other hand, carries its own load of practical and ethical dilemmas. Among these is the question of reciprocal responsibility between homeless informants who trust an advocate researcher, based on their common activism, enough to reveal potentially dangerous information—hidden camping places, crimes committed, etc.—and the researcher's desire to report as accurately and extensively as possible what s/he has discovered about the lives of their "subjects." Finally, the question of what to study is a dilemma. Above all, advocate researchers, who overwhelmingly operate from a structural perspective in understanding and explaining homelessness, must confront the issue of why it is we spend so much time studying those who are rendered homeless by the decisions of elites and so little time studying the elites and their decision-making processes.

Relations between homeless *activists* and housed *advocates* involved in anti-homelessness work are framed by implicit and explicit power and privilege differentials, resulting in a series of issues which must be navigated (Rosenthal

1996). These come into play for (housed)[1] researchers who are participant observers—*advocate researchers*, as I will call them here—as do a number of other practical and ethical questions tied to the research enterprise itself.

Relations Between Researchers and Homeless People

In earlier works (Rosenthal 1994; 1996) I have discussed at some length the tensions related to differences in power and privilege that arise between activists and advocates within anti-homelessness movements. Housed advocates share homeless activists' goal of justice (however defined) for homeless people, but since they are not themselves homeless, they may "lack the urgency we have," as one homeless activist put it (Cress 1990, 16). Nonetheless, advocates often assume leadership positions in groups fighting homelessness, based on their "middle-class" resources, including education and connections to networks of power. Some such leaders then tend to speak for homeless people instead of with homeless people, concentrating their efforts on lobbying "respectable" segments of the society—religious groups, government officials, etc.—instead of a strategy of empowerment of homeless people themselves. All too often, the access to necessary resources that housed advocates and those in their networks enjoy virtually mandates that their vision of the struggle will dominate movement work.

These differences often lead to disagreements at the level of strategies and tactics, but are also the elephant in the room on a micro level. All relations between homeless and housed people are played out against the background knowledge of both that the latter can escape the misery of homelessness at any time they choose while the former cannot. Envy, guilt, and issues of how to maintain trust are thus virtually inevitable, even where both activist and advocate think of themselves as comrades fighting a common fight.

The same is true, and perhaps even more so, for advocate researchers. Aside from our (typical) financial ability to quit the field of battle, we are clearly involved in an enterprise that will have a private payoff for us—publication, promotion, reputation, and so forth. We may say with all sincerity that our primary goal is to support homeless people with the skills we have at hand, but there is no denying that these less collective goods are also at stake. Homeless people, particularly at first, are understandably suspicious of researchers who might say they are comrades but who may take the knowledge and suffering of homeless people, turn it into a product they can sell on the intellectual market, and move on. Relations of equality require some form of reciprocity in what people bring to and get from the relation. Homeless people want to know what they will get in return, on both an individual and collective level, in exchange for the raw data of their lives that they provide to researchers.

This set of dilemmas yields no single easy answer; the dilemma itself is of structural origin and cannot simply be done away with by having our acts together. But the extreme worries of exploitation and violation of trust may be diminished when advocate researchers demonstrate through deed that we are in the struggle for the long term; that we are there to listen, not pontificate; and that we operate on the principles of reciprocity, expecting to give and receive as equally as we can within the bounds of a social context we do not control.

Rejecting Objectivity

Beyond those dilemmas which are tied to relations with homeless people, advocate researchers encounter issues which are tied to the enterprise of research itself, although these are often complicated by the fact that we are working on homelessness. A basic question is the stance we take toward our investigation, beginning with epistemological assumptions about objectivity and its attainability. It is by now, I would argue, well accepted in social science work that researcher objectivity is a myth (Behar and Gordon 1995; Clifford and Marcus 1986; Ferrell and Hamm 1998; Fine 1993; Marcus and Fischer 1986). All researchers begin with biases, assumptions, interests, and so forth that influence what we study, how we study it, what we hope to find, and thus what we do find. We may try to understand what these are and how they are affecting our work, but the very nature of assumptions is that they are largely hidden, and their matter-of-factness is so complete that we don't realize they are just assumptions. We simply cannot be aware of everything which influences our perceptions.

Given this understanding, some argue in Weber's voice that our goal must still be to strive toward a neutral "scientific" objectivity (1958), while others say with Marx (1968, 30) that objectivity should not even be our goal: "The philosophers have only interpreted the world, in various ways; the point is to change it." Mainstream social science has always insisted that the former path is correct, but advocate researchers begin with Marx's orientation. If researcher objectivity is always a fiction, impossible to achieve and only disingenuous to conceal, then better to openly declare our allegiances from the beginning and admit where our sympathies lie.

The decision to be partisan, however, isn't just a strategic decision about how best to deal with the unattainability of objectivity. It rests as well on a belief that neutrality in a world in which some groups have far more resources than others is itself immoral, an alliance with the powerful through omission at the very least. All research is ideological, either supportive of or resistant to existing social relations; those that don't challenge a given set of social relations in effect sanction and support those relations. That the advocate researchers' ideological agenda is openly declared doesn't show us to be invariably more "subjective" in our work, I would argue, but more conscious of our context in a social system in which the unequal distribution of power and other resources may appear to be a fact of life, eternal and inevitable, but is always the result of human actions—including those of researchers.

Yet there is no denying that an open declaration of support for a group—homeless people, in this case—presents important problems for an advocate researcher. In the first place, it invites dismissal of our work by opponents and those we seek to influence. There is a great irony here: one of the ongoing frustrations of social scientists is our belief that public policy is so often more influenced by the emotions, prejudices, and uninformed perspectives of everyday citizens and their representatives than the underlying realities we work to uncover. (Consider notions about the very existence of homelessness. When the modern wave of homelessness first surfaced as a public issue in the early 1980s, the overwhelming response of the public and public officials was to attribute homelessness entirely to the personal problems of homeless people. It took a decade of social science research before public opinion began to tip toward a more structuralist perspective, an understanding of the roots of the explosion in homelessness in societal trends in affordable housing, deinstitutionalization, and so forth.) Yet to the extent that our audience feels we are biased, our ability to say there is an underlying structure that needs to be understood—or anything else for that matter—is undercut. The irony is that those social scientists who are less openly self-reflexive about their own inevitable subjectivity appear more trustworthy than those who more honestly admit their allegiances, affecting the validity of their work in the eyes of policymakers.

I am speaking here, I would repeat, of *appearances*. Being an advocate researcher, of course, isn't a license to knowingly or cynically distort evidence, present falsehoods, or otherwise engage in research practices that any other researcher would not engage in. The difference is merely an open declaration of where our sympathies lie and how our research interests and agenda derive from those sympathies. But because the myth of scientific objectivity remains so strong in public discourse, my point is that we risk appearing less trustworthy than researchers who maintain a stance and appearance of scientific detachment and impartiality. Since public policy is often our bottom line—that is, we hope our research will affect public policy on homelessness, moving it toward more just, humane, and productive directions—when identification as an advocate researcher undercuts our claims to provide important insights, we have given away our only claim for why policymakers should consider our research as a basis for their deliberations rather than whatever ideas about homelessness are politically popular in a given time and place.

But let me move a step beyond appearances and openly admit that there are also precisely the dangers in advocacy research that opponents claim: that we may be blinded to the truth through our over-identification with one side of a struggle, or even that we will deliberately distort our data to support the political results we want to see.

Here is an example of the first danger. When I was researching homelessness in Santa Barbara, California in the 1980s, one of my interviewees was a guy I called Ray in the resulting book, *Homeless in Paradise* (Rosenthal 1994). Unlike almost all of my informants, I hardly knew Ray before I began interviewing him, but I had seen him around a lot at veterans' functions, knew he was a mainstay of the veterans' group, and I needed a few more veterans' voices to fill out that part of my research. Ray's story turned out to be useful, colorful, and gripping, and I was very glad to have found him. I hadn't followed my usual procedure of first hanging out with my interviewee for some time, a way of making sure I had some context for understanding the story and also, to be blunt, a way of having some confidence that what I was hearing was reasonably factual. But Ray's credentials made up for this, I felt. To doubt him would have been to doubt my friends in the veterans' group and other street people who had recommended and introduced him to me. To be honest, I don't remember worrying about it.

Ten years later I went back to Santa Barbara to explore writing a follow-up to *Homeless in Paradise*, an investigation into what had happened to my forty-four oral history respondents to be called *Ten Years Down the Road* (a project I eventually dropped). When I tried to track Ray down through the veterans' center, I was dismayed and devastated to hear from my friends there that not only had Ray permanently blown town, but that he had done so because it had been discovered by the other vets that Ray was a total fraud. He had never been a vet, but simply collected a reservoir of veterans' facts, details, and stories from vets he hung out with at veterans' centers across the country. Though his stories may still have been "true" (albeit second-hand), the inescapable fact is that he had passed himself off to me as someone he wasn't, and I had believed him in great part because I wanted to believe him. He looked as I expected him to look, he told stories that fit with what I had heard from other vets, and so, blinded by my assumptions and beliefs, I hadn't subjected his account to the same controls (i.e., familiarity based on months of interaction) I normally required. Of course it is entirely possible that I could be similarly misled by people I had known for months, but as I argue in *Homeless in Paradise*, I think familiarity with a respondent makes this considerably less likely (1994, 173–95). In any case, my political and ideological stance was (and is) that there is no reason to assume homeless people are invariably less reliable than housed people in what they tell an interviewer, and so I trusted his information more than I should have, as it turned out.

It is possible as well that my political beliefs and commitments—including being a core member of the Santa Barbara Homeless Coalition throughout the entire period I was researching homelessness—led to the second danger, that of distorting or shading the data in the service of a political need. When I began my research in the early 1980s, it was standard among citizens and political officials to subscribe to the conventional vision of homeless people as entirely responsible for their own situation, generally attributed to substance abuse. As I began my work and reading of the literature, I saw not only how inaccurate this characterization of homeless people as universally drunks and dopers was, but also how much this stereotype limited possible political responses. If homelessness was purely the fault of the homeless person (and substance abuse was widely considered an individual moral failing rather than a disease), the community had no responsibility to use public resources to respond. But if homelessness was largely attributable to social forces greater than the individual, then a political response was morally mandated.

In *Homeless in Paradise* I made these points about the relation of substance abuse to homelessness: (1) substance abuse may also be a result of homelessness as well as a cause; (2) substance abuse is a serious problem among some subgroups of the homeless population, but a negligible factor among others; (3) for some people, especially among street populations, substance abuse is a very serious problem, a cause of original homelessness and/or a complication for escape; (4) but even among those subgroups where substance abuse is most prevalent, it is not the primary issue in either becoming or remaining homeless for most members of the subgroup. These conclusions were based on what I was seeing, as far as I knew. But how much was my sight affected by my clear understanding that local officials would never take responsibility for doing anything at all for homeless people as long as they believed and/or could argue that homelessness was due to irresponsible people abusing drugs and alcohol? I did not consciously distort any evidence I had, but did I see it as clearly as I could have?

When I returned ten years later to explore the follow-up book, I sat for an hour or so with an old friend, Ken Williams, a Welfare Department worker who had long been the outreach person for street people. Over the years Ken and I had often talked together, and occasionally worked together when our concerns about a particular person overlapped. While generally supportive of the work I did, I knew that Ken felt I had either underappreciated or consciously softpedaled the devastating effects of substance abuse among the street people he worked with. I, in turn, felt he didn't fully appreciate how little a factor substance abuse was for other subgroups and how much of a barrier the image of homeless substance abuse was to political progress. As I left, Ken told me he would like me to go over to the Salvation Army before I left. "There's something at the Sally you should see," he said. "Just go in and ask anyone where 'The Wall' is." So I went over and found The Wall, a series of oak-tag posters covered with memorials for every street person who had died over the past few years. There were almost a hundred memorials when I visited. And I knew almost at once why Ken had sent me. In the last line of each was the entry, "Cause of death." And over and over, that cause was related to drugs or alcohol.

In my desire to achieve a political end—the de-demonizing of homeless people as all drunks and dopers, recasting them as largely victims of macro-processes they had no hand in creating—had I helped to minimize the issue of substance abuse among street people? Did I bear some responsibility for the deaths of some of the people I sought to help because I had airbrushed their situations to highlight what I thought would play best politically? Even now I find it hard to know the answer to that. I know, only, that biases of any kind that distort rendering an accurate picture of the real situation of homeless people—in all its complexity, with all their diversity, as it varies endlessly from moment to moment and person to person—carry risks, some of which we do not even see at the moment we are doing our work.

The Dangers of Neutrality

Advocacy, then, carries with it dangers—to the research and to the group one advocates for. Yet despite the cautionary tales I am relating, there are many ways in which the "neutral" alternative also carries its own dangers. I have previously voiced my belief that a moral question is involved, a choice of consciously or unconsciously accepting social relations as they exist or challenging those relations. But there are practical problems as well, ways in which a putative neutrality may also distort research among homeless people. Above all, it seems obvious that firsthand testimony from homeless people is an essential component for understanding homelessness, and yet why should homeless people trust an interviewer with such personal information if that interviewer appears to be a representative of mainstream society, i.e., likely not a sympathetic friend? In *Homeless in Paradise* I argued that advocacy carried with it a tradeoff: "Greater immersion into the world of homeless people in return for a possible loss of objectivity. . . . The friends I made through these political efforts became my best informants, not simply in reporting their own lives, but in directing me to others (often more hidden) who might shed light on areas of homeless life I had not seen before" (1994, 189). It was precisely because I became known in the local area as the guy doing *advocacy* research that some homeless people sought me out to tell me their stories and others agreed to be interviewed when I approached them.

Let me return to the story of Ray to illustrate this. While my advocacy stance led me, perhaps, to accept his testimony too uncritically, it could also be argued that my usual advocate stance might well have made this deception unlikely if I had had the same relationship with Ray that I did with others. That is, it might well be said that mistake was not caused by my stance as an advocate researcher so much as the fact that I had *less* interaction with him prior to our interview than I had with those I worked with in the Homeless Coalition, some of whom I knew for years before interviewing. The access to their lives that advocacy led to—political work together, casual hanging out, long philosophical discussions about the state of the world, etc.—was my best guarantee that they would not want to deceive me, and that I could not easily be deceived. My advocacy gained me entry into their daily lives.

This ground-level view, I want to argue, is an essential component of an accurate rendering of homelessness, or any other social phenomenon. It is instructive in this regard to look at the history of social movement theorizing in the United States. Until about 1960, social movements were largely regarded as a subset of "collective behavior," a category that included fads, panics, riots, and so forth, and generally attributed to the irrational activity of participants under the sway of emotion brought on by crowd situations. This ludicrous academic approach to social movements was rejected by a new wave of theorists in the 1960s, most of whom had themselves participated in the civil rights movement or other social movements of the time, and who were therefore informed enough of the on-the-ground reality of movements to dismiss the prevailing academic orthodoxy, framing social movements instead as simply another form of political activity carried out by rational actors for rational reasons. Homelessness, for all its structural causes, cannot be thoroughly understood without an intimate firsthand acquaintance with how it is experienced by homeless people. Advocacy and subjectivity here, perhaps ironically, are far more likely to lead to a rounded, "objective" view of homelessness than detached methods of survey and observation ever could.

Conclusion: Dilemmas of Advocacy

The entrée that advocacy facilitates, however, also brings some ethical dilemmas with it. Most important of these is the tension between our responsibility to homeless informants who trust an advocate researcher enough to reveal potentially dangerous information—hidden camping places, crimes committed, extent of drinking, etc.—and our desire to report as accurately and extensively as possible what we have discovered about the lives of our "subjects." One of fundamental reasons to do research in the first place is to convey the reality of homelessness to those who have not experienced it, to serve as a bridge between homeless and housed populations. Like any researcher, we want to do our job well, convey the experience in its entirety rather than airbrushing the picture. Even a pragmatic, policy-oriented approach may argue that information that may inconvenience particular homeless people (revealing where they sleep illegally, for example) may be of service to the greater homeless population—i.e., by conveying the information to the housed population that the lack of decent shelter is compelling citizens to spend their nights in parks, construction sites, and other unsafe environments. And, as we have already seen, withholding or shading information may adversely affect those we want to help in ways we may not understand at the moment we make these decisions.

But despite all of this, our first responsibility has to be to our informants. This is so, most obviously, because we routinely promise them confidentiality and assure them no harm will come to them personally from anything they tell us, but it goes far beyond that kind of formal agreement. We are involved in a reciprocal relationship in which we give some things to get other things. If one of the prices of getting candid information is that we occasionally have to withhold some of it which we think otherwise deserving of being revealed, so be it. There is no simple answer to this dilemma, only different ways of balancing claims on our information.

I close with one last dilemma, one I rarely see discussed in the literature. Much of the work advocate researchers do is ethnographic work, typically contextualized in structural data and arguments, but almost always conducted among homeless people. This makes sense in that we believe it is so important for the voices of homeless people to be heard in the debates about homelessness, and so crucial to provide that ground-level view of the situation. And yet, most of us regard homelessness as created by structural causes and the accompanying decisions of elites who preserve that structure as a given of political life. Why is it, then, that we spend so much time studying those who are rendered homeless by the decisions of elites and so little time studying the elites and their decision-making processes? Is it simply our desire to make homeless people visible? Could it also be that it is easier to gather that information than to gain entrance to the world of decision-making?

One of the great contributions of advocate researchers, concerning homelessness as well as other social problems, has been to insist on creating a fuller picture of the issues by seeing it from the point of view of those suffering from and struggling against the problem, ensuring their voice, too, is heard. In the same way, however, we need to include those who make the decisions and create the policies that frame the lives of homeless people. Gaining their trust, entering their circles, and reporting their lives, will, no doubt, produce its own package of dilemmas for the advocate researcher.

Notes

1. In this work I have assumed that researchers are themselves housed. Though this is not invariably the case, I write about it this way because: (1) it is usually the case; and (2) it is the situation I am familiar with as a housed advocate researcher. Many of the issues associated with being a *homeless* advocate researcher are quite different, requiring a different manuscript and a different author. Note also that housed researchers can advocate for a population using non-participant methods, but this too lies outside my experience and interest here.

Chapter 3
Homelessness and Drag
Kathleen R. Arnold

Abstract. Judith Butler has argued that performance and repetition are crucial to understanding identity as well as subverting it. Butler focuses on how femininity is performed and reinforced through appearance: clothing, makeup, hair style. Drag is a way to subvert identity not by replicating an authentic model but by denaturalizing the original. Something new is created in this parodic repetition rather than a mere replica. In the process, what is taken to be natural is radically deconstructed. In this essay, I will explore the drag performance homeless individuals must enact in order to be taken seriously and yet, how this performance reaffirms conventional stereotypes and hierarchies that justify the marginalization of the homeless at the same time. The repulsion and attraction to homeless dress—the homeless in *drag*, performing their homelessness for the public—crystallizes these binary modes of operation and double binds that the homeless are in. Conventional debates and neoliberal discourse reflect these contradictions, calling upon us to instead explore the homeless as political agents who can exercise positive rights and advocate on their own behalf.

Judith Butler (1990) has argued that performance and repetition are crucial to understanding identity as well as subverting it. Butler focuses on how femininity is performed and reinforced through appearance—clothing, makeup, hair style—and behaviors associated with appearance. Drag is a way to subvert identity not by replicating an authentic model but by denaturalizing the "original." A woman or man in drag shows that what is taken to be the original is a caricature and that all identity is constructed through performance and its repetition. To put it differently, something new is created in this parodic repetition rather than a mere replica. In the process, what is taken to be natural or authentic is radically deconstructed.

In this essay, I explore the drag performance homeless individuals must enact in order to be taken seriously and yet, how this performance reaffirms conventional stereotypes and hierarchies that justify the marginalization of the homeless at the same time. I focus on an experience I had nearly two decades ago as a housing advocate in a homeless shelter, when the residents and I dressed up as "homeless" to participate in a political protest in downtown Boston. A second personal experience mediates my memories and analysis: the difference between the welfare and shelter systems in Boston at the time and Washington, D.C., where I moved shortly after. I believe the subversive elements of drag in the Boston model positioned the homeless as political agents far more than the system in D.C., which was based more on a social work model and created an individualized, pathological subject.

I particularly think of Butler's work when remembering a picture that was taken of me and a toddler from the homeless shelter where I worked in 1990. Butler's analysis of gender and drag is highly relevant to not only the image of the homeless but also questions of authenticity. The picture was taken by the *Boston Globe* and was one of the only ones taken in the report of the protest mentioned above, which was on behalf of low-income housing and homeless rights. I do not know what the intentions of the photographer were that day, but the picture itself was a provocation of sorts and an affirmation of stereotypical images of the homeless. On the one hand, it most likely confirmed stereotypes about homelessness and poverty: a young white woman with long hair, wearing thrift shop clothing and a baseball hat, holding a sign in one hand and the hand of an African American girl of four in the other. At the same time, it challenged readers by: representing women as homeless rather than men; depicting an interracial relationship instead of presenting a monolithic, racialized image; and portraying the homeless as political agents rather than the conventional view that they are apathetic.

What is interesting about the *Boston Globe* picture is that the publication of that photograph suggested that I was the homeless person by virtue of my appearance, while the homeless women with whom I worked who were "dressed up as homeless" were not. At this time, I was a housing advocate in Dorchester, Massachusetts; I was just out of college, naïve (as you can already see), and it was my first "real" job. The shelter was an emergency shelter that housed roughly ten families, all headed by women, who often stayed an average of six months. It was located in a one-mile strip in which a murder occurred nearly every day that I worked there and at a time when poverty and homelessness were increasing in this area. When the shelter residents and I heard about the protest at Government Center, we all decided to go. The women decided they wanted to dress up to "look homeless" and encouraged me to do the same. This fact in and of itself is telling: the idea that to be taken seriously as homeless, one must look homeless. Just as being a woman must be "authenticated" every day through outward signs of femininity, the homeless are pressured to conform to stereotypical images in order to be accepted as authentically poor. For example, it has been found that beggars who look too neat are perceived as begging under false pretenses—thus, there is a motivation for the homeless to actually look ragged, unshaven, and unclean on occasion. And in fact, there is a constant pre-occupation among city dwellers and politicians with giving money to people who are not really homeless, who are begging and yet not truly poor, or who may use the money for the wrong thing. Of course, appearance is even more complicated because if an individual truly dresses as homeless, according to conventional views, s/he is also perceived to be part of the hardcore (that is, undeserving) homeless rather than an individual or family who are temporarily displaced due to fire or natural disaster.

But my story should challenge this superficial method of judgment and un-derlying normative demand that the homeless "dress homeless" in order to be believed. First of all, unlike the homeless women with whom I worked, I didn't really have to "dress up"—I already wore thrift shop clothing, including a man's overcoat, on a daily basis. At the time, I thought this was not only fashionable in an alternative way but also a challenge to shelter workers who tried to establish their class superiority to the homeless. The shelter residents were far neater, wore makeup and jewelry and would not have been caught dead in my clothes. The one article of clothing the women foisted upon me was an NWA (Niggers With Attitude) hat. Although I listened to rap, I didn't know what the group was. In contrast to my "already homeless" look, the residents sifted through bags of donations to get the right look. (This, of course, says something about what peo-ple think is fit to donate to the homeless: old or ripped clothing, dirty socks, worn sneakers.) As they altered their appearance to *look* homeless, the women were laughing uproariously. Not only were these homeless women dressing in drag to challenge images of authenticity (and yet to pander to conventional views of the poor), but they were also engaging in what Butler (1990, 146) calls "subversive laughter."[1] Both drag and subversive laughter mock the idea of an original while showing that the normative pressure to dress homeless can be challenged by informal political agency.

And so, perhaps because I was wearing my real clothes and perhaps because I often spent time with the little girl, the photographer took our picture, which ended up on the front page of the newspaper. That the photographer chose to take a picture of a young white woman holding an African American girl's hand I think is telling. As discussed above, the picture implies a mixed-race relation-ship, single motherhood, and young motherhood—all transgressions that have justified the stereotype of welfare recipients as being disaffiliated, irresponsible, lacking in self-discipline, and able-bodied but poor. The picture can also be viewed as subversive in Butler's sense—and it was. The photographer could have taken the picture to illustrate diversity and to push readers to think about race, youth, and homelessness. It could have been a provocation in a historically racially divided city. From another point of view, even though I was dressed in my own clothing, I was also in "drag." The simultaneous authenticity of the picture along with its drag performance should challenge the idea of any monolithic conception of the homeless, not to mention the notion of an original.

A few days after the protest, the same women who gave me the hat teased me about wearing it and having it imprinted in a major newspaper. As they explained, NWA sang violent songs full of misogynist lyrics. They had set me up and this became the subject of jokes and teasing for another week or two. Again, they employed subversive laughter in a homeless shelter, a site of normative social demands and bureaucratic forces that often positioned them as subordinate. Indeed, these homeless women defied all stereotypes about the poor and homeless: that they are politically apathetic, ignorant, and can only comprehend conventional views. Clearly, they wanted to dress in drag in a political protest that they cared about to both uphold and challenge images of the homeless. To Butler, this is the most subversive of all moves: using the very material or actions that subordinate a group as the condition of their resistance. They also demonstrated a sophisticated view of matters of race and gender when explaining the "meaning" of a group like NWA and why it was so funny to see the picture in the newspaper. Finally, although most of the women had never traveled very far outside of their neighborhood, they were not intimidated by occupying public space normally associated with white elites (something the homeless are rarely allowed to do legally), protesting in a "foreign" area, and traveling into new territory.

Unlike the unavoidable physical markers of gender and race (granted that these categories are largely socially constructed), homelessness is truly a performance, whether of "authenticity" (which Butler aptly challenges) or "drag" and therefore, subversion. The performances of race and gender also matter in evaluating the homeless performance. As much as homeless garb, a racialized and gendered image often confirms conventional beliefs about public housing, homelessness, and welfare. That some of the homeless must perform this drag show on a daily basis has ties to the recent past. Historically, the poor have been viewed as unkempt and pathological in various ways, but since the Chicago School made the poor and homeless an object of study, making poverty a pathology that could be examined "scientifically," unkemptness no longer just means unkemptness. Appearing homeless signifies disaffiliation, drug addiction, crack use, alcoholism, single motherhood, irresponsibility, lacking a work ethic, and a host of other social ills. The circumstances that brought about this shift in views are ignored and instead, the image has been naturalized and dehistoricized. For this reason, homeless conditions are mistaken for innate personality traits. Moreover, when the social sciences have made the homeless an object of study to be understood from a distance and when an elitist norm of rationality is applied, appearances matter more and local truths—as Michel Foucault (1984) would say—a lot less. The history of the margins is excluded and a monolithic norm of behavior is applied. The more the object is studied, the less the context matters.

For instance, in the 1980s and 1990s, neoliberal policies became more predominant and so the structure of labor relations began to change. A lot of affordable housing stock had been lost in the 1960s and 1970s and combined with changes for workers—less stability, increasingly lower relative wages, the loss of benefits, and the decline of unions—economic anxieties increased. The War on Poverty in the 1960s and 1970s became a war on the homeless by the 1990s. Public space for the homeless began to shrink as local ordinances increasingly banned life-sustaining activities. Shelters, which were often filled to capacity, frequently adopted punitive rules in conjunction with harsher local legislation. Shelter residents were often not allowed to store their belongings and so the individual with a shopping cart or the "bag lady" increasingly came into the public eye. The contraction of public space without a corresponding expansion of alternatives for showering, access to toilets, and sleeping inevitably leads to an unkempt appearance, more significant health problems, and the criminalized homeless person who tries to survive in the public space s/he is simultaneously excluded from. To put it simply, many of the homeless have had no means to maintain a neat appearance. Further, this unkempt appearance could serve as a sort of security system—repulsing would-be rapists or robbers. And as discussed above, unkemptness validates one's authenticity when requesting money or aid.

However, this image not only creates divisions but also obscures them. In contrast to the singular image of homelessness, there are divides in the shelter system: more men are on the streets and/or utilize emergency shelters, while more women are in longer term shelters (including the emergency shelter in which I worked, where stays averaged six months). Thus the splits are between poor men and women and those who face the streets versus those who reside in temporary shelters. For those on the street, local ordinances continue to marginalize them and deny them access to public facilities, if these facilities even exist, and thus the appearance of "street people" must be seen as one type of drag performance coerced and enforced by circumstance. Alternatively, if the homeless in more permanent types of shelter appear homeless, this can be a product of shelter rules or a conscious decision to "perform poverty" in exchange for aid.

In all cases, however, they are conforming to a public image that demands that these individuals appear poor. Additionally, it is interesting that the majority of the homeless are "invisible" in some sense—whether it is women and families staying in emergency shelters or homeless communities who reside in trailer parks, campgrounds, urban squats, and under bridges. Nevertheless, only one image of the homeless is prevalent: the dirty, scruffy, smelly individual who begs for money on a street corner or sleeps in a doorway. The image of the homeless is never mediated by the acknowledgment of these circumstances—the gaze continues to be on the "other," effacing the "self."

Perhaps as neoliberal ideas have increasingly guided public policy and poverty is progressively seen as a problem of individual responsibility and shortcomings, the mainstream want the poorest to *perform* their poverty—to be a spectacle that mitigates tension and brings the focus away from broader economic trends. The homeless in drag enact a performance that is supposed to "prove" that they are poor from individual failures. Anxieties about the weakening employment contract and greater polarization of wealth, outsourcing of jobs and loss of steady medical care, can all be mediated by the homeless. The *spectacle* of homeless poverty can reassure the middle class that they will never sink to these depths.

Nevertheless, this drag performance is a double-edged sword. The individual who looks truly homeless is an object of pity but also fear—thus, it is demanded than an individual looks homeless in order to be treated as such but this same person is not allowed to approach someone at an ATM, sit on a park bench, sleep on a public beach, or lounge in a library on a cold day. Some local ordinances have also ordered that the homeless not misrepresent themselves through wearing a military uniform if they never served in the military, for example. In contrast, the individual who hides his or her homelessness may not be publicly repudiated but may not receive outright charity or aid.

This contradictory demand of the homeless is paralleled by contradictory ideas about economic class in the United States. Clearly, the United States prides itself on the American Dream and myths of financial mobility. However, there is just as strong of a tendency to see the poor as permanently so, as the rhetoric of "broken windows" and a culture of dependency suggest. If stereotypes about race and gender are added to these beliefs, the tendency to naturalize poverty in conventional debates and images is strengthened. It logically follows that the idea of social mobility is central to American national self-understanding, and thus the Supreme Court refuses to recognize poverty as a suspect classification because it is a circumstance that can change. However, the image of the homeless reveals a much more static reality: homelessness is interpreted as a pathology, a permanent condition, and an expression of individual failure.

This desire to see the homeless as suffering from permanent conditions that caused their homelessness and yet to express a belief—tacit or not—in economic mobility is a contradiction also reflected in laws at the federal and local levels. The very poor are viewed as being responsible for their own condition and thus, laws tend to be punitive in nature, often cutting off eligible recipients for "non-compliance" and yet suffering from crippling pathologies that are treated as if permanent. The repulsion and attraction to homeless dress—the homeless in *drag*, performing their homelessness for the public—crystallize these binary modes of operation and double binds that the homeless are in. Conventional debates and neoliberal discourse reflect these contradictions.

If all of this is true, how subversive is the drag show performed by the women I worked with if status quo views are merely reaffirmed? Or is the value of subversion for the group itself—not letting themselves be defined by the outside world, participating in a protest in the center of the city, and not remaining confined to a shelter in a deadly neighborhood? My answer relies on another personal experience, and I would like to suggest that the shelter system's perspective of homelessness matters. Just as the context of reception matters when examining how immigrants fare in a host country, the way a city's workers—from welfare caseworkers to housing advocates to the police—treat the poor and homeless is also important in determining the meaning of the homeless' actions.

In Boston, I was hired in a shelter to be a housing advocate. My job was first to help the women navigate the bureaucracies dealing with housing and housing subsidies. But it was also to dispense legal information to prevent homelessness from occurring again. As I filled out intake forms for each of the families, they were required to discuss the reasons for the loss of their homes. In all of the cases, they had been treated illegally, unfairly, or their homelessness was the product of insufficient services. For example, one woman had been behind in rent and had discussed this with her landlord and yet one day she came home and there was a lock on her door. All of her possessions were outside when she and her three young daughters arrived home. Unbeknownst to her, this was an illegal action. Others lost their housing because they were behind on their rent. Still others had been "doubling up" in apartments or public housing and therefore, violating the leases of these dwellings and putting the tenants at risk. Another woman had failed to "recertify" her apartment in public housing, meaning that she had not signed the annual form required to confirm that she still needed to live in her building. Eviction on these grounds is also illegal, but when someone has been evicted from public housing, they are technically barred from it for life.

One woman—one of the most charismatic women I have met—had just been released from federal prison and because of state cutbacks, there were no programs to help her and her children find housing. They lived in an abandoned building until they moved into our shelter. Yet another woman had simply "aged out" of foster care and become homeless—this has become the norm for a significant number of foster children. My job was to give them legal information about their particular circumstances to help prevent future abuses. Housing advocates regularly met to exchange political and legal tactics to protect their "clients" and grouped together to participate in political protests, voting drives, and show videos like "Housing Not Bombs." Nearly all of our interactions with homeless residents treated them as citizens—rights-bearing individuals—who needed more information to protect themselves. Together with some of the residents, we filed discrimination suits at the Massachusetts Commission Against Discrimination (granted that this was largely symbolic, as the wait list for cases was several years long). We also discussed racial discrimination when looking for new housing.

This is not to idealize the shelter system in that city at that particular time. The way the shelter residents were treated by some welfare workers and people outside the neighborhood—particularly prospective landlords—shocked me. The very causes of homelessness leading to their situation are evidence that societal forces were going against them. Nevertheless, the shelter system and even the role of the housing advocate also positioned them as citizens: as individuals with inalienable rights and duties who just needed more information in order to secure more stable housing. This served, I think, as a buffer against the outside world: media images, police disrespect, open racism, and sexism. The shelter residents responded positively to the message that they had rights and that they deserved to occupy public space just as much as anyone else. When we watched the video "Housing Not Bombs," many of them cried. During the voting drive, they all signed up. All of us attended the protest described at the beginning of this chapter together. And all have since procured stable housing.

After about six months at this job, I decided to move to Washington, D.C. for personal reasons and thought that I would find a position in a shelter based on my experience in Boston. Homeless advocates like Mitch Snyder had radicalized the debate on homelessness in this city and I was excited about the possibility of doing even more advocacy work. But after a year of looking, I was never offered a job. Ironically because I spent a full year looking for a position and had interviews for nearly every job I applied to, I was able to "tour" the shelter system—from the House of Ruth shelters around Capitol Hill, to Jubilee Housing in Adams Morgan, to Catholic Charities in various sites inside and outside of the city, and many others in and around the D.C. area. Time after time, I was told that I didn't get the job because I didn't have social work experience. Ideally, they wanted someone with a Master's degree in social work who would work long hours for low pay. In nearly every visit, different programs like Alcoholics Anonymous were emphasized. As I explained my position in Boston, many of the directors thought it was very interesting—in the same way that it is interesting that some people eat with their hands rather than a fork and knife. The social work model, centered on a homeless figure who was thought to be poor due to his or her pathologies, permeated this system.

Later on, while I was in graduate school at University of California, Los Angeles (UCLA), I interviewed some shelter workers for a class on homelessness. They, too, emphasized that shelter residents could only help themselves when they admitted their issues and enrolled in self-help programs. Religious doctrine mixed with these programs to create an apolitical understanding of homelessness. In one shelter, I mentioned that in Washington, D.C. I had to stay on people's couches while I worked part time jobs in my quest to find a housing advocacy job. The worker insisted that I must have had problems with drugs or alcohol if that was the case.

Conclusion

In the midst of an affordable housing crisis that still exists today, an economy that increasingly divides poor and rich, and inadequate medical care for most Americans, these systems still want to blame the homeless and treat them as former citizens who have abdicated their rights in exchange for aid. The Boston system was not ideal, but in terms of analyzing how subversive a drag performance can be, the context of reception was far more open there—even if it had its contradictions and tensions—than in D.C. or Los Angeles. Homelessness was politicized, discrimination was challenged (if not defeated), and housing and child welfare issues intersected with an understanding of rights. The shelter systems in D.C. and Los Angeles at the time, in contrast, forced the homeless to stage another drag performance: one in which they had to admit to pathologies, show that they had internalized ascetic norms, and submit to their "superiors." Elliot Liebow's work on the homeless in D.C. (1968) evidences that shelter residents challenged this sort of thinking and thus, the system did not push them down entirely. Nevertheless, it must be asked what would happen if a shelter system treated the homeless as political agents first and foremost? What if their possessions were seen as private property and their appearance merely that: *appearance*? What if their cardboard boxes were not bulldozed and they were allowed to engage in free speech, approaching all other individuals in public spaces? The drag show of poverty and homelessness would be from one political equal to another, a new enactment of freedom of speech, a provocation to discuss and debate rather than exclude and expunge. Public space might become truly public and poorer individuals a crucial part of the landscape rather than a group to be cleaned up and cleared out.

Butler's analysis reminds researchers and advocates to denaturalize the homeless image and to understand the pressures the homeless are under to simultaneously conform to this representation of homelessness (i.e., pathology) if they want help at the same time they are expected to appear "normal" (i.e., housed) if they want to inhabit public space, work, or even keep their children. Rather than fixating on the homeless alone, we must ask how laws, shelter rules, interpersonal interactions, and racism, sexism, and class bias lead to a distorted view of the very poor. Today, instead of exploring the circumstances that lead to these contradictory messages or analyzing external circumstances forcing the homeless to carry bags, not shower, urinate in public, or look unkempt, appearance is taken as an unchanging reality, marking the abject.

The treatment of the homeless as political agents who can exercise positive rights and advocate on their own behalf is not the dominant model in shelter systems, the media, or academic writing. But I believe that if only basic needs are met, issues of political inequality and limited agency will never be addressed—political action and status must always come first. Then when the very poor perform a drag show, it will foster democratic debate and questioning rather than the reiteration of second class citizenship.

Notes

1. The full sentence reads: "Hence, there is a subversive laughter in the pastiche-effect of parodic practices in which the original, the authentic, and the real are themselves constituted as effects."

Chapter 4
Writing the Streets: Dilemmas of Depiction
Trenna Valado

Abstract. Most scholars who study the topic of homelessness are aiming, in part, to draw attention to the economic, social, and political roots of homelessness, with the explicit or implicit goal of effecting change. Yet the very act of writing about homelessness often sparks dilemmas for scholars. How can we present the realities of street life, such as the prevalence of mental illness and drug use, without reinforcing negative stereotypes? Will our findings be used to further legitimate the criminalization of homelessness? Is it possible to discuss the nuances of street life accurately without either romanticizing the positive aspects or overly dramatizing the negative ones? How do we examine the role of personal choice in homeless people's lives while still emphasizing the need for comprehensive social services? Primary among the many issues that arise in the writing process is whether and what to advocate for in terms of recommendations to ameliorate homelessness. As scholars, do we have an obligation to suggest and advocate for changes that are realistic within the wider economic, social, and political context, or should we instead offer radical critiques that delve into the underlying causes of homelessness? At the same time, it is sometimes unclear what we should be advocating for given the diversity of the homeless community: for those few who choose an outdoor lifestyle, it seems largely an issue of personal freedom and the curtailment thereof in contemporary society, whereas for those who want to escape the streets, it seems more an issue of the restrictiveness and inadequacy of current social service provision. This chapter explores these and other dilemmas that arise during the process of researching and writing about homelessness.

When I started thinking about a topic for my contribution to this volume, many things came to mind very quickly. After all, research on homelessness, and indeed any research involving people, especially marginalized ones, is rife with ethical issues, including considerations of if/when/how to engage in advocacy. I could write about how I presented myself and my research to homeless individuals, whether you can truly obtain "informed consent" for research with ultimately unknown outcomes, whether to pay people and the implications of doing so, how to set boundaries with participants, whether it is justified to do research that may not in any way improve the lives of the participants. The list could go on, but the point is obvious—where to focus, what to mention, and what to prioritize are all ethical considerations.

Despite this plethora of ideas and issues, I just could not get started on the actual writing. I thought a lot, and read even more, but I kept avoiding the writing process. Then I fully realized why—the very act of writing is itself an ethical issue. How do I depict the "players" in my research? What is my point? What is it all for? It is a paralysis that has kept me from writing much of substance on my research since completing my doctoral dissertation several years ago. In *Writing for Social Scientists*, Becker (2007) discusses the fear of writing, especially in terms of having other people read your work. I experience some of this fear every time I write about homelessness, or indeed about any important social issue. How will my writing be used, and more fundamentally, will it be used at all? Can I convey my thoughts clearly enough that they will not be perverted into a condemnation of homeless people, social service providers, or other well-intentioned people involved in trying to minimize homelessness? What, if anything, should I be advocating for? This chapter aims to shed light on some of the myriad issues that arise during the writing process, focusing in particular on the dilemmas of depiction that anyone doing social science research must face.

Portraying Self/Methods

Perhaps I should begin with some background on my research. I initially became interested in the topic of homelessness while I was pursuing my Master's degree in archaeology. I lived in Tucson, Arizona at the time, where there was a growing controversy over homeless people's presence in public spaces. I was busy analyzing prehistoric Native American settlement patterns while the city proceeded to pass a series of ordinances designed to oust homeless people from various venues—a ban that prohibited people from sitting or lying down on sidewalks in commercial districts, a ban on solicitation from roadways or medians, a ban on camping on city property. All of this led me to wonder where exactly homeless people were supposed to go and how they were dealing with the various restrictions on their use of space. Suddenly, the geographical movements of people long dead seemed much less deserving of scholarly attention than those of the homeless people with whom I interacted on a daily basis. So I finished up my thesis and moved into the realm of applied anthropology to pursue my doctoral studies.

I focused the ensuing research on homeless people's use of urban space, a topic I soon came to realize had attracted the attention of scholars from numerous social science disciplines (e.g., Amster 2004; 2008; Duncan 1983; Ellickson 1996; Evans 2001; Hoch 1990; Mitchell 2003; Rosenthal 1994; Rowe and Wolch 1990; Ruddick 1996; Snow and Mulcahy 2001; Wolch et al. 1993; Wolch and Rowe 1992; Wright 1997). I became involved with a county-wide coalition of social service providers and began talking with service workers from various agencies. I also interviewed law enforcement officials, city and county employees, and representatives from business coalitions, all with the goal of better understanding the issue of homelessness from multiple perspectives. But ultimately the main component of my research consisted of spending lots of time with homeless people in public locations throughout the city and the surrounding county. I conducted formal interviews with sixty individuals, twenty of whom I hired as Research Assistants to document their experiences through photography and journaling.

I offer this background as an entry point to discussing the challenges I later faced in writing about my research methods. When I set out to summarize my methods in my dissertation, I presented the standard spiel: interviews, hundreds of hours spent hanging out with people and accompanying them in their daily activities, enlisting people as Research Assistants, all intertwining to achieve the laudable goal of "triangulation." But then I felt compelled to add the following to my account (Valado 2006, 102–03):

> It is difficult to express the relationships that developed: people offered to and did protect me; they guided me through a landscape that is too often visible yet so rarely seen; they laughed and sometimes cried with me; they shared not just their resources but also their darkest memories and brightest hopes; and then they almost always thanked me, not for the meager compensation for their time (several individuals could have made more money in the same amount of time by pursuing their usual trades) but for listening and just as equally for wanting to listen. Even people who I did not formally interview often talked at length with me about their lives and experiences. In addition to sharing the bleak side of homelessness that the literature so often portrays, they also showed me the positive aspects: joking with friends on a sunny warm day in the park; decades-long bonds between travelers who meet up yearly in Tucson; street families providing the love and acceptance that an abusive "home" never did; and the pride that inspires people to hold their heads high despite society's judgment. Amid this, saying that I triangulated data gained from participant observation, interviews, and the efforts of the Research Assistants seems a rather dry methodological statement.

The point I was trying to make by discussing my methods in such a personal way is that I do not believe that the integrity or validity of research findings can be based on a simple, objective description of data collection activities. Instead, some provision must be made for the actual experience of collecting data, for how "close" one gets to research participants. I again quote rather extensively from my dissertation, mostly because I do not believe I can rephrase it much better today (Valado 2006, 104):

> I cannot claim to truly comprehend the experience of homelessness. No one who has not lived it can—no amount of participant observation or number of nights spent sleeping on the streets can replicate what it is like to have no alternative. But I can say I understand the contradictions that street life entails: the constant harassment by day versus the quiet solitude of a clear night; the struggle to make ends meet versus the freedom of having no commitments; the denigration by social service agencies versus the camaraderie and support of peers. I felt the draw of the positive aspects: I had moments of wanting to "go native," and I was saddened when I left behind new friends in each research location. This, more than any statement of methodological techniques, makes me confident that I was at least moderately successful in seeing homelessness through the eyes of homeless people themselves.

Talking about my research in this way was then, and is still now, a deeply ethical issue for me. My goal was to understand homeless people's experiences as well as I possibly could, because I felt a deep commitment to convey that information accurately. I certainly did not intend to simply chronicle individual life stories, to let people "speak for themselves." Instead, I wanted to use their stories to highlight the ways in which the economic and social transformations associated with neoliberalism have left many people without a space (both literally and figuratively) in contemporary cities. Thus the personal tone I chose to use in discussing my research methods was an attempt to convey my belief that I successfully retained the essence of people's stories in the process of disarticulating them for analytical purposes.

Portraying Others: "The Homeless"

In writing about people who are experiencing homelessness, one of the first issues that arises is terminology. The word "homeless" carries so many connotations, such as safety, security, belonging, and family. Thus, labeling someone as "homeless" implies a lack of these things, even when those one is referring to may not feel this sense of deficit. The term "homeless" is actually a relatively recent label, having been popularized by researchers and social service providers in the 1980s amid a surge in homelesssness that resulted in increased diversity among the homeless population. Prior to this, people who would now be called "homeless" were labeled in a variety of ways: beggars, bums, hobos, tramps, transients, vagrants, vagabonds, and perhaps more charitably, mendicants or itinerant laborers. The term "homeless" emerged, in part, as a way to draw attention to the underlying structural causes of the growth in homelessness, particularly the increasing lack of affordable housing and living-wage jobs.

Yet many people who meet the standard definition of "homeless" espoused by the U.S. Department of Housing and Urban Development[1] do not actually consider themselves homeless. Of the sixty people I interviewed during my research, only thirty-two referred to themselves as "homeless." The remainder used a variety of terms to describe themselves, including living out, sleeping out, traveling, street tramp, street soldier, and home-free. In writing about the research participants, I tried to respect this by using these and various other terms to describe people who were living outside. This was especially essential when referring to people who explicitly said that they had a "home," regardless of where the place they described as home was located. The self-appellations offered by participants were linked to many other aspects of their lives, including whether they expressed a desire to stop living outside. And this fact raised another important issue that became problematic when I set out to write about my findings, namely if and how to discuss the role that "choice" played in the lives of research participants.

For many social service workers, simply the idea that someone might "choose" to live outside is automatically considered evidence of mental illness. At the same time, suggesting that some individuals do choose an outdoor lifestyle runs the risk of providing fodder for the "blame the victim" perspective on homelessness (i.e., the idea that homeless people are ultimately responsible for their situation due to a variety of poor choices) and for cuts to social services. This is such a sensitive subject that I automatically feel the need to toss in the caveat that the vast majority of people experiencing homelessness are not doing so by choice. But the truth remains that a small percentage of individuals do describe living outside as a matter of choice. Should we dismiss this as evidence of mental instability or avoid discussing it for fear of how it may be perverted, or should we instead try to unravel why this might be the case? Given that most depictions of homelessness emphasize the intense suffering that many people experience (and for good reason), it seems almost unfathomable that some individuals might choose the lifestyle. But this neglects the fundamental fact that street life can be the preferable choice out of an array of unappealing choices or even the best conceivable choice for some people. Marvasti (2003, 53) makes a similar point in his nuanced critique of ethnographic studies on homelessness:

> The assumed importance of being part of mainstream society is so great in Liebow's text [1968] that he is astonished that more homeless people do not take their own lives. Inverting this assumption of a universal sense of normality involves viewing the status of homelessness from the subjects' point of view. For example, it may be that some homeless people find it astonishing that members of mainstream society are so attached to their status—or as I once heard a homeless man say. 'It sucks to be a citizen.'

The preceding discussion of choice reflects my own struggle about how to discuss the topic in my writing, and there are several other aspects of the causes of homelessness that present similar conundrums. Primary among these are the issues of mental illness and substance use. It is undeniable that many people who live outside exhibit signs of mental illness and that a significant percentage of the homeless community partakes in intoxicants to some degree. What is less clear is whether these things can legitimately be considered the "cause" of their homelessness. Marvasti (2003, 26) makes the following argument, which is equally applicable to substance use: "Two issues complicate the task of attributing mental illness as the cause of homelessness. First, there is the issue of how street survival strategies may be labeled as antisocial or pathological by inadequately trained researchers and poorly designed research projects. . . . Second, the critics of the mental illness approach have pointed out the issue of causal order, questioning which came first: homelessness or mental illness." Despite the seemingly obvious causal fallacy in operation here, many social service workers and members of the general public attribute homelessness first and foremost to mental illness, substance use, or a combination of the two. This leaves researchers to struggle over how to talk about these subjects without feeding into the widespread "individual pathologies" perspective on homelessness that typically focuses on personal behaviors or attributes while neglecting the underlying structural causes of homelessness. Complicating things even further is the fact that causes often imply solutions—so if the "cause" of homelessness is mental illness or substance use, then surely the "solution" is more and better services. Yet this approach, which has dominated public policy in the United States for decades, has clearly been ineffective (to be generous). The point is that any researcher who hopes to better the lives of people living outside is faced with the dilemma of whether to gloss over topics that represent an important component of many homeless people's experiences in order to avoid implicitly legitimating failed public policy.

Another issue that presents problems in writing about homelessness relates to service use, or more specifically, the non-use of services. Numerous researchers have cataloged the myriad reasons that some people shun the social service system (Baxter and Hopper 1981, 15; Koegel et al. 1990, 102–03; Rahimian et al. 1992, 1321; Rowe and Wolch 1990, 198–99; Wagner 1993; Wolch et al. 1993, 161; Wright 1995). The complaints that such individuals express range from the practical (e.g., concerns about safety and sanitation) to the ideological (e.g., perceiving service providers as "poverty pimps"). Many people also report feeling abused and degraded in service settings (Buck et al. 2004, 519; Marvasti 2003; Underwood 1993, 298; Williams 1996; Wright 1997, 44–52) and thus may avoid services in an attempt to preserve their dignity (Hopper 2006, 219; Wright 1995, 46). Despite these valid reasons why some individuals avoid services, their reluctance or refusal to accept proffered assistance is often viewed as stubbornness or ungratefulness by service providers, who may lump them into the category of "service resistant" or "hard to serve." Many researchers, of course, hope to counter this perception by shedding light on street people's experiences with the social service system. But even talking about non-use of services runs the risk of having one's insights pulled out of context and ultimately used to legitimate the idea that the reason people remain homeless is simply because they refuse to accept help. Even more dangerous, perhaps, is writing about those individuals who frequent social services but do not have any intention of using them to get off the streets. These people who "abuse" the service system already serve as the archetype for groups that seek to cut funding for social programs, and the possibility of providing fodder for such rhetoric should give any researcher pause.

This concern about reinforcing negative stereotypes continually emerges in research on homelessness, and I could offer more examples, such as how to discuss violence and illegal behavior among street people. But instead I want to shift focus to talk about an issue that I struggled with throughout my writing process, namely the overarching tone that is used to present findings. Marvasti (2003, 40) touches on this issue in his analysis of literary works about homelessness: "Perhaps the most common textual constructions of homelessness takes the form of romantic accounts. Here, homelessness is represented as exotic and as the last bastion of authenticity in modern life." He is speaking of accounts that emphasize the freedom of life on the road, the sense of escaping the fetters of responsibility and conformity. In contrast, much of the scholarly work on homelessness paints a very bleak picture, emphasizing the physical and mental hardships of living outside. There is certainly no doubt that street life is hard and that highlighting that fact is important. Yet my research left me feeling that such portrayals do not accurately reflect the realities of homelessness. The people I interacted with during my fieldwork expressed both deep suffering and profound joy. Perhaps it is my anthropolgical gaze that gives me a sense of unease when I read the many scholarly depictions of homelessness that almost seem to contain an implicit assumption that poverty is synonymous with misery. In my own writing, I wanted to find some way to talk about both the positive aspects and the hardships of street life, to seek some middle ground between romanticizing and dramatizing homelessness. At times, it seemed like it would be more efficacious to speak solely of the suffering in order to engender sympathy and support for homeless people, but total neglect of the positive aspects seemed like an oversimplification and even a betrayal of the research participants.

Many of the dilemmas I faced in trying to write about people who live outside are partly rooted in the broader issue of diversity. The label *homeless* groups together such a huge array of individuals that any attempt to talk about them as "the homeless" becomes problematic. To illustrate my point, I offer a few details from my research. The sixty individuals I interviewed ranged from teenagers to senior citizens, whose length of time being homeless varied from less than one month to several decades. They reported at least seventeen different reasons for becoming homeless, and used twenty-four self-appellations to describe themselves. They came from twenty-seven states and five countries. Some of them used services intensively, whereas others avoided them completely. Most stayed in Tucson throughout the year, while a few migrated around the country seasonally. Given such diversity, it is hardly surprising that trying to discuss their lives and experiences in a meaningful way is a very challenging endeavor.

Portraying Others: "The Public"

Another very diverse group that often gets homogenized by a label is "the public." This includes people who have only passing interactions with homeless people as well as those who are intensively involved with them on an almost daily basis. I am particularly interested here in the latter group, which is itself very diverse, including social service workers, government representatives, law enforcement officials, and business owners. The voices of these groups are rarely included in scholarly accounts of homelessness, despite their substantial impact on the lives and experiences of people who live outside. I tried to remedy this in my own research by conducting interviews with individuals in the various groups, becoming involved in a county-wide coalition of social service providers, volunteering with providers who do outreach to urban campers, and riding along with city police officers and county sheriff's deputies.

I initially believed that such activities would be quite difficult, that I would be confronted with opinions on homelessness and homeless people so diametrically opposed to my own that I would be frustrated and even infuriated. But what I experienced was something quite different. I found myself understanding their points of view and the constraints under which they operate. As such, it became very important to me to represent their perspectives as accurately and respectfully as those of the homeless research participants. I really did not feel like I had any models for how to do this. Much of the scholarly literature painted the issue of homelessness almost in terms of "good guys" and "bad guys"—the poor helpless street person taking on the Goliath of the harsh, unsympathetic "system." And this simply was not an accurate framing of my own findings. So I struggled to find a way to discuss my research that demonstrated both the problems inherent in the system and the powerlessness of many of the individuals who work within the various systems that affect homeless people.

One manifestation of this dilemma was the issue of causality. As I mentioned in the preceding section, many social service workers seem to attribute homelessness to mental illness or substance use, and the same could certainly be said of law enforcement personnel and other groups. But the key word here is "seem"—when I first asked people about the causes of homelessness, they did immediately refer to these and other individual-level factors. However, when I probed deeper and observed more extensive discussions, it quickly became apparent that they understood that these "causes" were actually the proximate causes of homelessness rather than the root causes. In other words, many of the people who regularly interacted with street people believed that certain personal attributes, such as mental illness or substance use, could precipitate a bout of homelessness, but that the underlying reasons for homelessness were related to broader structural issues of entrenched poverty and inequality. It really should not be surprising that service providers and law enforcement officials have a nuanced understanding of the forces at work in the production of homelessness. They are, after all, often the first to encounter newcomers to the streets and thus see the variety of the homeless population, including children and families. In essence, although the "system" may ultimately operate in a way that is malicious toward homeless people, it is critical to note that the individuals making up that system often have the best of intentions and do not necessarily agree with the policies they are tasked to enforce.

A few examples might help illustrate my point here. Several scholars have documented that service providers often work with homeless people to construct service-worthy identities that will help them gain entry into various services (e.g., Hopper 2006; Marvasti 2003). This frequently entails "fitting" them into categories for which services are available, including the categories of "mentally ill," "addict," or both. But doing this does not mean that the workers actually buy into the individual-pathologies explanation of homelessness. In reality, it is more a case of expedience than endorsement—service workers are confronted with people in need of immediate help and seek to get them that assistance, even though doing so may result in inadvertently reinforcing the notion that personal behaviors or attributes are somehow the cause of homelessness. Similarly, officials within the City of Tucson government recognized the underlying causes of homelessness and tried to take steps to both combat these causes and prevent further deterioration of conditions for those who were already homeless. The city instituted a living wage for contractors and hoped that this would serve as a model to encourage businesses to raise wages, thus preventing people from becoming homeless. The City Council also thwarted initial attempts to pass legal ordinances that would restrict street people's use of public space, such as the aforementioned sidewalk ban. In addition, social service providers and city representatives worked together for several years to try to find some place to establish a legal camping area for homeless people after razing a large encampment on city land due to persistent pressure from neighborhood groups.

Many of the seemingly powerful groups that have a role in policymaking recognize the systemic contributors to homelessness, but they often feel powerless to enact policy changes that would address the underlying causes. This was clearly demonstrated through my involvement in a committee that was tasked with developing a plan to end homelessness in ten years. The committee, which was formed when the federal government began encouraging communities to create these plans, included not just social service providers but also city, county, and state representatives, business owners, and law enforcement officials. A recurring topic of debate among the varied committee members was how to refer to the plan. Although this may seem like a trivial issue of semantics, it actually revealed a deep ambivalence about our endeavor. Several people, including myself, objected to the use of the term "end." I was by no means the most vocal in pointing out that no amount of funding for job training, drug treatment, behavioral health care, or other services was going to resolve the underlying problems of lack of affordable housing and living wage jobs. Some people wanted to scrap the whole notion of "ending" homelessness and instead refer to it as a plan to "minimize" homelessness.

The core issue here was that many of the committee members realized that the structural causes of homelessness would keep operating to push people onto the streets and that social service "solutions" were never going to be adequate to end homelessness. Yet the committee certainly did not have the power to effect change in the structures producing homelessness, and so we did our best to propose expansions in service provision that might help some people avoid or escape the streets. This experience, among others, led me to write a section in my dissertation entitled "a strange equilibrium," in which I noted that no one seemed happy with the current situation but no one could figure out how to change it. I discussed the phenomena in specific reference to homeless people's use of urban space, but it is equally applicable to almost every facet of homelessness.

Many of the contributors to this volume emphasize the importance of "studying up." Through my own work I came to fully recognize just how critical it is to make an effort to understand the perceptions of the different groups that impact the lives of homeless people. Without this wider context, I could have offered many critiques—of the failures of the social service system, of the fundamental injustice of legal ordinances restricting the use of public space, of the intolerance and misperceptions of neighborhood associations and business coalitions. While all these things are true, there are complex reasons behind them that are essential to comprehend in order to ultimately challenge them. It is one thing to point out the flaws in the system and quite another to offer ideas for remedying such flaws. In my opinion, research that stops at the former is ethically questionable. Moving beyond mere description, and into the realm of advocacy, requires working with the various groups that have a stake in the issue of homelessness. But this also makes advocacy much more complicated, because it can sometimes lead to doubts about exactly what we should be advocating *for*.

Advocating for What?

When I began my research on homelessness, I had strong beliefs about the underlying causes of homelessness but only a vague notion of how I might ultimately use my findings to try to better the lives of homeless people. I never struggled with whether I would engage in advocacy, in part because my intellectual underpinnings in applied anthropology explicitly guide me to conduct research for the purpose of addressing social problems. I naively thought that I would reach some determination about what to advocate for through the research process, when in fact I became more befuddled as my research progressed. There were so many important avenues for advocacy that picking one to concentrate on seemed nearly impossible. At the same time, trying to advocate for too many different things seemed likely to be ineffective. In short, a big part of the dilemma I faced in terms of advocacy centered on the fact that there were myriad things that I could conceivably advocate for in regard to homelessness.

One possible focus of advocacy relates to service provision, in particular increasing access to and availability of services. This was the most common type of suggestion offered by the homeless research participants. Many of them tended to buy into the "blame the victim" perspective on homelessness, and thus they focused on remedies that were essentially iterations of the more and better services approach. Social service providers, not surprisingly, also focused on service-based "solutions" to homelessness, noting the need for additional funding for various populations and programs. Both groups made valid points about various aspects of the service system, and it was interesting that the ideas for change that they espoused were very similar despite differences in terminology. Aside from the expansion of almost every type of service already available, the research participants also emphasized the need to simplify the process of obtaining services. Some of the problems they reported included strict eligibility requirements for various services, the specialization and dispersion of services, an abundance of rules that clients had to adhere to in order to remain enrolled in services, and the unrealistic expectation that full integration back into the housed population could occur within a matter of months. All these factors made it challenging for people to access the services they needed and to remain enrolled in those services. It also contributed to "service fatigue," in which some individuals simply gave up on the service system as a viable way to escape homelessness.

Advocating for changes in all these aspects of the service system is certainly a worthwhile endeavor, and this is where much advocacy is in fact focused. However, it neglects the underlying structural factors that continue to produce homelessness. Simply put, for each person who gets off the streets, there are others who become homeless. Given this, it also seems important to advocate for the basic human rights of those who do end up living outside. Cities throughout the United States continue to criminalize homelessness by passing ordinances that restrict the use of public space and the unavoidable activities that people must do in the course of daily life, such as urination. These ordinances are not only fundamentally unjust in that they punish people for being homeless, but they also compromise people's ability to escape homelessness. In Tucson, for example, it is illegal to sleep in parks without a permit or to sleep on other city-owned land. This means that people often get citations for sleeping outside despite the fact that there are not nearly enough shelter beds to accommodate the entire homeless population. Based on various factors, these citations can elevate to the level of felonies, thus impeding people's ability to access jobs and housing. Clearly, advocating for the repeal of such ordinances would be a first step in gaining some rights for street people. Similarly, it would seem reasonable to advocate for the right to sleep on public property or in abandoned buildings.

Again, while this type of advocacy may help improve conditions for people who are homeless, it does not confront the underlying causes of homelessness. This brings us to yet another possibility for advocacy, one that calls for changes in the very structures of society. Many other countries have minimized the number of people who end up homeless by building more affordable housing, providing basic healthcare, expanding social welfare programs, raising the minimum wage, and protecting the rights of laborers. These comprehensive attempts to ameliorate the deleterious effects of neoliberalism are often linked to a national right to housing that obligates the government to attempt to provide housing for all citizens. When the government is unable to do so, occupation of abandoned public or private buildings may be considered a valid response, and several countries have laws protecting squatters' rights.

These are all laudable efforts, but there is something even more fundamental at work here. What about the people who do not "fit" in the neoliberal world? In the process of trying to bring all labor into the market system, neoliberalism has squelched informal jobs, migratory labor, and various types of undocumented self-employment. And in trying to make all space highly profitable, neoliberalism has demolished most of the areas where low income people could access inexpensive lodging, food, and other resources. This means that some individuals do not have a place (both literal and figurative) in contemporary society. At the same time, certain people may want to opt out of an economic system that they feel is exploitive and unjust. In both cases, it seems that advocacy efforts would best be directed at challenging the legitimacy of neoliberalism rather than simply trying to mitigate its effects.

With all these possible avenues for advocacy, it may be apparent why I struggled with the issue in my writing. Above all, I wanted my advocacy efforts to be effective. This urge pulled me toward focusing on the problems that could actually be addressed at the local level, such as service provision and legal restrictions. In this context, I believed I could offer some feasible recommendations for change that were sensitive not only to the expressed desires of homeless people but also to the constraints faced by policymakers. Yet such recommendations felt inadequate, because they did not address the underlying structural causes of homelessness that were largely beyond local control. While I certainly had the option to advocate for both practical and transformative changes, I thought that offering a radical critique of homelessness might result in dismissal of my research by the groups who could enact policy changes.

In the end, my dissertation did advocate for just about everything discussed above, and I attempted to distribute it to all the different individuals involved in my research. I hand delivered copies to numerous people and donated archival quality copies to local libraries. I also wrote special "short reports" for the police department and the county-wide coalition of service providers, each of which was tailored to their interests and reflected the experiences and recommendations of local homeless people. I presented my findings and recommendations in various venues, and some of my ideas were incorporated into the county's plan to "end" homelessness. All these efforts were aimed at making my findings accessible to both homeless individuals and policy makers, which I believe is an essential aspect of advocacy.

Conclusion

No one studies homelessness for fun. Although it may be an interesting topic, nearly everyone who pursues it as a subject of research seeks to bring about some sort of transformation through their work—transformation in the lives of people who are homeless, transformation in the systems that serve (or fail to serve) them, transformation in the perceptions of policymakers and the wider public. It is precisely this desire to effect transformation that makes writing about homelessness so challenging. Scholars must constantly ask themselves if they are accurately depicting the perspectives of the various groups that have a stake in the issue. At the same time, researchers need to think about how their work might be used and take steps to maximize the accessibility and utility of their findings. This is not to suggest that everyone who studies homelessness must engage in advocacy—that is a personal choice that each individual must make for themselves. But what is not, or should not, be a matter of choice is the obligation to produce writings that can be used for that purpose. To do otherwise is to seek profit from the hardships of others. When studying pressing social problems, there is no room for the luxury of "objectivity" or "neutrality."

My own desire to effect transformation led me outside academia and into program evaluation, where I get paid to make recommendations to improve social service programs. In this venue, I do not have to struggle with being neutral, because the work begins with the assumption that systems are flawed and need to be changed. It does not lend itself to the radical critiques that might lead to real transformation in the economic relations or the racial, ethnic, and gender inequalities that underlie many social problems. The recommendations I make are, and must be, feasible, resulting from a negotiation between the researcher and the client, in which only practical recommendations are acceptable. In some ways it is very satisfying work: my recommendations go to the people and groups who have the power to make policy changes, and I sometimes get to actually witness my suggestions being implemented. In other ways, it is very frustrating work: the recommendations I make are never enough and there is not much room to go further. Yet this in itself is enlightening. I speak directly to those who enact public policy at the federal level, and I see that they too have limited power to effect structural change. Such transformation will have to come from somewhere else.

When I reflect on my prior research through this lens, I feel certain that it did not make any lasting impact on the problem of homelessness in Tucson. But I do think that it sparked, at least temporarily, a little understanding between groups that are often at odds over the issue. And maybe that is how substantive change will someday begin—with a sense of solidarity that inspires collective action to redress the injustices that produce and perpetuate poverty.

Notes

1. The U.S. Department of Housing and Urban Development recently updated the official definition of homeless to include the following categories: "(1) Individuals and families who lack a fixed, regular, and adequate nighttime residence and includes a subset for an individual who resided in an emergency shelter or a place not meant for human habitation and who is exiting an institution where he or she temporarily resided; (2) individuals and families who will imminently lose their primary nighttime residence; (3) unaccompanied youth and families with children and youth who are defined as homeless under other federal statutes who do not otherwise qualify as homeless under this definition; and (4) individuals and families who are fleeing, or are attempting to flee, domestic violence, dating violence, sexual assault, stalking, or other dangerous or life-threatening conditions that relate to violence against the individual or a family member" (Office of the Federal Register 2011, 75994).

Part Two
Relationships and Ethics

Researching such a multifaceted and stark issue as homelessness is, as we have seen, rife with ethical dilemmas at almost every turn. Beyond issues of whether and how to be an advocate for people in marginalized and impoverished states of existence, there are also the more micro-level ethical issues attendant to being a relatively privileged researcher vis-à-vis other human beings who have not been as fortunate. Should a researcher offer to buy lunch for someone they have interviewed? Is it okay to give a homeless person five dollars, or cigarettes, or other materials, when they have been helpful to the researcher? Who owns the final product of the research, and who profits from it? These and other similar queries strike at the heart not only of homelessness research, but also at our larger interactions with one another in an increasingly complex and polarized world.

The dedicated scholars and compassionate researchers brought together in this section explore these ethical issues through the lens of relationships, presenting compelling examples to illustrate their own processes and considerations. Michael Rowe begins with a cogent analysis of ethical issues such as status, function, and power in the context of his many years of work in services-oriented research, asking us to consider ways in which researchers can strive to ameliorate harsh conditions without, in the process, making promises that are difficult or even impossible to keep. Jürgen von Mahs reveals the initial awkwardness in approaching homeless people and the benefits of being open to serendipity in navigating the many roles of the researcher, exposing his own doubts about and stresses from the nature of the work, and concluding in the end that both immersion and distance can have their virtues. Kurt Borchard describes entering the field with a basic premise of doing no harm, only to soon realize that it is a standard that is not fully attainable given the unpredictable nature of life. He thus calls upon researchers to be open to new ways of sharing their findings while acknowledging that we are always engaged in an ongoing learning process. Julie Adkins delves deeply into the essential issues of power that pervade the field, grounding her analysis in an intensive case study that admits inquiry into various roles and relationships within the homelessness milieu and developing a complex synthesis that bridges many of the ethically oriented dichotomies and contradictions inherent in doing this sort of research.

The issues explored here are broad-ranging in their implications, yet they also remind us plaintively and poignantly that, at the end of the day, the ultimate concepts being studied are essentially *relationships*, from the interpersonal to the sociopolitical. We exist in relation to one another, to the structures that condition our life choices, and to the larger environment (including the built environment). Every interaction in this complex web of relationships poses ethical queries and dilemmas—that is, if one is paying attention, at least. The authors here take that implicit first rule of social inquiry (Pay Attention!) to heart and, in the process, provide crucial guidance for upcoming researchers preparing to embark on their own work—work that will undoubtedly change their lives, and perhaps even the world around them.

Chapter 5
Planning and Managing Ethical Dilemmas in Homelessness Research
Michael Rowe

Abstract. My research on homelessness has included programs aimed at helping persons who are homeless and have a mental illness, a substance use disorder, or both. More and more over the past fifteen or so years of doing this work, I've come up against the unsettling thought that these interventions can help and hurt people at the same time. They have shown some successful outcomes as measured quantitatively and as stated by participants or observed qualitatively. but they can also raise people's hopes for jobs, acceptance and valued roles as community members, and more, and not deliver on the implicit or explicit promises they have made. There aren't any easy solutions to this problem of which I'm aware. I suggest. as a provisional approach, that by embracing such dilemmas—facing the likelihood that they're present from the outset or will emerge at a later point—researchers, working with others including people who are homeless, service providers, and administrators, may be able to modify their negative impacts. I discuss some of these dilemmas and possible responses to them, including the idea that attention to the ethics of services research can push researchers toward advocacy and systems change.

Before becoming a sociologist I worked in social and human service agencies for runaway and neglected youth, released offenders, and people with drug addictions, mental illnesses, or both. I went back to school and was in my third or fourth year as a graduate student in sociology, hunting for a dissertation topic and a job to support my family when I heard that the Connecticut Mental Health Center in New Haven was looking for someone to run an interagency homeless outreach team. The New Haven team would be one of eighteen in the country that the federal Substance Abuse and Mental Health Services Administration

(SAMHSA) was funding as part of a national research project on services for people who were homeless with mental illnesses. I got the job and stayed with it until federal funding ended six years later. During this time I also conducted qualitative and ethnographic research on the encounters of homeless people and outreach workers, and since then I've continued to do research that has included services for people who are homeless or at risk of it. Thus the research ethics I'll talk about are bound up with programs, interventions, and services. I hope these considerations have some relevance to other homelessness research, but I make claims only for the kind I write about here.

The gist of what I have to say comes down to four points. First, homelessness services research is bound up with ethics because it involves people who are deprived of resources and privileges. Second, research involving close contact with people who are homeless is ethical at its core because relationships are ethical at their core, being built on trust, and there is a power differential favoring researchers. Third, services research on homelessness brings into play ethical dilemmas that go beyond the purview of Institutional Review Boards. Fourth, researchers should embrace responsibility for managing ethical dilemmas in advance, while engaged in, and following completion of, data collection, even if these dilemmas seem unmanageable at bottom by virtue of their place in the structure of things. This managing and planning may involve stakeholders at personal (homeless persons, service providers, and researchers), institutional or systemic (mental health and other social service bureaucracies), and sociopolitical (representational-legislative, local community, and society at large) levels.

It's a fair guess to say that for many researchers, "ethics" conjures first the image of their Institutional Review Board. Protection of human subjects from dangerous or shoddy research is certainly an ethical concern, and scrutiny of human subjects research is the proper work of a group of one's peers and fellow citizens. Yet the review board process can loom so large as to become a separate, daunting process tacked on to the work of designing the study and can threaten to narrow the researcher's gaze. That is to say that since the concerns of Institutional Review Boards are the concerns of researchers in deal-making or deal-breaking ways, they cast long, if mostly benign shadows over other ethical questions.

While running the New Haven outreach team, I also studied the encounters of homeless people and outreach workers. Mental health outreach work has many predecessors and influences, going back at least as far as the Bible tract missionaries of the 1820s who reached out to poor urban dwellers whom they saw as being at risk of losing touch with agrarian values and falling prey to urban vice and godlessness (Boyer 1978). More directly and recently, outreach has been influenced by the assertive community treatment (ACT) model for persons with chronic mental illness who do not do well with office-based care. In the ACT model, an interdisciplinary team provides a range of engagement, medication monitoring, case management, and other services and supports for persons whom clinicians have assessed as being "hard to serve" and likely to drop out of treatment. ACT teams were not designed to serve homeless people, though.

Experience with homelessness starting in the late 1970s and early 1980s showed that many people living with mental illness on the streets and in emergency shelters avoid contact with mental health professionals because of previous difficulty gaining access to care, clinician's demands for treatment compliance, fear of being hospitalized, and other reasons. The response in some local systems of care was to find clinicians and case managers who were willing to leave their offices to look for people who were homeless and have mental illnesses, and persuade them to accept mental health treatment, housing, help with entitlements, and other goods and services (Rowe et al. 1996).

Outreach workers and teams have developed a set of principles to define their work. These include not making promises you can't keep and keeping the ones you make, meeting potential clients on their physical and existential turf as opposed to demanding they come into the clinic, building trust with them over time by making contact with the person first not the patient, and offering them choices among a range of services rather than requiring motivation for treatment as the price of gaining access to other goods. There are exceptions and shadings to these rules, but they are the rules.

I began to see tensions and potential contradictions between the bedrock principles of outreach that guide the work, and the institutional and social contexts of that work. Making promises that you can keep, for example, implies that the promise workers give is what they say it is, with no strings attached of which the two parties have not spoken. This promise is embedded in the trusting relationship that the two parties build together. In addition, contact with the person first not the patient implies that workers know what the promised goods mean to persons who are homeless and, therefore, understand the consequences that having, or not having, these goods will bear for them. But there are problems with these implications and assumptions.

Boundary encounters host negotiations over both identity and tangible goods. The very tenets of outreach imply the valued status of homeless persons in the eyes of outreach workers. This conferred status, in turn, encourages hope for a positive social identity to go with the tangible goods for which homeless persons are negotiating with outreach workers. Yet promised apartments may come with the baggage of poverty-stricken neighborhoods and social isolation, and with the baggage of second-class, or program, citizenship built around mental health professionals as opposed to full membership in the larger community.

Now, many homeless persons may conclude that, all things considered, they are still getting a pretty good deal compared to what they've got now—life on the streets or an emergency shelter and the stigma of homelessness to compound that of mental illness. Or they may consider that the non-citizenship of homelessness and refusal of program citizenship leaves them with an identity more positive than the one outreach workers are offering them to go with their ticket out of homelessness (Rowe 1999). Or, as I implied above, they may be disarmed by what their relationships with outreach workers appear to promise for their futures, and end up being disappointed with the results.

Such a summary as this risks oversimplifying and homogenizing the collage of episodic homelessness, episodic treatment, trauma, and threadbare social support that is the life of many persons who are homeless. It also risks overstating the roles of outreach workers. My point here, though, is to touch on the nature of these encounters and relationships and to suggest ways in which ethical dilemmas may arise from them.

Building a relationship with the person not the patient implies that outreach workers make themselves known, too. Their encounters with people who are homeless and the services they deliver signal who they are not only as workers, but as people. Like homeless persons living at the margins of society, outreach workers live at the margins of social service institutions. They help people gain access to goods and services these institutions offer, without asking their clients to pledge allegiance to those institutions. Outreach workers, if they are successful on the street, come to be seen as people who know that "to live outside the law you must be honest" (Dylan 1966). The law and its codifications are a poor substitute for your own honesty and ethical actions, and the law and its codifications don't work on the street, anyway.

But workers are backed up by, and carry with them, the social and organizational elements of status, function, and power, and the parties to boundary encounters have unequal power. If persons who are homeless can walk away from workers, workers still dispense the services that homeless people accept or decline. The stakes for workers are their pride and belief in who they are. These cushion them against the inevitable frustrations of working with people who spurn their help, and from the sense that the goods and services they offer are a drop in the bucket of social and economic problems that are drowning the people they work with. The stakes for homeless people are far steeper, of course.

Outreach workers serve two masters—they are client advocates and gatekeepers to services, outlaws and bureaucrats, even if the unlikeliest bureaucrats you will ever meet. Leaving their clinics and mental health centers, they carry with them an internal office containing funding, professional, legal, and procedural guidelines that mark off the boundaries of the encounter. "Wearing an innovator's hat," I wrote elsewhere, "the outreach worker pushes bureaucracy out into the community. Wearing an official's hat, the same worker directs street-level encounters into traditional channels" (Rowe 1999, 63).

The range of services that workers offer dovetails with the principle of client choice. These, taken together, suggest that what is left of the self-esteem of their clients will not be damaged in accepting the goods and services they choose. Yet accepting help recursively creates a supplicant, even in one who has been persuaded to accept the goods that he or she refused initially. The deal sealed with a handshake, the outreach worker opens a file on a new client and starts to process him or her through the mental health system. Kim Hopper (2006, 223), characteristically, gets it right in summing up the dilemmas of what he calls the "committed work" of outreach:

> What's at stake in these unheralded gestures of care and connection is nothing less than the quiet protests of the welfare state's own workforce. In these pockets, at such moments, one can glimpse a restive moral sensibility at work, opposing the law of necessity in the name of compassion, questioning what slowly, inexorably, and falsely has assumed the status of fact, destabilizing convention by appeal to an old uncommon decency. This is civil disobedience in the service of inclusion. But—and here's the awful rub—such opposition redeems rather than undermines the state's offer of assistance, and it does so without revealing its own secretly corrective ministry. It meets that refusal of the service-wary . . . with a refusal of its own: standing alongside them, not in judgment or simply in compassion but (there really is no other word for it) in solidarity—and then working the system on their behalf. The upshot may be resistance co-opted, line workers hyper-exploited, and system betrayal delayed rather than averted. Or, put differently, a battered system keeps chugging along, secure in its "institutional bad faith," riddled with tensions and antagonisms that work against collective action, and propped up by the secret ministry of its own reluctant agents.

There is also the risk of individual bad faith in the sense that the worker who, living outside the law, must follow the dictates of his or her own conscience is, at the same time, an agent of institutional bad faith. And outreach workers cannot look to their compatriots or to the team as a whole for a buffer against this complicity. If the team and its leadership, which stand between them and the institution as a whole, codify the ethics of outreach, they only echo workers' convictions, lend moral support to shore up their faith in the work, and help them stave off burnout from it. They cannot justify to workers their role as "reluctant agents" of the mental health or social welfare system.

The following story is one I've told too many times, a measure of the impact it had on me, and more than once in print, but not quite in this form. Jim was a mid-fifties working class white male in the mid-1990s when outreach workers first sighted him. Then, he was an unknown person, probably male but maybe female, who slept on the ledge of a highway bridge for Interstate 95 about four feet below a few thousands trucks and cars each night, and half a dozen blankets with his neon yellow sneakers sticking out at the end of the mound of them. Workers left him alone when they saw him at 6 a.m. on the morning outreach run. They didn't want to wake him so early and they didn't know who they'd be waking, so they thought it best to come back later when he, or she, was up. When they did, though, the person with the yellow sneakers was gone. Eventually they found him at the public library downtown by looking at people's feet under the table.

Jim was a hard guy to reach out to. Walking into his ken, I felt as though I was walking into an anti-magnetic field of despair that sat in him, pushing me away physically as much as emotionally. He didn't deserve any help, he said when it was offered. Over time, outreach workers pieced together parts of his story. He had grown up in a large working-class family in Pittsburgh. In his late teens he'd had an inappropriate relationship with a younger female cousin and was ostracized from his family. He joined the army, got a general discharge, and then began a life of drifting up and down the East Coast, taking odd jobs and then losing them because of his drinking. He'd had little contact with mental health clinicians.

Jim made it up to the New Haven area some time before the outreach team found him. His sister, who lived in a small town outside New Haven, agreed to take him in, but kicked him out a couple months later because of his drinking. He came to New Haven and slept on ledges on the underside of one highway bridge after another, often with other bridge buddies. He was not working and had no entitlement income. He ate at soup kitchens and kept warm during the day in the public library when it was open. One of the outreach workers, Antoine, who had his own history of homelessness and drug use, was able to build trust with Jim:

> After getting to know this guy, I knew it was better for me to talk to him after he ate. It wouldn't do any good before. He was just a grouch, he would rebel and wouldn't want to hear anything. He was struggling with being able to feed himself. He didn't want to be involved with you if he hadn't eaten (Rowe 1999, 63).

Antoine moved slowly, taking his cues from Jim.

> I observed his survival tactics. I noticed that he picks up bottles. One of the things I did was collect some bottles. I brought the bottles down, using that as a conversation piece. He took the bottles. I observed that he had ripped up blankets so I offered him a blanket. He took the blanket. Every time we got together I had something to offer him. As time went on we became friends. I think the most vital piece that put a hook in him and drew him closer to me was that I would listen to him. I never asked him for anything, I always brought something *to* him. When he had been approached on the street they always wanted something *from* him (Rowe 1999, 63).

Over the course of a year of meeting with Antoine, Jim agreed to see the outreach team's psychiatrist, applied for entitlement income, which he was awarded, and finally, lo and behold, agreed to accept a subsidized apartment that Antoine had found for him. The day he moved in was a day of celebration for the outreach team. This was a great thing for Jim, and it was clear we all could walk on water.

Two weeks later Antoine came into a team rounds meeting and said Jim had told him he wanted to go back to sleeping under bridges, because at least there he had some friends. The temporary fix in Jim's case was to have Antoine spend a little more time with Jim, but for me Antoine's announcement in the team meeting was a eureka moment, one that went far beyond our strategic decision about how to cushion Jim's jump from homelessness into housing. Outreach workers, I saw, could find and build trust with people who had learned not to trust anyone who had anything to do with mental health systems. They could help them get income through entitlements or paid work, get primary medical care and behavioral health treatment, and find housing. What they could not do was help people who were homeless become neighbors, valued community members, and citizens in the sense of having strong connections to the five Rs of *rights, responsibilities, roles,* and *resources* that society offers its citizens, and to *relationships* available to them as part of the associational life of their neighborhoods and communities (Rowe 1999; Rowe and Baranoski 2011; Rowe et al. 2001).

This notion of citizenship became the impetus for research that would take up a good chunk of my time over the next decade and a half. First, I worked with persons who had been homeless, providers of services, and other community members on a community-level approach to facilitating community acceptance of homeless persons who were making their way into housing. The project was far too ambitious for its time, but it was a first attempt to address that aspect of citizenship that concerns what society, and the citizenry as a whole, was willing to do for its new or prospective citizens (Rowe et al. 2001). This project also set the stage for three others.

The first, the Leadership Project, trained people who were or had been homeless to serve internships on boards of directors of agencies that served homeless people, based on the idea that "representation of the governed" would be an empowering experience for the students, who might use it as a launching pad for work and valued roles in the community, and might help improve services for homeless people at large (Rowe et al. 2003). The second, the Citizens Project, was geared toward persons with serious mental illnesses and criminal justice histories, usually with co-occurring substance use disorders and often in association with homelessness. The project involved nontraditional classes geared toward the five Rs followed by "valued role projects" in the community—training for police cadets on what it's like to have a mental illness and be approached by a police officer on the street, for example—and wraparound support from peer mentors. The third involves community-based participatory research leading to development of an individual outcome measurement of citizenship (Rowe et al. in press).

While engaged with these projects, my colleagues and I also conducted research on peer-based mental health outreach services for people with histories of a lack of engagement in treatment and, often, homelessness, and peer services for homeless women with substance use disorders. (Lawless et al. 2009; Sells et al. 2006; Sells et al. 2008). This research, while not directly inspired by the citizenship agenda, is not inconsistent with it.

There is a common theme among these projects related to the ethical dilemmas of services-based research, but let me return, first, to my original argument. The ethical dilemmas of services research have to do with providing tangible and intangible goods and services—resources, relationships, identity transitions, and others—that appear to be stepping stones to other goods and to a higher social status that may not materialize for people in the way they hoped. Such services-based research involves implied promises to participants, the implications of which emerge for them in the course of their participation. The intervention that researchers evaluate goes so far and no farther, but even if the intervention is intended only to give a jump start to participants, researchers likely did not take into account some of the personal, system, and social factors that would come into play for participants. In my case, Jim, who inspired our citizenship-based interventions, came, ironically, to characterize the problem with them.

The Leadership Project has been a modest success. High dropout rates for the first two cohorts decreased with later ones, and those who did complete the training usually went on to complete successful internships on boards and action groups, including a statewide coalition of emergency shelters and the New Haven Mayor's Special Commission on Homelessness. Those with more education and less severe, or no, substance use disorders fared best of all. Most participants had a good experience with the class and internship, many stayed on and become full-fledged board members, and board members generally were pleased with their contributions. Up to now, we have not had the resources to study the effects of their participation on the boards and their work over time.

Beyond these results, though, and more pertinent to my topic in this chapter, there was a common theme among a number of participants in the Leadership Project that can be summarized as, "This has been great for me. Now I'm ready to get a job." Often, the job people wanted was in social and human services. Other times it was a job, period. In either case, we had no mechanisms in place to help people make this next step. Reasonable people could disagree on the realistic expectations of next-step help for participants in small-scale projects like this one, but the point I want to make here is that we were unprepared for participants' readiness to take the next step beyond the one our intervention helped them reach, and so had limited help to offer them for taking it.

There was a similar theme with the Citizens Project. The main finding, published and under review regarding clinical outcomes, was that participants in the Citizens intervention had decreased drug and alcohol use and increased quality of life compared to those in the standard services group (Rowe et al. 2007). But there were other findings, too. Many of those who stayed through the classes and completed their valued role projects, and even some who didn't make it all the way, talked about the transformative power of the experience. The theme of having finished something important for the first time in their adult lives was a strong one for graduates, and the theme of readiness to take the next step—a job and stronger connections to the local community and community members outside social and behavioral health systems of care—was prominent, as well. In addition, this group intervention that we had conceptualized, initially, as a vehicle, a tool for helping individual participants "make it" in the community became, for participants, a small community that nurtured, supported, and challenged them in their ventures into larger community life (Rowe and Baranoski 2011).

The complementary theme to this nurturing community was the loss of it for each cohort and participant when the intervention ended. Graduates were welcome to come back and visit a class, attend a weekly pizza party, and meet now and then with a peer mentor or the project director, but it wasn't the same. A number of people did go on to school or jobs, and for a number of others the Citizens Project was a stepping stone to the Leadership Project. Still, the Citizens Project, beneficial as it has been for many participants, at least, has seemed to leave some with that same question of "What's next?"

The peer staff research has yielded some positive findings regarding client outcomes, including peers' special ability to build trusting relationships with their clients (Sells et al. 2006). The ethical dilemmas associated with them involve mostly peer staff hired for projects that are participating in the studies. Here again, work—the wish to continue as peer mentors after the intervention ends, to find full-time peer or other work in social and human service settings, or to find other competitive employment—is the next step. And here again we, as well as the local mental health service system, have had limited next-step help to give.

There is a risk of putting responsibility on research and researchers that belongs to service systems, yet while the degree of responsibility of researchers and the ethical dilemmas associated with them can be debated, the responsibility and the dilemmas seem to me to be real ones. Now, one could make at least two additional objections to the dilemmas I have posed in this chapter. First, I could be charged with ignoring my own message that "programs" can only do so much to facilitate homeless people's community integration and citizenship. After that, community acceptance backed up by substantial resources and opportunities, along with advocacy and other efforts, need to take over. There is truth to this, but the potential for setup or misrepresentation, even when unintentional or unknowing, remains and can crop up in many forms. Second, one could say that I strain at small dilemmas in the face of huge social and economic barriers when such programs as those I write of do, in fact, provide resources and supports to people who have little of either. Yet the argument I am making is not that these interventions are more harmful than helpful, but that they contain, or can foster, dilemmas that are not inconsiderable for participants.

Conclusion

If homelessness services research can become tangled up with ethical dilemmas, what can researchers do with this knowledge? How can they investigate potentially effective interventions and undercut the chances that those interventions, even the relatively successful ones, may leave some of their participants with high hopes and limited options? I have no cookbook answers, but will offer a few thoughts.

Research Design. The first opportunity that services researchers on homelessness have to deal with the ethical dilemmas of their interventions is to try to tease them out in the research design period. What are the upstream effects that the intervention's success or failures might have on participants, services systems, or communities, and what would it take to put into place resources or plans that could address these? Are there modifications to the research design that could be made to help address such likely or possible dilemmas without, in the process, eviscerating the intervention? An example might be a large research grant to fund a number of outreach programs for homeless people across a state, and researchers' assessment that, while the services are likely to help homeless people, the infrastructure to follow up on these gains is shaky in many areas. Researchers, or those that fund them, might require commitments from local homelessness, behavioral health, and social service systems to put into place certain services or resources as a condition of competing for the grant. SAMHSA made like requirements for states applying to be sites for the Access to Community Care and Effective Services and Supports (ACCESS) research demonstration project.

One might say that there are a number of other considerations, before ethics, that better describe this strategy, including getting more bang for your buck and enhancing the likelihood that your research will be successful. I would say that ethics, service planning, and research design are not entirely separate domains, and that ethical considerations may be methods without necessarily compromising the principles that make them ethical. Ethical, and practical, considerations such as the capacity of the local socioeconomic and service system structures, can be considered and decisions made or commitments required of prospective site sponsors without compromising research designs.

If researchers pursue their dilemmas by attempting to ferret them out in advance, the plans they make in response to those potential dilemmas might reduce their impact on research participants. Once ethical dilemmas are enumerated, a number of ethical responses could be made, from the decision to delay the research until certain conditions are met, at one end of the spectrum, to the decision to go ahead with the research as swiftly as possible, reasoning that the need is so great and the potential effectiveness of the intervention so compelling that the ethical risks associated with proceeding must be taken, at the other end. Involving people who are homeless in the planning process, along with service providers and others, can help researchers come to such decisions. Many home-less people are remarkably eloquent about their experience of homelessness and services aimed to help them. People who are or have been homeless, including those with histories of mental illness, substance use disorders, and criminal jus-tice histories can also be integrated into research teams, and their attention to ethical as well as research questions can enrich and improve the study (Rowe et al. in press).

Midstream Dilemmas. What about ethical dilemmas that arise in the middle of the project? For me, these occurred about a third of the way through the six-year ACCESS project, via Jim and others. We responded, modestly, with the first and subsequent citizenship-based interventions. Here, I would point out two key elements in this coming upon of ethical dilemmas. The first is the im-portance of participant observation, ethnography, and other qualitative work in exposing the shape and reach of ethical dilemmas, which are also problems, ultimately, of facilitating "good outcomes" for participants. The second is that different researchers may have different roles to play in addressing these ethical and practical dilemmas. To the extent that these dilemmas look beyond the work to systems of care, the community, the labor market, and other domains, princi-pal investigators are likely to need to take the lead, or work with others with such expertise in trying to address the problems their interventions are helping to uncover and, in some sense, create.

Next-stage Research. Having uncovered certain ethical dilemmas in their research, what can researchers do to address these dilemmas in next-stage re-search? First, these dilemmas should be considered part of the research findings, and deserve a more prominent place in articles based on the research. This, of course, would require that journal editors be open to giving space for such find-ings. Second, and more particular to subsequent research design, the ethical di-lemmas that arise during a research project can suggest the logical responses to them. Our overreaching with the original, community-wide citizens intervention, which took on the huge task of facilitating community acceptance of and tangi-ble help for persons who were making the transition from homelessness into housing, was a lesson we learned well. In a later, first attempt to seed the estab-lishment of what we called a "Citizens Council" composed of people who were and had been homeless, one which we hoped would, ultimately, take on some of the tasks the original Citizens Project had set for itself, we designed a far more modest intervention involving peer training of service providers and laying the groundwork for continuing the council after private foundation funding ended. In any event, we were only partially successful with these objectives, but this time not for lack of focus on the ethical and practical dilemmas associated with them.

Beyond Services Research. Another lesson to be learned from the ethical dilemmas of services research is to look beyond services and services systems for responses to homelessness, toward other social and economic pathways for people and building coalitions for change to overcome structures of subordination. If assertive outreach work impinges upon advocacy, then there may be room for further partnerships at the margins between service providers and anti-homelessness advocates. Cohen and Thompson argue that homeless mentally ill persons should be seen first as impoverished and disenfranchised, rather than diseased persons, and that mental health workers should see advocacy for basic goods and services as a central ingredient to their practice. By doing so, workers may become part of a larger constituency to address political questions of rights and equity. Programs that are open to all homeless persons, they suggest, should be considered as an alternative to those that target a disabled subset of the homeless population (Cohen and Thompson 1992).

About the encounters of homeless people and outreach workers, I wrote:

> The homelessness or lack of structure of boundary encounters suggests the possibility of transformation on both sides, even of partnerships between homeless people and outreach workers to advocate for social change. There is danger in the margins, as Mary Douglas (1976) has written. Here, the structure of ideas which shapes and guides a society breaks down. The gaze of Reason herself, studied from afar, may appear not as disinterested, as turned away from common pursuits, but as "a look of concentration, a look of one who is privately engaged in a difficult, treacherous task" (Goffman 1959, 235), that of defending her vast empire (Rowe 1999, 4).

I would not want to push services research too far into advocacy, because in doing so we might lose sight, a little bit, of individuals who need the help of the goods they offer. As ethics go, these interventions, if they are fraught with ethical dilemmas, are so because they are ethical at their core and thus are filled with ethical content, much of which is positive. This is "committed work," and we need that too, even when the commitment is fraught with contradictions and danger.

Chapter 6
A "Buddy Researcher"? Prospects, Limitations, and Ethical Considerations in Ethnographic Research on Homeless People in Berlin
Jürgen von Mahs

Abstract. In this paper, I will reflect on my experiences in conducting ethnographic research among single adult homeless people in Berlin, Germany. My longitudinal ethnographic approach to the study of homeless people, and therein particularly the effects of social policy on homeless people's exit chances, is modeled after the concept of a "buddy researcher" who is actively involved in the daily lives of homeless people yet maintains his/her role as a researcher. In this paper I will discuss both the strengths and the weaknesses of this approach with particular emphasis on ethical and practical problems I encountered throughout my fieldwork. Specifically, I address difficulties with identifying and approaching homeless people, doubts on my part about the legitimacy of the chosen research approach, problems generated by the proximity to homeless people (e.g., experiencing a role change from researcher to advocate), and dilemmas about dealing with troublesome information (e.g., about criminal behaviors, domestic abuse, sexual problems, drug and alcohol abuse). In writing this chapter, I hope to provide some guidance along with some well-intentioned warnings to future researchers who wish to explore this promising approach to the study of homelessness.

In this paper, I will reflect on my experiences in conducting ethnographic research among single adult homeless people in Berlin, Germany, to assess the effects of social policy on homeless people's exit chances and in so doing shed light on the intriguing question as to why the nature and extent of homelessness are similar in Germany and in the United States—and durations of homelessness even longer in Germany despite the fact that Germany has a much more comprehensive and generous welfare system.[1] My longitudinal ethnographic approach to the study of homeless people is modeled after Snow and Anderson's (1993) concept of a "buddy researcher" who is actively involved in the daily lives of homeless people (I lived in a homeless shelter for one month) yet maintains his/her role as a researcher. In this paper I will discuss both the strengths and the weaknesses of this approach with particular emphasis on ethical and practical problems I encountered throughout my fieldwork. Specifically, I address some of the problems I came across in rather chronological fashion, including difficulties with identifying and approaching homeless people and entering the field, doubts on my part about the legitimacy of the chosen research approach, problems generated by the proximity to homeless people (e.g., experiencing a role change from researcher to advocate), dilemmas about confidentiality when dealing with troublesome information (e.g., about criminal behaviors, domestic abuse, sexual problems, drug and alcohol abuse), distinguishing between true and false information, and dealing with stress during the research. In writing this chapter, I hope to provide some guidance along with some well-intentioned warnings to future researchers who wish to explore this promising approach to the study of homelessness.

I must admit up front that at the time of conceptualizing this study and entering the field, I had relatively little guidance in how to actually conduct ethnographic research on homeless people. The PhD program in geography I had entered at the University of Bamberg provided little academic support in terms of methodological issues or the study of homelessness. Knowing about these academic constraints, I received most theoretical and methodological guidance from prior experience in conducting primary research on homeless people in the context of an evaluation of a homeless service project in Los Angeles (Dear and von Mahs 1997) and my affiliation with research conducted in the context of the Los Angeles Homelessness Study when I was a graduate student at the University of Southern California (USC) (Koegel 1988; Rowe and Wolch 1989). Further inspiration came from existing publications in English (Baxter and Hopper 1981; Hopper and Baxter 1982; Miller et al. 1998; Snow and Anderson 1993; van Maanen 1988) and in German (Bauer 1980; Girtler 1990; Schneider 1998). In hindsight, a book like this one—dealing with research experiences, methods, and ethics around the study of homelessness—would have saved me a great deal of trouble, since I believe that my problems and concerns have surely been experienced by other researchers on homelessness before me. Some more seasoned ethnographers reading this chapter will probably chuckle and think, "been there, done that."

The following will lay out some of the problems I encountered and how I solved them, along with some recommendations for novices and experts alike.

Entering the Field and Approaching Homeless People

Most ethnography textbooks—few of them explicitly on homelessness—discuss in great length the process of immersion or entry into the field and the problems that may befall ethnographers, including, among other things, lack of communication, rejection, hostility, and even racial tensions (Desjarlais 1997; Fetterman, 1989; Hopper 2003; Miller et al. 1998; Neuman 2002; Schneider 1998; van Maanen 1988; Warren and Karner 2005).[2] I was therefore aware of such problems in general. Yet, since I am by no means a shy or reserved person—most people consider me outgoing and sociable—I would have expected few problems informally talking to homeless people and thus gaining entry into their lifeworlds. Moreover, my prior research experiences with American homeless people (through the referral by my advisor Michael Dear) was rather unproblematic and I experienced no noteworthy difficulties in talking with and interviewing homeless people at Genesis I, a homeless advocacy project in downtown Los Angeles (Dear and von Mahs 1997).

Still, much to my surprise, in Berlin I found myself in the very difficult situation of needing to both identify and approach homeless people and to start informal conversations, especially in public spaces, subways, or railroad stations across Berlin. As a matter of fact, I recall being chastised by a potential respondent at a busy city square who informed me, visibly angry: "Hey, asshole. I may look that way but I am not homeless and I work odd hours. These are my work clothes. You should not prejudge" (unidentified pedestrian at Nollendorfplatz, field diary, entry on December 7, 2007, translated from German by the author). It is evidently difficult to readily identify people as homeless, as most homeless people, especially sheltered folks, do not resemble stereotypes of homeless people and remain unnoticeable in public and private spaces. Yet, even when easily finding homeless spaces and after identifying homeless persons as in fact homeless, I found it, in the absence of common ground and shared experiences and without referrals by third persons, quite difficult to start any conversations. Many people sensed that I wanted something from them and consequently hesitated to talk with me or even blocked any approach. In other cases, I simply could not bring myself to walk up to individual people or groups.

Fortunately, I was able to escape the predicament of not being able to approach potentially homeless people in public spaces by changing strategies. I decided to focus my investigation exclusively on homeless service users and their problems with accessing and receiving case-appropriate assistance in designated homeless service facilities, including a transitional shelter, a day center, and a homeless street newspaper agency, all places that were frequented by homeless people and where I could establish contact over time, in a less obtrusive fashion. There was, in the end, no need for a street homelessness control group.

In each of these case studies—transitional housing unit, day center, and homeless street newspaper agency—I employed methods of participant observation, informally mingled with people, and carefully got to know enough of them well enough to initiate formal interviews. To this effect, I actually lived in a shelter for one month, which allowed me to carefully and patiently get to know neighbors, gain their trust, and eventually interview them.[3] Despite unforeseen problems, which I discuss below, I was able to get to know and interview thirty-two homeless people and include the experiences of twenty-eight of them over the course of one year into the overall analysis. I was further able to get a fairly reasonable cross section of Berlin's homeless population in terms of age, gender, and nationality, although because of low case numbers I could only peripherally deal with the experiences of women (four respondents), foreign nationals (four respondents), or people with disabilities (four respondents, including two women).

Although I eventually overcame the obstacles, I recall my initial experiences as rather negative and discouraging. To ease future ethnographers' entry into the field of homeless spaces and homeless lives in their function as researchers, I recommend the following:

1. If you maintain your identity as a researcher, introduce yourself and your intentions and have a good, well-rehearsed story line with which to approach people. Be forthright with people. They know or sense that you want information. If possible, "practice" with a homeless person you already know.
2. Start the conversation easy, with something both of you can identify, such as the location, setting, or the day's headline news.
3. Have a few pointed questions for a potential respondent that are easy to understand yet broad enough to get an overall sense about the person and about whether or not to solicit an interview. Keep things simple and try not to sound too rehearsed or academic. Use informal, everyday questions.
4. Give respondents room to elaborate and choose the direction of the conversation.
5. Find out, at the end of the conversation, if a person is interested in a more personal, in-depth follow-up. If you can, invite the person for coffee or a quick meal.
6. Try to find gatekeepers—people who know people—and ask for referrals to other potential respondents. Get to know a person first before making such inquiries.
7. Consider compensation for participation. I was prepared to pay each interview partner the equivalent of $7 for an interview, which respondents greatly appreciated. Paying for their time is also a way to show appreciation and that the information is "worth" something. Not a lot of people

actually listen to homeless people rather than talking down to them, so being given the opportunity to talk and tell their story was, for the most part, appreciated, and information was provided freely and voluntarily. And a few bucks can be survival for a day.

8. Informed consent must be granted, and people should know their rights and that their anonymity is protected.

Once I entered the field and found opportunities to approach people and solicit interviews, I encountered other, unexpected problems during my time living in the shelter and doing my research at the other locations.

Ethical Dilemmas:
Doubts about the Research Approach

Very soon upon moving into the homeless shelter, I was overcome by grave doubts about the rightfulness of intervening in homeless people's lives by sharing their space. In my research diary I noted on February 14, 1998, a Saturday evening: "This is not right. I come in here with all my knowledge (what is that anyway?) and pretend I can gain some inside information. The last thing those guys need is me around. I can choose to go home any day, but those guys, by default, can't. They are not awarded that privilege." And it was difficult even in the intimacy of closed quarters to make contact. There was a seemingly long period of hesitation, of "checking out" one another, of getting a "feel" for the person. I could not escape the impression that the shelter residents were a bit doubtful about me and my objectives. I found it awkward to engage in small talk in the hallway or the common cooking area, often preferring just to watch and not say much. The desire for space and silence was, initially at least, mutual.

Fortunately, I was able to break the ice relatively quickly, and once I did so with the first few people in the direct vicinity of my room, I was eventually able to gain the trust of entire groups and thus gain entry. Very helpful was my immediate next door neighbor Sachse, who invited me to his room on my third day in the shelter, curious about my motives once I introduced myself and my goals. We had a very nice conversation and sat together for an entire afternoon. Later that day, he invited me over to a group evening with a few other residents to watch a soccer game on TV together. It also helped that a few days later, during my third formal in-depth interview, my respondent, Bob, 24, told me upon hearing about my doubts: "Stop it, man. We actually talked about you, you know? We think it's good what you're doing. At least you're trying to see things from our perspective. The damned politicians certainly don't. And, besides, if we can help you get a dissertation out of it, why not? Good for you." (Bob, Wohnheim Trachenbergring, personal interview February 25, 1998, translated from German by the author). These reassurances, along with getting more comfortable with homeless people, helped me carry on and eventually overcome my doubts. With some shared experiences—e.g., previous encounters in group settings, meeting at the supermarket, riding the train together—it became easier to start conversations. In this way and with the help of referrals and a few good words by previously interviewed people, I was able to snowball my way through the shelter.

I experienced similar problems in the other research locations. At the day center, I spent my entire first visit and lunch by myself. There was generally little conversation, aside from a few tables with what seemed to be regulars. On my second visit, I was able to start a conversation with two very nice and chatty middle-aged women. Again, the ice was broken. Eventually a single man, curious about the stories, joined in, and in this way I established first contact to, as it turned out, a group of regulars.

At the street newspaper agency, it was coincidence that ensured my entry. At a vendor assembly meeting, a young woman noticed my Franconian dialect and told me her boyfriend is also from Franconia, a region in northern Bavaria. A few minutes later, the boyfriend entered the room and turned out to be an old acquaintance of mine from my high school years in Erlangen, in southern Germany. We last met at my eighteenth birthday party and lost touch a few weeks later when he was arrested on aggravated assault charges. In the meantime, he had, through many detours, arrived homeless in Berlin, contacted the street newspaper agency, and advanced in the organization by becoming the elected vendor representative of the agency's board of directors and an occasional author of articles. He volunteered to establish contacts to fellow homeless street newspaper vendors and took me with him to work. This certainly made my life a lot easier. (We are still in contact!)

Despite having eventually broken the ice, I kept the quandaries associated with making and maintaining contact in mind when proceeding in my empirical research. And, to be honest, I still have problems with approaching homeless people on the streets despite the familiarity and rapport I have established with many homeless people. I would think that the best precaution is simply to expect a certain extent of unease and discomfort initially. There is a reason for this, in that there are, inevitably, status differences and power relations (gender, race, class) at work that skew the relationship between interview partners. Let's not forget that we, the researchers, are in a situation of advantage and privilege, and are perceived as such when looked at from the vantage point of a homeless person. We can go home, they cannot.

Role Reversals:
Participant Observer or Social Worker?

Another problem with the concept of a "buddy researcher" and the close proximity to homeless people is that respondents know very well that a researcher possesses knowledge about service provision, options, and facilities. Perhaps inevitably so, respondents turn to you for help or to request assistance. Homeless respondents certainly knew about my expertise and began turning to me for advice. This posed a particular dilemma since it is typically a primary responsibility of the researcher not to affect the outcomes of one's study unless the approach is deliberately conceptualized as "social action research," which mine was not.

To give an example, in a number of my interviews, respondents discovered through a question of mine that they were insufficiently informed by welfare agencies about the availability of a subsidized monthly public transportation pass (half-price monthly ticket, twenty-five Euros). Without this knowledge, twelve of the twenty-eight respondents had accumulated substantial fines with the private collection agencies that collect the fees and charge interest on behalf of Berlin's transit authority. I know of at least seven respondents who, understandably upset, returned to their welfare case workers to inquire about public transportation passes. All were issued a discount ticket and thus were able to prevent future fines. In this way, I unintentionally affected the course of events by having saved some people money.

Seven respondents overall had asked me quite specific questions about welfare law or service programs. While I did not dispense any negative or potentially harmful information, I did not decline requests for help, but I always referred respondents either to the social workers in the facility or to other appropriate services for further information, especially if questions involved issues that I felt I was unable to address or resolve.

Reminding myself about my responsibility as a researcher and my personal obligations toward helping people whenever possible allowed me to accept the fact that my presence and interventions might very well change the course of events. Still, I do firmly believe that all things considered, my role seldom truly affected people's choices and behaviors or the ultimate outcome of events.

Positionality

A researcher should be acutely aware that one's presence—the aura of researcher and brain-heavy professor or nerdy grad student—always creates expectations and sometimes even suspicions and fears on the part of the observed. Potential respondents should be put at ease and made aware that interviews are not interrogations and are not about seeking confessions of broken lives, but are conversations about their lives, experiences, hopes, and dreams. Not only is there nothing wrong with this, it is even imperative that one's own self is part of the conversation. For instance, telling a story about your own life and your own problems may give the respondent an opening, and lead to the realization that he or she does not sit across from a dominant, more articulate intellectual but somebody who is at least trying to listen.

In the end, however, the social distance that remains between observer and observed also has a good side in that it serves to protect one's personal life. It is a barrier against getting hurt, taking too much interest in respondents, developing friendships, or simply getting depressed in light of all the personal misery. A certain extent of distance is also good for another thing—dealing with "sensitive" information in rational ways.

Dealing with "Sensitive" Information

When I conducted the semi-structured interviews and essentially gave respondents the opportunity to bring up issues of their own choosing, I learned about quite troubling information that sometimes even involved unsanctioned or criminal behaviors. At times, I was not sure what and what not to believe. There is obviously a range of possible ramifications of the information people provide or even the behaviors that people engage in. I have experienced both the more subtle and more threatening examples.

For example, it became quite clear that many informants, particularly older males, had overtly xenophobic and racist attitudes. In an attempt to locate themselves in a social hierarchy, some homeless people perceived foreign nationals and ethnic minorities as "threatening, job killing, and unassimilated welfare spongers" and even blamed them for their situation. Moreover, foreigners and recent immigrants were, incorrectly, often accused of receiving preferential treatment and higher benefits from the welfare state whereas the "Germans" got shortchanged. The "teacher" in me, of course, was interested in setting the record straight and I started to argue with people, but they were quite insistent on their misinformed opinions.

My worst experience, also related to xenophobia, involved a potential brawl with a gang of young Turks. When I was accompanying FTW (a tall and intimidating long-haired and tattooed homeless fellow) on an errand, he began picking an unprovoked fight with a group of five young men of Turkish descent. Only with the help of another homeless man who joined us and my meager knowledge of fundamental Turkish was I able to drag FTW away from the scene and prevent a fight, after which I almost got into a fight with FTW myself.

Another example of sensitive topics involves the use of alcohol and drugs. The issue of substance abuse among homeless people is often used in support of a more conservative "tough love" approach to combat homelessness. Moreover, portraying homeless people as drunks provides right-leaning politicians and commentators with ammunition to legitimize political inaction and funding cuts, and to demonize both the service sector and the homeless themselves. A self-proclaimed left-leaning scholar like me would do anything not to provide fuel for what I perceive as a self-serving, potentially damning portrayal of homeless people as addicts and the political and cultural ramifications thereof. But let's face it—two-thirds of my respondents had an alcohol problem (older males) or substance abuse problem (especially cannabis among younger people) when I interviewed them, which is a finding that corresponds with medical studies on the health of homeless people in Berlin (Podschus and Dufeu 1995).[4] The omnipresence of alcohol or drugs in the shelter frequently initialized group activities involving the consumption of substances. I inevitably spent many evenings in such settings and, needless to say, stories often became more glamorous and exaggerated and discussions more heated as the evening and alcohol or drug consumption went on. Conversations during substance-enhanced meetings often revealed information that people would not necessarily want to make public had they been sober. Things like participation in illegal activities; substance abuse problems; criminal activities; domestic violence; or sexual problems, preferences, and practices were among the topics that came up in substance-enhanced conversations, along with ridicule, affirmation, and rejection by other homeless people in the group.

I also had a hard time dealing with information potentially implicating homeless people themselves or third parties in criminal activities ranging from shoplifting, petty theft, and nonpayment of alimony and childcare costs, to grand theft, drug dealing, and prostitution. I have encountered a number of people who were engaged in such activities or had information about real criminal activity. I proceeded to draw the line where other people's health and well-being were adversely affected. Fortunately, I was not put in the position of having to involve authorities and, in so doing, breach the terms of informed consent and of not disclosing private information to others.

Future generations of ethnographers should simply be reminded of the severity and magnitude of oftentimes problematic information, behavior, or actions on the part of the people they wish to study. One has to bear in mind that homelessness is an enormously multifaceted problem that affects people from all walks of life, yet does so quite differently for each individual. We may, in fact, know quite a bit about structural root causes, policy deficiencies, and individual problems and behaviors, but we will never really know how all these factors interact to affect individual homeless people's lives, behaviors, and choices unless we talk with the people to understand their social worlds. And this is precisely the great opportunity that ethnographic research on homeless people has to offer. Qualitative research is able to move beyond the statistical significance of variables or the strength and direction of social relations; it allows us to get a comprehensive picture of the multiple interactions that affect individual homeless people and their daily experiences and how this relates to broader societal processes.

Taking Sides and Making Judgments

The previous section on sensitive information already alluded to a big problem: unless we are talking about shared experiences, most information comes directly and in an unfiltered fashion from the respondents. How can we tell if people are telling the truth? Many people, homeless or not, tend to exaggerate and embellish past experiences. So how credible is information? Unfortunately, there are no ground rules to follow other than using one's own best judgment. One possibility to get to the root of the credibility of a story is to rephrase the question and address the issue again in a casual fashion on a later occasion or in a follow-up interview. If you suspect false or inaccurate information, avoid any blame and don't make accusations—simply ask for a clarification, or say you were not sure you understood.

A similar problem concerns contradictions when other people are involved (he said, she said) and a researcher is forced to assess which perspective is probably correct. For instance, I once accompanied a respondent to the welfare office so I could, in his words, "see for yourself how I am being treated there." Indeed, while sitting outside the office door, I overheard a rather loud and unpleasant conversation between my respondent and the case worker after which, screaming, the case worker threw my respondent out of her office. On a later occasion, I had a chance to talk to the case worker, who, without revealing specifics for reasons of client confidentiality, painted a completely different picture of the respondent as unreliable, late, unfriendly, and uncooperative. A "hopeless case," she told me. To get to the bottom of it, I had a couple of informal conversations with the respondent around some of the issues. Upon his own admission, it turned out that the case worker had a point. He did miss appointments, got irritated and impatient fast, and often failed to comply with directives. His assertion that the case worker was rather unfriendly turned out to be true: friendly, she was not.

Ultimately, it does depend on the ethnographer's skills and intuitions to detect potentially incorrect or false information and to take measures to find the "truth." At the same time, however, I am convinced that most of my respondents answered questions truthfully and from their own, free perspective. I very rarely had reason to suspect otherwise and typically managed to get the necessary clarifications. I do, in the end, believe that I was able to get an abundance of useful and truthful information that would allow me to examine personal experiences of homeless people with public policy from a variety of angles and viewpoints. Yet, doing all the work—i.e., constantly having to be on, and always being surrounded by the often discouraging atmosphere of shelter life—does take a toll on a researcher's life.

Information Overload and Stress Management

A final problem that I would like to address is that of stress associated with this type of ethnographic research. In-depth ethnographic research can, at times, be incredibly overwhelming both physically and emotionally. Any ethnographer must come to terms with the fact that she or he is forced to lead a double life—one as your own self (academic and private worlds), and one in the new life-world of homeless people (homeless world). One is required to make constant role changes, flip between these two worlds. Moreover, one's academic and personal worlds do not stop, especially when one has social ties such as children, partners, parents, friends, or work obligations.

The amount of stress and aggravation obviously depends on the actual research approach and the duration and the extent of involvement. In my case, living in the shelter for over one month and thus having more or less 24/7 exposure to the life-worlds of homeless people, the stress level was high. For one, I was constantly on the move, rushing from appointment to appointment, interview to interview. There was simply very little downtime and such downtime was still typically in the context of the homeless world. And usually I would sit with my laptop during downtime, especially in the evenings upon completion of my daily activities. Then I would reflect on the day in my research diary or transcribe notes from interviews that I could not tape. I also often needed to prepare for the next day or make phone calls.

Aside from the actual workload, the in-depth immersion in the homeless world has psychological effects, as I already mentioned in the context of doubts about the research approach, methods, and the close contact. It also becomes an issue if one gets to know some people quite well and thus begins building personal relations. This makes one vulnerable to becoming emotionally and psychologically affected by homeless people's misfortunes and the omnipresent injustice that surrounds their lives. I myself began to internalize some of the negative impressions, and there were nights when I did not sleep well (which is rare) and my own consumption of alcohol and cigarettes increased quite a bit.

It helped in my case that I had once worked for over a year as an assistant nurse in a psychiatric hospital. This experience taught me how to be compassionate about patients and still maintain a protective boundary. My nursing experiences also helped with assessing people's physical and mental health conditions, and with distinguishing between fact and fiction in the colorful stories the respondents told me.

Given, of course, that not all aspiring ethnographers can capitalize on previous clinical or other field experiences, I would certainly recommend to novices—besides considering all the well-meaning advice from this volume—to take a course on qualitative research methods and a course on homelessness before embarking on any ethnographic quests to study homelessness. It pays dividends when starting a complicated ethnographic research project on an especially complex societal group such as the homeless. Many textbooks (e.g., Warren and Karner 2005) address some of the concerns that have been raised in this chapter and others in this book, but do not necessarily point out how difficult, time-consuming, and stressful research on homelessness—a particularly multifaceted problem—really is.

A final thing that helped me cope with stress and the depressing homeless milieu is the fact that I had the opportunity to occasionally escape the environment. One of my best friends lives in Berlin and we met weekly, giving me a chance to decompress and get a refresher in my "own" life by going out, playing darts, or taking extended walks just talking. I would think it is important to plan some downtime outside the homeless world. Go to the movies, a dinner, talk with friends. Simply get some distance every once in a while.

Conclusion

All things considered, I regard this ethnographic research approach and project as very successful, and I have gained a lot both personally and professionally. This research succeeded in providing a rich set of data that allows more in-depth investigations into welfare regime theory, homeless people's interactions with the state, the geographies of homelessness, life and social networks in homeless shelters, advocacy and self-help through street newspapers, and policy recommendations, along with multiple possibilities for trans-Atlantic comparisons. I have started to write up the results of this research in a number of reputable journals and book chapters.[5] In the end, I have been able to accomplish most of my major academic objectives, including:

- Verifying the utility of ethnographic, case-based analysis to shed light on the effects of public policy on homeless people's long-term life chances;
- Providing a sound typology of life-course groups that showed nuances in effects of social policy and other policy measures based largely on the extent of previous social and economic integration in the city and the nature and existence of exacerbating social problems;
- Confirming the tenor of welfare regime theory in that Germany's welfare system is more generous and comprehensive than that of the United States, yet pointing out flaws in the local implementation of social policy and the adverse effects it has on homeless people;
- Explaining how policy—often contradictory in objectives—more often than not displaces homeless people, contains them in service ghettos, and provides only minimal and uncoordinated assistance. Such socio-spatial exclusion further aggravates homeless people's life circumstances, often keeping them trapped in chronic homelessness;

- Providing an explanation for long durations of unemployment and homelessness due to the German welfare regime's characteristic of fostering an insider-outsider dualism, protecting social insurance contributors yet merely managing the long-term excluded and unemployed through subpar shelter provision and welfare payments;
- Emphasizing the virtue of social work over mere administrative practice; case workers in mainstream welfare and labor offices barely accounted for the multiple needs of their clients, whereas dedicated, informed social workers with ample experience were able to provide the concerted assistance needed for some respondents to exit homelessness for good;
- And despite the critique of the German approach to homelessness, still maintaining that a more comprehensive welfare system—albeit flawed at the local scale—is preferable over a dysfunctional, patchy, and exclusionary liberal welfare system such as that of the United States, in which people remain exposed to the most brutal aspects of unfettered capitalism.

These accomplishments notwithstanding, there are, of course, a number of limitations to the study. First, it is impossible to ascertain whether the findings are representative of the local homeless population overall. Surely some groups, most notably women, families, and foreign nationals, remain insufficiently considered in this research. This limitation inevitably affects the overall persuasiveness of the argument. It is, however, a start that lays bare all of the different factors and how they interact, so that homeless people's struggles and efforts become understandable and the true, cumulative effects of public policy become transparent.

Second, the lack of representative data will not satisfy the expectations of policymakers who implement reforms, since they need "hard" data to justify funding increases or changes in administrative policy. While I certainly would have liked to triangulate my ethnographic data with the results of quantitative inquiries such as, for instance, a panel study, I did not have the resources at the time to do so.[6]

In terms of my future research, I am considering replicating the ethnographic methodology that underlies my research in Berlin in a North American city, along with triangulation with more extensive survey research that may provide us with an even better comparative understanding about exit from homelessness and the effects of policy intervention. Through triangulations and thus quantitative evidence, this anticipated research will allow for making policy recommendations en route to a more responsive local welfare state, thus overcoming one limitation of the current study.

While this research has allowed me to generate data that I can publish for a while and has allowed me to pursue an academic career and thus helped me professionally, it also has helped me personally. I am extremely grateful to the twenty-eight individuals who shared their lives and life stories with me, and in so doing enriched my own understanding of and appreciation for people and the enormous potential they have. My experiences were often upsetting, sometimes heartwarming, occasionally funny, but never boring. I gained a lot of respect for the ways homeless people deal with extremely adverse circumstances, and despite all that maintain their sense of identity and self. I do not think that I would have gained all these profound insights any other way. The pursuit of an ethnographic strategy proved to be flexible enough to allow me to make adjustments and informally experiment with approaches to see what worked and what did not, how to approach and select people, or how to bridge communication problems. Flexibility is the ultimate survival tool for ethnographers who conduct research on homelessness. Nonetheless, a book like this one with tips and insights on how to conduct research among homeless people would have certainly helped me back in the days and prevented a lot of trouble, including easily avoidable and time-consuming hassles and worries on my part.

Notes

1. For more information on the rationale behind the study and the main results, see von Mahs (2005).

2. Three of the publications, Desjarlais (1997), Miller et al. (1998), and Schneider (1998), do explicitly address problems with ethnographic research pertaining to homelessness but were not available to me at the time when I conceptualized my research approach in 1997.

3. In November 1997, I met with Uta Sternal, manager of the Wohnheim Trachenbergring, a midlevel shelter providing transitional housing to single homeless adults. During the conversation, I inquired about the possibility of staying at the shelter to conduct research. Mrs. Sternal accepted my proposal provided beds were available, and I paid a nominal fee. I consequently moved in on February 12, 1998, and stayed at the shelter for four weeks.

4. In this context, it is important to point out that while approximately one-third of my respondents had an alcohol or drug problem at the onset of their homelessness, which thus constituted a contributing factor to becoming homeless, over two-thirds had a substance abuse problem at the time I interviewed them, which was, on average, 1.5 years into their experience with homelessness. This indicates that homelessness had either created or exacerbated people's problems with alcohol or drugs, especially in shelter settings (von Mahs 2005).

5. I am just finishing writing a book (von Mahs, forthcoming) and have recently completed, with Don Mitchell, a special edition on a potential "Americanization of Homelessness" (von Mahs 2011a; 2011b).

6. For U.S. studies that have used panel studies to inquire about exit from homelessness, see Koegel (2004), Wong (1997), and Wright (1996).

Chapter 7
Ethics and Studying Homelessness: Tales from the Field
Kurt Borchard[1]

Abstract. The ethical imperative of research on human subjects is "do no harm." The idealistic and abstract standard it sets, though, is difficult for a field researcher studying homelessness to achieve. Here I present several examples from my own research where I made decisions with ethical implications. The dilemmas I faced had no "one right answer." and a decision at the time was necessary. Although good things have come out of my research, I can also never know all the possible harm I might have caused. I argue that the ethical researcher stands by his or her decisions but admits and learns from errors, makes plans to reduce chances for harm, and educates others about mistakes made. The best standard of ethical research of homeless people is a self-reflexive researcher who thinks hard about the question. "will I harm my subjects?"

For anyone studying homelessness in an academic or university setting in the United States, it is standard practice to consider the ethical issues involved in one's study. In graduate school, I completed a required report for an Institutional Review Board (IRB) that outlined the possible risks and benefits of my first study, which was an ethnography of homeless men in Las Vegas (2005). My human subjects were homeless men and homeless service providers, whom I both conducted interviews with and observed as a participant observer. When I later used these same methods to study homeless men and women for a second book (2011) as a professor at a different university, I completed new reports for the IRB.

For both universities, part of my approach to meet the standards included writing an informed consent statement that introduced me to my potential subjects. The one-page statement said why I wanted to conduct the study, how long I would be studying homelessness, where I would be studying it, and what would happen to the results. It also told potential subjects that participation was voluntary, and that the confidentiality of the data and the subjects was guaranteed, which meant that I would destroy the tape recordings of our interviews and change all participants' names on any final reports (as I have in this paper). Furthermore, I wanted to double-check my findings with those I studied; I told subjects I would be happy to provide copies of my initial reports to them, and looked forward to any comments and suggestions.

Announcing these practices to my university IRB and to my subjects and carrying them out allowed me to meet my institution's guidelines for ethical practice during my study. The maxim for ethical research practice, though, is captured in the phrase "do no harm." Following these practices could not prepare me for several other situations where I did not have sufficient time to reflect on how to act in relation to my subjects or come up with a solution to ensure no one was harmed. I therefore want to share these tales from the field where I was faced with situations and decisions, especially those I still reflect upon. I hope that sharing such incidents might better prepare another researcher for the ethical pitfalls he or she will certainly encounter. At times I made a decision in a moment because I needed to. At other times, I was able to take more time to prepare a better, more ethical practice, or think carefully about the pros and cons of my previous actions. When I consider whether my actions might have harmed a person or persons I studied, and what my responsibility is to my subjects, I realize that the ethical questions I faced in real situations gave me epiphanies affecting how I think about conducting research today.

In the first two sections of this chapter I focus on ethical questions involving my relationship to my subjects. I first consider dilemmas in my role as a participant observer of and ethnographic researcher on homeless people, and how my use of monetary incentives might have affected my research findings and relationships with subjects. I next discuss how my choice of clothing did not clearly distinguish me as a researcher to the homeless people I was studying, perhaps confusing possible subjects when I at times shifted from a participant observer to an interviewer.

In the third section of this chapter, I focus on ethical questions concerning who benefits from research on homelessness. These questions concern my relationship to my subjects, but also the ethics of my relationship as a researcher to my university and community. I discuss publishing research results in both academic and popular outlets as an ethical practice. I also consider the ethics of homeless researchers who might benefit materially from their research.

The Researcher Role and Use of Incentives

The first incident I will discuss occurred after I conducted an interview with Bill, one of my research subjects. Since our initial interview, I had been giving him small tokens of my appreciation (meals and a few dollars). I had asked him if he would be willing to keep a journal for my project. I bought him the pen and journal, and said he could write about anything he wanted. I had asked him if I could please make a Xerox copy of his entries for the purposes of my research. He agreed.

A few weeks later, I ran into Bill and asked him if I could copy the journal. After we traveled together to a copying center and made the copy, I took Bill back to his newly arranged shared apartment. While I drove he suddenly turned to me and said, "So, is this journal all I mean to you?" I was caught off guard, and hesitated to speak. He said, "Never mind. Your silence speaks volumes." I tried to talk to him as we rode, but I have a hard time remembering exactly what I said. I remember feeling upset, confused, and fearful. I remember it didn't go well.

Looking back, I wanted to explain that he did mean more to me than simply the journal, but that I didn't know how to express that. I liked him, but I also knew that he was a research subject for me, and I was afraid of becoming friends with any homeless person because I felt I did not have the resources as a graduate student to help him. I had not thought about the boundaries I would have between my interview subjects and me. I frankly worried about how much he would ask from me. I also wondered if I was supposed to simply document his condition as a homeless person, or if I should attempt to assist him out of homelessness, and if so, to what extent. I later wondered, to what extent do the roles of researcher, activist, and friend overlap in fieldwork like mine? Also, if I were to provide material help and/or friendship for Bill, then shouldn't I do the same thing with other homeless people I interviewed? Would the results of my study change through friendships with subjects?

The type of fieldwork an ethnographer can conduct depends in large part on the local context where such work will occur (Emerson 1983). Doing fieldwork with homeless people in Las Vegas usually did not allow me opportunities for extended interviews, observations, or even interactions with a single subject over time. Homeless people are by definition nomadic. I found it difficult to follow the approach of a typical fieldworker, which is to develop rapport with single individuals or small groups over time (Buford 1990; Emerson 1983). In Las Vegas, several of the charitable institutions homeless people used had strict curfews and rules regarding visitors, further limiting my ability to contact and/or interact with subjects. I found that my subjects' temporary housing arrangements, be they in a shelter or a car or outside or staying with a friend, were also unstable. At times I could regularly meet with a subject at a soup kitchen, for example, but I understood that such agreements could be broken because of any number of unexpected problems a subject might have, including transportation difficulties and changing schedules. Such unpredictability and difficulty in following a subject over time was why I decided to ask some subjects to keep journals in the first place, allowing me better insight into someone's daily routines and regular thoughts. To supplement these journals I decided to conduct as many one-shot interviews as possible, and observations of homeless people, primarily in and around shelters. A few subjects such as Bill, though, seemed willing and able to interact with me more. Yet these subjects still left me with larger questions of how I should treat them.

Elliot Liebow and Mitchell Duneier have also written about if, when, and/or how they as researchers chose to intervene in the lives of their poorer research subjects. At times, their subjects asked for money. In *Tally's Corner*, Liebow (1968) describes how some subjects "exploited" him simply because he had more resources than they did. He noted that in the circle of men he studied, anyone who had resources could expect to be approached by others to share. In *Sidewalk*, Duneier notes how some magazine vendors and panhandlers he studied came to regularly ask him for money. Duneier (2000, 355) states:

> The questions for me were: Could I show my deep appreciation for their struggles *and* gain their appreciation for my purposes as a sociologist without paying for some simulacrum of it? How could I communicate my purposes as a researcher without dollar bills and small change in my hand? (emphasis in original).

Duneier says that later he did learn how to say no to such requests, "and to communicate the anguish I felt in giving such an answer" (2000, 335). He describes both the practical ways he tried to improve the lives of those he studied, the friendships he had with some subjects, and how he ultimately decided to share his advance and royalties with several of his key subjects. He concludes (2000, 357) that, "I would like to think that whatever respect I ultimately get will be based not on what I did or didn't give in the way of resources but on whether the people working and/or living on Sixth Avenue think the work I did had integrity, by whatever yardstick they use to take that measure."

I only saw Bill once after our car ride, but his question has haunted me for over a decade. Bill helped me realize the stark inequality of every personal encounter I had while I conducted research. Bill was asking me about the extent to which my interest in him was instrumental versus expressive, or an exchange-based versus a personally based relationship—was I simply using him for what he could tell me about homelessness, or did I care about him as a person? I was left wondering if these positions were mutually exclusive, and if not, what balance could I find between them? Was Bill's comment representative of how some, most, or all homeless people felt about my interaction with them? In my first research project concerning homelessness, I rarely was able to hang out with groups of homeless people, and frequently would meet a man for a single extended interview, often never to see him again. Was I harming homeless people that I interviewed by not seeing a need specifically to try and meet again after the initial encounter, or by becoming more personally involved in their lives? Or would my involvement, perhaps, cause unanticipated, harmful consequences? Is friendship what some, or most, of my interviewees wanted, or just Bill? I felt I had been open and honest with my informed consent statement about what I was doing as a researcher and why I was doing it. I wondered if perhaps Bill was trying to manipulate me into saying we were friends so that he could ask me for more material assistance.

In my original IRB form completed for my university, I had said that I would at times purchase food or other small items for research subjects as incentives for those subjects to participate. The use of small incentives for interviewees is a common practice in survey-based research (Dillman 1978). I did not explicitly state the incentive I might provide, though, on my informed consent form. I had worried about providing explicit incentives because, similar to Duneier, I did not want to be perceived as "buying" interviews; I was afraid that some people would want to participate minimally only to receive some money or food. I wanted to abide by the basic journalistic practice that you do not *pay* people for interviews. The compromise I reached in my first few years of interviewing was that if a meal or a pack of cigarettes seemed likely to facilitate an interview with someone by making the person or our time together feel more comfortable, I would offer that up front. I also knew that homeless people need money, so after an interview was complete I would frequently try to give an interviewee five dollars as a way of saying thank you. Some homeless people I spoke to, though, altruistically said they wanted to participate because it might help someone else in the future (though not one of those interviewees refused any money I offered).

Other researchers have dealt with the issue of providing a material incentive in varied ways. Amir Marvasti (2003) discusses how he would give cigarettes to people he would talk to in the shelter. Although some homeless researchers might criticize such a response as enabling or contributing to a homeless person's health problems, Marvasti notes that the long-term effects of smoking are among the least pressing problems faced by homeless persons. Snow and Anderson (1993) do not explicitly mention giving incentives systematically to their research subjects, but do discuss bringing food and hot drinks around to homeless camps, and imply that they at times shared alcohol with participants. Wasserman and Clair (2010) note that they gave food, toiletries, supplies, and sometimes cash to their homeless subjects.

Some criticize the idea of giving homeless people small amounts of money for an interview based on a belief that homeless people will act irresponsibly with it. I often think that homeless people are infantilized by social service agencies, because those at the agencies often act as if they know better what a homeless person needs than the person themselves. I believe that since in the

United States homeless people are seen as individually responsible adults with the right to be homeless, they also should be seen as having the right to make up their own minds about what to do with cash. I did not purchase alcohol for respondents because I tried to avoid interviewing someone drunk and, in the discourse of Alcoholics Anonymous, I did not want to be an enabler. Although I initially agreed to purchase cigarettes for interviewees, I soon stopped because I felt guilty. I rationalized that once I had given someone money *after* an interview, that person could buy whatever he or she wanted. Everyone needs cash for small things, and after meeting several interview subjects who had little or no cash on them, I thought it was ethical to give an interviewee five dollars after speaking to him or her. I also think of the five dollars as a way of thanking an interviewee for sharing their stories and showing that I appreciate their time.

In one specific instance, though, I did not offer an interviewee five dollars. During our interview, Bruce discussed his alcoholism in depth, including the delirium tremens he experienced from alcohol withdrawal. After interviewing Bruce I realized that he would only use any money I gave him to buy more alcohol. He had asked me for thirty cents earlier in the interview, which I gave him before I fully knew his problem. He was able to buy one large beer with it and some other change. I thought later that that might even be good in the short term for him to have the alcohol, as it could keep him from experiencing delirium tremens. He said he wanted to get up the next day, and I thought any more beer might prevent that. In Bruce's case, nothing he said during our interview made me think that giving him more money would help him. He admitted to being out of control.

My role as a researcher versus being more of a friend toward my subjects was something I learned to negotiate individually with each person I interviewed. I learned that I liked some interviewees I spoke to more than others, and that how I felt toward an individual should be my guide in trying to befriend him or her. I also learned that it was equally important to spend time with homeless people I didn't like or had difficulty relating to, because those people had important experiences and shared important insights with me on homelessness as well. In the last few years I have been interviewing homeless people, I generally have tried to stick with a standard of five dollars as a "gift" after an interview or extended period of time together, but again I decide on a case-by-case basis. Once a man I had interviewed all day, Jerry, had soiled himself in front of me, and asked me for ten dollars so that he could buy a bus pass so he would have a safe place to sleep all night (Borchard 2005, 52). I gave him the money in part as an emotional reaction to his accident and the humiliation he must have felt being with me when it happened. I later realized though that, as an alcoholic and a smoker, he might well have been tempted to use the cash for something else. It was a tragic situation, but I gave him what he requested.

Like Duneier, I hope that those I interviewed feel that my work has integrity. I also know that, for many of my interviewees, they had far more pressing concerns than following up on my work. Also, my work did not really help them materially. The fact that so many people have agreed to share their lives with me, even if it was in the hopes of gaining greater friendship or assistance than I thought I could offer at the time, says volumes about *their* capacity for human decency, and the need we all have to connect with others. In trying to help rather than harm my subjects, I hope I was a good listener and offered an ear when an interviewee was looking for one.

Dressing Down to Fit In

A second set of ethical concerns revolved around how I presented myself when I went into the field. I would usually wear an old T-shirt and jeans, a beat-up old jacket, and tennis shoes. Generally when I first arrived in an area where homeless people were hanging out, such as by a chain link fence near a shelter or in a yard outside of a shelter, I would pick a spot and wait, observing. Even though I was not homeless, I appeared as though I was in that context. I only later realized that my subjects could see my presentation of self as researcher deception (Adler and Adler 1994). Because this was a bad part of town, those in the area generally assumed that if a person was hanging out outside of a shelter with other homeless people, that person was also homeless. The homeless people in the area had no reason to suspect otherwise.

I went into the field as a participant observer, and then sometimes I would meet a homeless person I was willing to introduce myself to, whereupon I would shift into interviewer mode. The problem with being a participant observer in my early years of research was that I was shy and at times found it difficult to approach homeless people. I felt safer "hanging back," just being in the area and observing, without introducing myself. Ironically, I could justify my shyness at approaching homeless people through the practices taught to me in my qualitative sociology class that ethnographic researchers should be careful about entering a field. I was told that you do not go into a field wearing a shirt that said, "Hello! I'm doing ethnographic research," because you would create a variation of the Hawthorne effect (Babbie 1995, 236)—i.e., a researcher affecting the behavior of those being studied by his or her presence.

One incident in particular revealed how my presentation of self in the field might be confusing to those around me. Once while in the homeless corridor of Las Vegas, I was standing by a chain link fence, trying to grow comfortable enough to eventually approach a man for an interview. Another man soon came by and began giving a small box drink of orange juice to each of us standing on the fence. He soon tried to hand me a box. I explained to him that I wasn't actually homeless, but was a student from the University of Nevada, Las Vegas (UNLV) researching homelessness. I told him because I didn't want to deprive someone else of a drink, which I thought was the right thing to do. He raised his voice in response to my revelation, basically calling me a liar in front of the group. He said (in Borchard 2005, 216):

> Yeah. and I'm the president. Come on. man. You think you're too good to take my juice? If you was really a student at UNLV. you wouldn't be out here sitting with all these homeless guys. you'd be sitting in your warm dorm room. Don't act like you're above it. like you're better than us. Now. don't say anything. don't talk. I don't want no conversation. just take the damn juice.

I was surprised and confused by his strong response. I then took the path of least resistance: I took the juice and began drinking.

There were other problems with being low-key when entering the field and then slowly introducing myself to others. Once I sat at a picnic table where I was to meet a woman, Jessi, for an interview. I hung out and conversed with the men at the table for a half-hour, saying simply that I was supposed to be meeting Jessi, who they all knew. After they asked more about me, I said that I was a researcher studying homelessness, and that Jessi had agreed to let me interview her. One man then announced that it seemed I had been interviewing them for a half an hour, and should buy them all lunch. In the spur of the moment, I agreed. We ended up having a group quasi-interview over lunch, a spontaneous occurrence the dynamics of which allowed for interviewees to reinforce or disagree with what others had to say. All eight of the men at the table wanted to have lunch, but only five then wanted to speak in any depth about their experiences on record.

My incidents in the field studying homeless people taught me that I should be relatively up front relatively early about my status as a researcher *with at least one person present* if I had any plans to do more than simply observe. Few people like to learn that they have been observed for a long time without their consent. Although most people understand this intuitively, there is a special dilemma with regards to unobtrusively observing homeless people in public. Homeless people are by definition forced to live out their private lives in public space (Amster 2008). While housed citizens can withdraw from view when they want to do personal things, homeless people are particularly vulnerable to public observations of their private behaviors, and can be very resentful of intrusions into the private lives they are forced to live out publicly.

I have been heartened to discover that other fieldworkers studying homelessness have, implicitly and explicitly, faced similar dilemmas. In his study of African-American street vendors in New York City, many of whom were homeless, Duneier (2000) decided to work with one vendor. At one point during an interview where a participant held his tape recorder, Duneier briefly left, only to listen to the tape months later. Some of the African American participants had discussed Duneier, who is Caucasian and Jewish, in terms of Jewish stereotypes. Although Duneier tried to be explicit in maintaining his ongoing researcher status with this group, the participants had forgotten that the recorder was on, and thus it had recorded a conversation that captured some of the men's racist thoughts that they might not have wanted Duneier to know. Although Duneier advocated the use of real names in other parts of his study, in regards to this conversation "the participants, who forgot the tape was running, have asked me to conceal their identities in this instance" (2000, 336). In this case, even his explicit researcher status and visible racial difference did not prevent him from gaining some information that his subjects would likely not have told him.

In developing their ethnography, Snow and Anderson described what they called "listening unobtrusively to conversations among the homeless that arose naturally" as a technique for gaining information from homeless people (1993, 22). They mentioned two types of listening: "eavesdropping . . . and a kind of nondirective, conversational listening . . . when we were engaged in encounters with one or more homeless individuals" (1993, 22). The ethical issues involved in eavesdropping are not explicitly discussed in Snow and Anderson's work. The authors mention, however, that, "we positioned ourselves in relation to the homeless in the role of a 'buddy-researcher'" (1993, 22). One of the authors "hung out" with homeless people on a regular basis, made "daily institutional rounds" with them, and provided small kindnesses and listened to them as a friend. This buddy-researcher "tried to avoid distinctive dress by wearing old clothes similar to those worn by most homeless, although his were generally cleaner" (1993, 22). Snow and Anderson then note that, "It should be emphasized, though, that the researcher did not attempt to pass as a homeless individual. He frequently brought up his researcher status by mentioning his research and university affiliation and by asking [personal] questions" (1993, 22).

Snow and Anderson do not weigh in on the ethical issues involved in combining a method like eavesdropping with dressing to blend into rather than appear distinct from a group. Although they assert that the fieldworker in their pair did not try to conceal his identity as a researcher, it was possible that a homeless person (or persons) spoke candidly around him in institutional settings before (and perhaps long before) that homeless person came to know he was a researcher. If and how to disclose one's identity as a researcher in the varied contexts of fieldwork on homeless people, then, is an important ethical issue in such research. As homelessness blends public and private space, I believe it is crucial to consider carefully how a homeless person might feel about, for example, being listened in on when having a conversation, or having his or her photograph taken without explicit permission.

My solution to the dilemma of how I should present myself in the field is to try to explain my researcher role early on to at least one subject with whom I interact. "Dressing down" is a good idea to reduce the social distance between my subjects and me, but it becomes deception if the subjects with whom I interact directly think that I too am homeless. Honesty begets honesty, and that means I need to be up front with subjects so that they can make an informed decision about participating in my study.

Who Benefits from Research on Homelessness?

Daniel Kerr asks an important question in his study of homelessness, politics, and gentrification in Cleveland: "who benefits from homelessness?" (2011, 3). I will therefore consider a third ethical issue not often voiced by those who research homelessness: whether or not I was profiting or benefitting from studying homelessness at the expense of my research subjects. This issue did not seem particularly relevant when I studied homelessness as a graduate student. Once I had published books on the subject, however, I thought more about how I (and others) might be benefiting from or profiting from writing about homelessness.

According to Dolgon (2006, 116), "writing and research on homeless people has certainly become a cottage industry of sorts in the academy." He notes that the field had become so large that Sage Press had published a nearly one thousand page *Encyclopedia of Homelessness* in 2004. The idea that quite a lot has already been written on this subject also carries (at least for me) an implicit critique of the *purpose* of all this work. Is the goal simply to document the occurrence of homelessness? Is it to critique existing social structures? Or, is it to change those structures, to address those inequalities so that they might be overcome?

Since there is so much published now on homelessness, and since homelessness itself does not seem to have abated, Dolgon's statements could also suggest that conducting these studies helps keep sociologists employed. Undeniably I, and other authors and researchers who study homelessness, derive material and professional benefits from studying this topic. As experts on homelessness, we benefit to some extent from the problem continuing (Wasserman and Clair 2010, 46).

The ethical issues of who benefits from homelessness, and in particular to what extent researchers of homelessness should benefit materially from their studies, often go unaddressed by the authors of such studies. In my selective review of recent ethnographic studies of homelessness (Borchard 2005; Kerr 2011; Marvasti 2003; Snow and Anderson 1993; Stephenson 2006; Wasserman and Clair 2010; Williams 2003) the authors did not discuss either donating a portion of their profits from their royalties or direct profit sharing with their research subjects. One notable exception is Duneier (2000), who states that he considered the vendors, scavengers, and panhandlers he studied to be "collaborators" in his work. For twenty-one such people who were central to his study, he "made a commitment to return the advance and a share of any royalties or other forms of income that the book might yield" (2000, 14).

A central issue is connected to ideas of profit sharing with participants in a study: how much profit is being made from such studies? In Duneier's case, the book was produced for a large commercial press. In my case and in the cases of Kerr, Marvasti, Stephenson, Wasserman and Clair, and Williams, the presses publishing the work were either smaller academic/commercial presses, or smaller university presses. Snow and Anderson published with a larger university press. Speaking for myself, if I were to calculate all the expenses incurred while doing years of fieldwork, producing transcriptions, conducting analysis, preparing the manuscripts, paying others to produce the parts I could not (photographers, cartographers, and indexers), shopping the manuscripts around, and other miscellaneous expenses, there would be a net loss. I have also found it hard to win external grants to conduct my research, because most granting agencies want to fund entities working to develop programs to address homelessness, not ethnographers who want to document its occurrence. Therefore, the majority of field researchers of homelessness, I believe, do not profit substantially from their studies. For researchers of social life working in university settings, publications are expected, but generally these can be on any topic of social importance. In my experience, studying homelessness was motivated more by interest than profit.

There are further considerations about if and how those who write about homelessness benefit from its existence. People are not motivated by one thing at a time. I am interested in critiquing social injustices, *and* in my own material existence. There is also an implicit dilemma for anyone who works for something seen as a noble cause (a "calling") but who also gets paid for it: some feel that those whose primary work should be to help others ought not to receive compensation beyond an arbitrary, but always low, standard. The idea of a "calling" then creates a discourse justifying the low pay that teachers and social workers, for example, often receive: ideas are promoted that "social workers shouldn't be doing that job for the money," or, "higher teacher salaries means fewer resources for the students—by requesting raises, those teachers are being selfish," for example. A double standard then exists for compensating those working in the helping professions or directly with poor people compared to those in business or even government.

The idea that a cottage industry now exists for homelessness studies might also be seen as perpetuating a false dilemma: either your academic work is solving a problem, or it is perpetuating it. Importantly, no one fully knows what impact their research will have on the field or on people's view of an issue. I could argue that perhaps we haven't written *enough* on homelessness, because it obviously isn't resulting in dramatic social change. It is possible that there is then a need to continually update accounts of poverty in the United States, because materially comfortable Americans refuse to accept their culpability in creating this life-threatening inequality. We need more books (and other media accounts) on homelessness and poverty in the United States, because such stories must compete with a media carnival of entertainment escapism, celebrity worship, and pundit infighting. We have yet to reach critical mass on the importance of addressing who benefits from poverty in this country, how poverty is reproduced, why it is reproduced, and what can be done to stop it.

It could also be argued that researchers conducting homeless studies should also serve as organizers to address this problem. I don't think that is crucial either. Academics certainly can be organizers, but academics can also motivate others to organize, or to write other, more popular works for different audiences that might inspire activism. To give one example, Amanda Haymond, a student at UNLV, contacted me after reading my first book. She wanted to produce a street paper for homeless people in Las Vegas. Within a year her paper, *Forgotten Voice*, was being published monthly. Homeless people suddenly had a regular media outlet to enact a public dialogue with each other, with those at the helms of city government, with those who manage charitable organizations, and even those in mainstream media organizations. I also began writing columns for *Forgotten Voice* where I discussed the lives of homeless people I had met and the social context in which homelessness occurs in Las Vegas. I was glad that my academic work played a small part in inspiring another person to organize a front-line, street-level response, empowering homeless people and bringing further local attention to the problem.

Other ways of presenting my research to a popular audience followed. Nearly a year after my first book was first published, I worked extensively with Margaret Anne Miille, a reporter with the *Las Vegas Review-Journal*, on an article about homelessness in Las Vegas and my research (Miille 2006). Her article began as a shorter piece, but after her editor grew interested in the topic the article grew into a three-page "In-Depth" section of the newspaper. Her article summarized many parts of my study and highlighted evocative excerpts for a lay audience. I soon realized that having such an article appear in the local newspaper with a distribution of over 200,000 copies would give my ideas, and the words of my research subjects, a readership that none of us had imagined. I also received many comments from readers of the article whose ideas about homelessness were changed because of the piece, readers who likely would never have picked up an academic tome on the subject.

An ethical maxim for homeless researchers should then be to either write about homelessness *in varied ways* and *for varied audiences*, or to at least work with others to disseminate their findings. *Not* writing about homelessness, I think, would be far worse. As a field researcher of homelessness, I do not believe you have to be an organizer or even an activist, but I felt it was imperative that my research had a larger audience. I thought carefully about what my intent was in writing a book about homelessness. I had made an unspoken promise to the homeless people I had interviewed to value what they had to say to me about their homelessness, and their stories. I realized that a book format would allow for a more extended, nuanced presentation of the complexity of homelessness, and a presentation that would be forceful for being *in homeless people's own words*. Several of the men and women who shared their stories with me believed that having a wider audience concerning their daily problems could only help to change the situation for other homeless people later. I am gratified that the audience for their words has been so large. The cumulative effect of retelling such stories might be an increased awareness of stark inequality in the United States, possibly leading to social movements or simply allowing an individual to reflect on how he or she should act.

Conclusion

Before entering the field as an ethnographer, I had vague thoughts about many aspects of my study. I thought about how I might appear to my research subjects. I had considered whether or not I should give an interviewee money or buy him or her something after an interview. I thought about what type of interaction and what type of relationship I would have with an interviewee. Although I had thought about all of these things, in the process of actually carrying out actions I learned that the decisions I have made were not so obviously "good" or "bad"—in practice, it was often impossible to conduct myself in a way where someone wasn't occasionally off-put, offended, or even hurt. The degrees of difficulties or harm I caused others through my research can be a source of endless internal debate and perhaps inhibit my ability to act.

During my research, I further thought about how I might publish the results of my study. However, I had not considered how publishing my study in book form could be seen as profiting from my research. I also had not thought about seeking out both academic and popular outlets for my research to give it the widest possible audience. Continued publication of research on homelessness in a variety of outlets, I believe, is an ethical response to questions about who benefits from continued research on homelessness.

The ethical maxim of "do no harm" is an abstract and idealistic standard. As a researcher and author, I respond: I have made mistakes. They were unavoidable. Not only was I learning about my subject, but I was learning about how I might learn and communicate about my subject. I *have* learned, and hope I will be able to further help researchers and homeless persons by applying what I now know. I am writing this chapter to provide future researchers a few real life examples that I did not have.

I believe that if I did my best to be ethical, that if I continue to review my actions, and that if I continue to do my best today, I can live with myself.

Notes

1. A version of this paper was presented at the annual meeting of the American Sociological Association in Boston, Massachusetts, in August 2008. I wish to thank Shaun Padgett for reading a draft of this work and offering helpful suggestions.

Chapter 8

Weapons of the Weak, by the Weak, and for the Weak: Negotiating Power Between and Among Homeless Persons and Service Providers

Julie Adkins

Abstract. Homeless persons have no power: they are arrested and jailed for sleeping in the "wrong" place. Homeless people have vast power: to frighten people away from downtown and to depress property values. Service providers and caring agencies have significant power over the homeless: to provide or to deny vital services. Agencies and providers have little power: they are at the mercy of donor restrictions, limited funding, and rules that they themselves did not write. In the midst of these paradoxes, negotiations for power are a constant presence—foreground and background—both in the lives of homeless persons and of those who seek to aid them. Based on extensive fieldwork in Dallas, Texas, this chapter examines the claiming and denial of power in a particular agency's clients and employees, and reflects on the author's own struggles with her role as both observer and "helper."

Call them clients, call them guests, call them customers, call them what you will;[1] but I suspect that the homeless folks I spend time with are alternately amused and angered by the civic discourse that calls them "powerful." The stories I hear from them are mostly about helplessness and loss: arrest for sleeping on the sidewalk, confiscation or destruction of personal belongings in police sweeps, theft and assault committed by other homeless persons, hunger, domestic violence, police harassment in ostensibly public locations such as the city library and parks, shelter rules so rigid that a resident cannot maintain a job without violating curfew, and/or other "program requirements" such as mandatory chapel attendance. And yet, according to many civic leaders and downtown business owners, the homeless are in fact quite powerful. They have the power, it is claimed, to prevent the revitalization of downtown areas by frightening customers away from businesses. Their presence, sitting or sleeping on city sidewalks, is believed to interfere with planners' and developers' ability to (re)gentrify downtowns with the sale and/or lease of expensive apartments, condos, and lofts. In fact, their mere presence in certain sectors is said to depress property values.

These claims have of course been made in many cities (cf. Gibson 2004; Mitchell 2003; Valado 2006); Dallas, Texas may be one of the few in which local-level research has been conducted in order ostensibly to "prove" such assertions (Weinstein and Clower 2000; 2006).[2] The ninth-largest city in the United States, with an estimated population of 1.2 million (according to the 2010 census), Dallas is reluctant host to a homeless population estimated at 5,000 to 6,000 Dallas's homeless tend to be clustered in the center city and, as one would expect, most of the nonprofit and government-related agencies that serve them are located downtown as well. (It remains a chicken-and-egg question whether the presence of those agencies has drawn the homeless into downtown, or whether the prior presence of poverty in the center city drew such agencies to locate themselves there.) Because of the clustering of these "helping agencies," downtown Dallas also serves as a magnet for homeless and at-risk persons from the suburbs that surround the city on all sides.

In these respects, Dallas is hardly unique among large American cities. Dallas, however, has burdened itself with an origin myth—the "city with no reason to exist," created as a "monument to sheer determination" by early entrepreneurial pioneers (Hill 1996, xvi) and governed wisely by business leaders for the good of all—that has made it particularly difficult for the city to deal creatively or compassionately with poverty in its midst. The implicit argument runs something like this: if early settlers arrived with "nothing" and somehow created a world-class city on the plains, how can having "nothing" in the present moment possibly be an obstacle for any person already privileged enough to live in such a place? The "power" of the homeless in Dallas is just this: their continued presence calls Dallas's whole story of itself into question. Ultimately, what the homeless cannot be forgiven for is their failure to abide by the myth and, thus, their power to tarnish Dallas's glittering image of itself (see, e.g., Graff 2008; Hanson 2003; Hill 1996; Payne 1994).

From within the large and complex urban space of the city of Dallas, I want to highlight and analyze power negotiations and the resulting ethical quandaries in just one microcosm: the soup kitchen, day shelter, and helping agency known as the Stewpot.[3] Begun in 1975 by the First Presbyterian Church, the Stewpot garners widespread community support in the form of both financial contributions and volunteer labor. The Stewpot serves a noon meal,[4] provides a safe place for people to "hang out" during the day (and even to sleep, though it has to be at a table or stretched out on the floor), employs six caseworkers to assist clients with particular needs, and hosts a variety of other programs and agencies that are available on a weekly or monthly basis with a regular schedule.

For a period of three years, my primary role at the Stewpot—in addition to being the onsite anthropologist and asking endless questions—was that of an "intake volunteer." In that job, I would sit at the front desk and "process" clients as they came through the line. This involved a number of activities: entering a client's name on the list to see a caseworker; answering questions about where the nearest night shelter can be found and giving directions; and handing out various necessities as they are requested, such as toiletries, pain medication, writing paper, feminine hygiene products, condoms . . . or, apologizing when a requested item is no longer available.[5] Each morning when the doors were unlocked at 8:00 a.m. there was already a long line of clients waiting outside, often extending from the Stewpot's corner site to the far end of the city block. Clients would hurry to re-form the line inside; there were rarely fewer than 100 people in line as the morning began, and it continued to grow for at least the first half hour as folks would trickle in after breakfast at a nearby shelter. It was unusual for the intake staff and/or volunteers to reach the last person in line before 9:30 a.m., by which time the casework list for the morning was nearly always filled with as many appointments as the staff could hope to see by noon. Clients continued to approach the front desk all morning, though, with various questions, requests, and demands; a normal morning involved anywhere from 200 to 300 separate staff-client interactions across the front counter. The pattern repeated itself in similar fashion when the Stewpot reopened at 1:00 p.m. after a one-hour lunch break, although there were normally fewer clients in the afternoon.

Although my visible role at the Stewpot was my volunteer "job," all of the staff there were aware that I was doing research and planning to write about my findings. The topic, as I described it to them, was "homelessness, and the City of Dallas's response—or appalling lack thereof—and the Stewpot as a lens through which to view the issues." Indeed, staff often brought me information and shared anecdotes that were not directly related to any work we were doing at the moment, in the interest of sharing as much data as possible. Some, but certainly not all, of the homeless persons that I encountered in the course of my work knew that I was more than a volunteer. However, here and in other publications, I report only on interactions and behaviors that were public in nature and overheard or observed by numerous individuals. At no time have I used (or will I use) information that was entrusted to me privately, as a volunteer, by any individual who did not also know of my research role.

In three years of deepening familiarity with the Stewpot and its operations, and having become a trusted member of the volunteer "staff," I observed not only what I expected to see—imbalances and negotiations of power between agency staff or volunteers and the clients—but also intricate negotiations between homeless clients themselves, and between and among the staff and volunteers of the Stewpot. These last are the most troubling to me, because they are largely invisible to the client population, who must nevertheless live with their aftereffects.

Between Agency and Clients

I begin with the power issues that are best documented in the research thus far, those between clients and service providers (cf. Rowe 1999).[6] At the Stewpot, these become apparent almost immediately as one enters the building on the ground floor. Staff and volunteers enter the building through different doors than do the clients, most often through a parking garage protected by an automatic gate and staffed by a security guard. The ground floor, although reasonably spacious in terms of the area available for clients to relax and/or wait, has clearly delineated areas where clients may not go unless invited or accompanied by a staff person (I will include volunteers under the rubric of "staff," to save time repeating). The so-called front desk where I sit to interact with clients as they first come in is behind a counter which stands nearly forty-eight inches high; a person in a wheelchair cannot begin to see over it. Thus, by itself it defines a clear barrier not only between "us" and "them," but also between "our" space and "their" space. Very early in my work, I became so uncomfortable about the privilege implied in *sitting* behind that high counter while my conversation partners had to *stand* on the other side that I began standing as well, sensing that I needed to do something to bridge the distance.

Obviously, even in my limited volunteer role, I have more power vis-à-vis the institution than do the clients. However, all of the staff I have observed do what they can to place relationships on as equal—or at least, respectful—a footing as possible. They make every effort to remember clients' names and to address them respectfully; in particular, new clients are most frequently addressed as "Mr. [Jones]" or "Ms. [Smith]," with the use of first names coming only after acquaintance has been made. Clients are invited to call caseworkers and other staff by their first names and often do so, though this is frequently modified, particularly by African American clients, to include a title along with the first name; e.g., "I need to see Mr. Ronny." Caseworkers' individual office spaces are arranged so that the client is always nearest the door and can choose to exit unobstructed. Occasionally these "equalizing" efforts have unintended consequences: in one case, a newly hired female caseworker received a little *too* much attention from some of her male clients, who chose to interpret her friendliness as sexual interest. For a period of several weeks following her hire, she had clients who insisted on seeing her daily whether they had a particular need or not, and she complained of inappropriate or too-frequent attempts at physical touching by several of them. Through a period of coaching, she became able to distinguish between claiming her own power in setting appropriate personal boundaries with clients while not making it an issue of the institution's power over them.

Even so, the balance of power clearly lies on the side of staff. Clients who become abusive, whether physically or verbally, are directed to leave the building at once, and are removed from the premises by a uniformed police officer if they fail to comply. Those who continue to argue and/or fight with the officer may be banned for a certain period of time, and may even be subject to arrest. Ejections and bans, temporary or permanent, may occur for other reasons as well; I have observed ejections stemming from a broad range of behaviors such as repeatedly blowing a loud whistle for no purpose except to draw attention to oneself, trying to start a fight with another client, and rolling a joint while seated at one of the tables in the waiting area.

But power is more commonly exercised in ways that are far more subtle, and are often invisible to clients and even to other staff who do not observe the behavior. Front desk staff and volunteers, like most "street-level bureaucrats" (Lipsky 1980), actually have a tremendous amount of discretion within certain areas. Front desk staff can, for example, add a client's name to the casework list even after it is "officially" closed, if they perceive a need that is urgent or unusual. Caseworkers will never know that the "maximum" has been exceeded unless one of them comes and counts the names, which they never do. Staff may allow a client to use the phone at the front desk, even though it's technically forbidden . . . or they may go "by the book" and refer the client to free phones at the nearby night shelter, or pay phones at the public library. They may agree to check a client's mail before or after the usual hours for the mail station, or they may not. They might take the time to look through the whole United Way directory of helping agencies to locate assistance for a client who needs something the Stewpot cannot provide . . . or they might not. When a caseworker asks front desk staff to "call for the next client," they are supposed to use the microphone to call the next name on the list . . . but on rare occasions, they will skip over names and call someone else first. Knowing individual casework staff personalities as they do, front desk workers may attempt to arrange that particular clients get seen by particular caseworkers—either because they need to see someone uniquely knowledgeable about given subjects (e.g., veterans' issues), or particularly sympathetic (e.g., a female caseworker for victims of domestic violence), or particularly rigid about following rules.

There seem to be (at least) two patterns operating in these decisions to bend or break the rules, but neither is what I had expected to find. That is, favors are not necessarily granted to those clients who are the most polite and articulate, or withheld from those who are aggressive or manipulative, although these behaviors occasionally enter into the equation as an additional factor to be considered.

Rather, staff seem most often willing to exercise their unequal power on behalf of the clients they perceive as the most power*less*. For the most part, this does not appear to be a consciously reasoned choice; it is rarely articulated and is certainly unwritten. Yet I find myself—and I see caseworkers doing the same—more willing to bend the rules for, or take extra time with, for example, a mother with a small child in her arms, an elderly client, a person who is newly homeless and clearly "lost" in the system, the young man who comes in dressed in a pink sundress, etc. Those whom the staff perceive as most vulnerable and most at risk on the streets are the ones on whose behalf they are most likely to exercise their discretionary and unequal power.

The second pattern is that staff also seem willing to bend the rules for clients whom they perceive as needing only one more little push to get themselves off the streets. For example, if a client states that he has a job interview later in the morning—and there is reason to believe he is telling the truth (perhaps he is more nicely dressed than usual)—the staff may try to slip his name higher on the list so that he can see his caseworker sooner rather than later.

Of course, staff and volunteers do not always exercise their institutional power in ways that would be perceived as helpful by the clients. Though it is far from politically correct to say so, some of the homeless are difficult and unpleasant people. And while there is widespread evidence indicating large-scale structural causes for homelessness in America (cf. Gans 1995; Hopper 2003; Lyon-Callo 2004; O'Flaherty 1996), it is equally true that many among the homeless—for a variety of reasons, not all of which they can control—act in ways that are not in their own best interest and that contribute to their status as outcasts. From the point of view of the front-desk staff, the most consistently irritating behavior (because of its frequency, and because it seems usually to involve interrupting) is the "Did you call my name yet?" query, which also takes the alternate form of "How far down the list am I?" There are a handful of clients who seem almost compelled to approach the front desk about once every ten minutes to ask, in one form or another, how much longer it will be until they are seen. Some of these are undoubtedly people with short-term memory problems, who literally do not remember having asked the question a few minutes previously, much less the answer they received. Others make frequent trips outside the building to smoke or to visit with friends who do, despite having been instructed to wait indoors until their name is called. Most, however, simply cannot bear to wait. A few are so anxious about the answer that they will break into line—in front of people who have not yet had a chance to speak with staff at all—to demand a response. Staff and volunteers have tried a variety of strategies to discourage this behavior—everything from answering "I don't know," which is clearly untrue, to telling a client that if they ask again their name will be moved to the end of the list. Afterward, though, staff guiltily debate among themselves about whether their irritation really stems from frustration with client behaviors that truly are problematic in their own right—imagine behaving in such a way while waiting for a job interview or a medical appointment—or whether it's just that they are too easily annoyed when they should be more understanding.

Though most power clearly lies on the side of staff and volunteers, there are some clients who have found ways to use language in particular to try to increase their limited power vis-à-vis the agency. Abusive or obscene language—which may be effective in some settings—only serves to get clients kicked out of the Stewpot. A subtler strategy is therefore needed. Since the Stewpot is a faith-based institution, disgruntled clients often choose to utilize religious discourse to express unhappiness when they have not been given what they wanted. One man, on being told that he would have to come up with half the fare for a bus ticket home before the Stewpot paid the remainder, stalked out of the caseworker's office saying, "I can't believe you call yourselves Christians." Others offer "I'm going to pray for you!" as a parting shot, in such a tone that it is clearly meant as a threat rather than a promise. And a few have mastered the art of saying "Bless you!" in such a tone of voice that it is clear that what they really mean is "F*** you!"

Between and Among Clients

A second place where I have often observed power negotiations taking place is between our homeless clients themselves. In many instances this appears as a question of "rights" and one client's perception that another is violating his or her rights. The most common source of friction has to do with a client's perception that someone is trying to cut in line ahead of them. Unfortunately, the setup of the room at Stewpot makes this inevitable: clients enter the building through a door that is to the left of the front desk, but must then walk past the desk to get in the line which begins on the right-hand side of the desk/counter. Newcomers almost always will come in the door and head straight for the front desk and its staff, not realizing that they must instead go to the end of the line. Fortunately, most "regulars" are patient with this kind of line-breaking: they know when someone is new and cannot be expected to know the rules. While those already in the line *do* expect that staff will send that person to the end of the line (which the staff indeed do), they do not shout and create a stir. It is a different matter altogether, however, when someone who "ought to know better" ignores the line and approaches the desk because they want something simple and don't feel that they should have to stand in line with those who are waiting to be put on the casework list. However, whether that "something simple" is just asking a brief question, or requesting a vitamin or a bar of soap, these line-jumpers elicit loud protests from those already standing and waiting. Tension also rises quickly when a person utilizes the voice-mail access phone for longer than the posted four minute limit. Some clients will confront the offender themselves; the majority are more likely to complain to the staff to intervene on their behalf. It is perhaps unsurprising that, among people whose rights are so frequently trampled by the larger society, there is great importance placed in this setting on each person's behaving as though s/he is no better nor worse nor more important than anyone else. Clients expect that Stewpot staff will support them in this belief.

A second, far subtler and more beneficent, negotiation of power takes place in the relationships of reciprocity that become established between and among clients. I have most often observed these in the form of generalized reciprocity (Sahlins 1972): "A" has been given food at some other location, and chooses to share it with B, C, and D, knowing that at a future date one of them will share a windfall with him (and he will have the "right" to claim it). Reciprocity often also occurs in a kind of "pay it forward" form. Those who have been homeless for a while and have learned how to negotiate the system often give advice and directions to newcomers, walk with them to the shelter they're trying to locate, tell them where the best place is to find a phone or a shower, and so on.

Finally, there are occasional episodes where one of the clients will attempt to get the staff police officer to intervene in a conflict occurring outside the building. Different officers have varied opinions on whether they believe it is appropriate to intervene in such conflicts; although in Dallas Police Department uniform, they are officially "off duty" and some understand this to mean that their right and obligation to intervene ends at the outside door. Nevertheless, it is not uncommon to have a client come in and ask the officer to come outside and deal with a person who just took their bundle of clothes, or to intervene in a fight between two people, or to arrest someone who is making threatening remarks. In this way, they attempt to enlist to their cause someone who is perceived as having power, especially when they feel they are justified and in the right.

Within the Agency and Among Staff/Volunteers

What was most interesting to me in my research and volunteer experience is the power negotiation—both overt and covert—that constantly takes place between and among the staff themselves, whether paid or volunteer. (This is rarely discussed in the literature; for exceptions, see Bridgman 2003; 2006.) While overall the agency operates smoothly and with little friction, there are frustrations and differences of both personality and opinion that occasionally manifest in staff interactions with clients. For example, in my second or third week "on the job," the volunteer who was training me became upset at a caseworker who refused to bend the usual rules in a specific instance: a particular client needed a Greyhound ticket to get out of town, but she did not have the one-half cost of the ticket that the Stewpot usually requires in order to pay for the remainder. Ronny, the caseworker involved, had the authority to make an exception but chose not to. Both Alan, the volunteer, and Marco, the security officer on duty, were of the opinion that the client would be at high risk on the street because she was young, female, petite, and attractive; and they felt Ronny was being unreasonable. Alan took $40 out of his own wallet and asked me to take the client to the back hallway where Ronny could not observe us, and give her the money. With very little hesitation, I did so.

A long-time—and only recently resolved—source of friction between frontline staff and behind-the-scenes policymaking staff had to do with the Stewpot identification (ID) cards. These are photo ID cards which include the individual's name, birth date, Social Security number, and signature, which the Stewpot created and began issuing many years ago at the request of the city.[7] Clients need only provide a Social Security printout with their number on it in order to have the ID made,[8] and these are honored by city offices and the Texas Department of Public Safety as one of the documents required to obtain an official state ID, a birth certificate, and other legal proofs of identity. In addition, quite a few employers have been willing to accept them as a temporary measure until a person can arrange for permanent ID, and the various nighttime shelters in Dallas also accept them as proof of identity. These ID cards are laminated in plastic and are quite sturdy—but this is of little help if the card is lost, stolen, or "disappeared" in a police sweep of homeless camps. Longstanding policy provided that a replacement Stewpot ID card could be made, but this second ID would be kept in the file at the Stewpot and the client would receive only a paper photocopy. Particularly after 9/11, however, city and state agencies became much more reluctant to accept the photocopy. In fact, whether or not the paper copy will be accepted depends entirely on which clerk happens to be staffing an agency at any particular moment—just as with Stewpot staff, some are more willing than others to bend the rules—and clients were understandably unhappy at the increasing difficulties and dead ends they began to encounter.

Front desk staff were the first to learn of government offices' unwillingness to accept the photocopied ID; clients would come in to pick up their Stewpot ID and then head straight for City Hall to obtain their birth certificate (which the Stewpot had also helped to pay for), only to be turned away by a city staffer who insisted on the "original" ID. Despite an increasing accumulation of anecdotal evidence, the Stewpot's director remained adamant for some time that the policy was not going to change. The issue was argued in staff meetings for several months before a change of policy eventually resulted. Now, those who want a second laminated Stewpot ID may pay five dollars and receive one; they can still have a photocopy free of charge (and future copies as well, since an original will then remain in the Stewpot's files). The first Stewpot ID remains free for any person who needs or wants one.

Many of the Stewpot's staff have been working together for longer than a decade, so it is not surprising that conflicts occasionally arise among them. In addition, a significant number of them are members of First Presbyterian

Church, so their lives overlap in other places and at other times than work. Their commitment to the institution helps them to overcome some of the friction that inevitably arises in such stressful work; it also appears to have the effect of keeping them committed to the Stewpot even though most of them could make much more money working elsewhere (even at other nonprofits). Even so, the longer I was involved the more concerned I became about a few ongoing patterns of individual staff behavior and intra-staff conflict that seemed often to have a negative impact on work with the client population.

Some conflicts are episodic and non-recurring: one morning, a client arrived five minutes late for a class because she had been on an errand given her by her caseworker, who told her it was okay for that reason to come to class late. Unfortunately, the senior caseworker was having a bad day, and chose this particular client to make an example of. Although Molly had told the client to come to class as soon as she arrived back, Ronny refused to let her in. My attempts at explanation on the client's behalf were unsuccessful; the client in this case was poorly served, having followed exactly the instructions she was given by one staff member while being denied services by another. She had to wait nearly two weeks before finally being able to complete the class.

More troubling to me, though, are ongoing feuds among the staff, most of which seem to involve Teresa and various other staff members. Teresa has worked at the Stewpot for more than twenty years, and, despite a gruff exterior, has deep compassion for the clients, many of whom call her "Mom." Her job description clearly involves client intake and the supervision of volunteers who assist in this process; it does not include casework with clients. While Teresa has a great deal of "street sense," she lacks any training for doing formal casework. Yet she frequently oversteps her boundaries by trying to assist clients on her own and/or arguing publicly with casework staff on behalf of particular clients. Both Ronny and Karl, the director, have counseled her about the matter in performance reviews, but behind their backs Teresa is adamant that she is "not going to stop helping clients."

Over the years, Teresa has become skilled at using "weapons of the weak" (Scott 1985) to impose her will occasionally on staff who otherwise "outrank" her. One example will have to suffice: on a particular afternoon as closing time was approaching, she noticed that there were still five people on the list wanting to see a caseworker. I assured her that all of them had been informed at the time they checked in (as "standby" clients) that we could not guarantee they would be seen that afternoon. Nevertheless, at five minutes before closing, Teresa called all their names over the microphone and had them come to wait at the table behind the front counter (i.e., in "our" space), thus "forcing" Ronny to attend to all of them before he could leave for the day.

In retrospect, at least, that episode was amusing. It had the added benefit of clearly siding with clients over and against the schedules and agendas of staff. In contrast, most of the time, at least insofar as I have observed, client needs are regularly pushed aside in the interest of Teresa's own agenda. As noted above, the casework list is normally filled by 9:30 or 10:00 each morning, even though the Stewpot does not close for lunch until noon. During the couple of hours remaining before noon, front desk staff and volunteers are—or should be—available to answer questions, give out hygiene items, and encourage clients who come in late to return after lunch to see a caseworker. On many mornings, however, when the last slot on the casework list has been filled, Teresa places a large "Closed" sign on the high counter at the front desk and either disappears into the back offices for extended periods of time or greets those clients who dare to approach with, "We're closed! What do you want?" This does not appear to be official Stewpot policy (i.e., stating that the intake desk is closed even though the agency is officially open)—indeed, Teresa does not "close" the front desk when Karl is nearby—but rather a means by which Teresa seeks to exert some control over her work environment. Clients are often difficult, their needs are overwhelming, and Teresa's job description does not empower her to do very much on their behalf. In this respect, it is perhaps understandable that she walks away from it, whether literally or figuratively.

Even so, this is the one and only situation in which I as volunteer lost my temper (publicly, anyway) in three years' time. One particular morning as I was busily writing my tallies and field notes, Teresa became frustrated with a difficult client and, as soon as he walked away, slammed the sign down on the counter and said, "That does it! We're closed!" Through gritted teeth, I fired back, "It's 10:00 a.m. We are *not* closed!" and yanked the sign away. This surprised me almost as much as it did her, as it occurred during a period when I was trying to limit my role to observing and not "working" as a volunteer. However, I paid for my outburst by having to work for about the next fifteen minutes, as Teresa stalked away while there were clients waiting to speak with one of us. I am not certain what set me off on this particular day as opposed to others on which I have sat silent while she has done the same thing. And I continue to struggle with what is appropriate in my role as an observer and/or a volunteer vis-à-vis an agency that has welcomed me into its midst but not solicited my opinions.

Conclusion

Within the overall structures of a city such as Dallas, nonprofits that serve the homeless arguably have only slightly more power than the clients they serve. Their resources are limited and never enough to meet the need; business interests seek to place limits on them in order to keep the homeless out of sight; and elected officials concerned about the city's "image" often perceive such agencies to be more a part of the problem than a part of the solution because they provide a place and an excuse for "undesirables" to congregate. Faith-based organizations like the Stewpot understand a part of their role as being "speaking truth to power," but even in a Bible-belt city like Dallas the voice of the faith community does not carry a great deal of weight when it challenges political and economic "conventional wisdom" and values. Within such a context, the small-scale negotiations for power I have outlined here take on a certain poignancy. On the one hand, neither the Stewpot's clients nor its staff and volunteers have a great deal of power to effect the kind of transformations that would help a large number of homeless to exit the streets permanently—or to keep them from ending up on the streets in the first place. On the other hand, people's lives are at stake.

I often question my role within the mix. Am I just one volunteer among many, who may choose simply to stop offering her time and energy if she becomes sufficiently frustrated with the staff with whom she must interact? Either as a volunteer or as a social scientist, is it my "place" to draw supervisors' attention to staff behavior that seems to be detrimental to the institution and to the population it serves? The Stewpot has no mechanism in place by which to solicit input and feedback from volunteers, so it is not at all clear whether such an intervention would be welcomed. Certainly, in my role as a researcher I can and do ask "innocent" questions that have not-so-innocent subtexts; e.g., "I'm curious about the decision to 'close' the front desk at 10:30 or 11:00," or "Tell me about how that decision was made, or how it frees up resources to do other tasks?" On the other hand, given that the Stewpot does tremendous good in the community (which I do not dispute), is it better for me not to "perturb the system" (Cassell 2002) at all, but only to observe and report?

There are additional reasons for which I feel the need to be extremely cautious in exercising or claiming power within the agency: staff and volunteers know me to be not only an anthropologist, but also an ordained Presbyterian minister of more than twenty years' experience. Thus, although I am "only a volunteer" within the organizational structure of the Stewpot, I am also a colleague of Karl, the director, and therefore his equal with respect to professional status. In addition, the Dallas church which I served until its closure in 2008 gave a gift to the Stewpot of $97,000 from the final disbursal of its funds. Thus, although for the purposes of research I might like to be considered "just" an observer and volunteer, my social location with relation both to the agency and to its "parent" church and staff makes this impossible. It would be naïve for me to expect that my ideas, recommendations, or even offhand remarks would be given no more weight than those of any other long-term volunteer or even "expert" outsider.

But the question remains: when is it time to stop observing and begin advocating? Even at the micro-level—within one helping agency—the answers are not always clear. Is it appropriate for me to claim my own power and to challenge a staff member who (it appears to me) is behaving inappropriately toward the client population? Is it my role to chime in on policies (such as the Stewpot IDs) that need to be amended in order to serve clients better? Should I take sides in staff disagreements when I have strong feelings about one side or the other? If I answer these questions affirmatively, will my ability to do useful research in this setting be compromised? If so, will that change how I answer the questions? In this setting, or in any setting where we find ourselves, which is the greater goal in the present moment: to increase useful knowledge over the long term, or to make an immediate impact on vulnerable lives? (For more on these issues, see Rosenthal's discussion in chapter 2.)

Scholars who work among and on behalf of the homeless—such as those represented in this volume—find ourselves at differing places on the continuum between noninterference and advocacy. It is perhaps not altogether different from the struggles faced by helping agencies to find a balance between charity and justice, between meeting immediate needs and seeking to change social structures in order to eliminate those needs. I would argue simply that, wherever on the continuum we find ourselves at any given moment, it is incumbent upon us to be certain that we enlist our own power—whether it is the power to describe and analyze, or the power to bring about change, or some combination—in ways that will increase and not decrease the power of the populations we are studying . . . in this case, regardless of their power in relation to each other.

Notes

1. There is much debate, among both scholars and care providers, about what term(s) should be used to refer to homeless persons in need of services. "Clients" is accurate in some regards, but emphasizes the inequality between giver and receiver. Locally, the Metro Dallas Homeless Alliance prefers the term "customers," which reminds providers that they are there to *serve* the population, but implies a certain level of free choice among multiple options that most of the homeless do not in fact have. "Guests" is often heard as well, especially for shelter residents but also in other contexts. In this chapter I use the term "clients" deliberately, as it foregrounds the unequal power between those who seek services and those who have the power to give or to withhold.

2. My use of quotation marks around the verb "prove" is deliberate: these studies, though useful in some aspects—i.e., their survey of current efforts to assist the homeless in Dallas and other major cities—are problematic in terms of their research methodology. The first (Weinstein and Clower 2000) establishes a negative statistical correlation between (a) property values in Dallas's southern downtown sector, which are considerably lower than those in the northern downtown sector, and (b) the presence of homeless people in the southern sector—and concludes from this that the presence of homeless persons *causes* property values to be depressed. The second (Weinstein and Clower 2006) is problematic in at least two ways. First, it asks only about business owners' perceptions of whether customers are frightened away by the presence of the homeless; it makes no effort to survey customers who regularly shop downtown (or who avoid shopping downtown) to ask them whether this perception is true. Second, and most egregious, its *sole* research method is to survey downtown business owners—the very group that funded the study in the first place, creating potentially significant conflict of interest.

3. The Stewpot and First Presbyterian Church are the actual names of the referenced institutions. Given that the specific Dallas context is crucial to my ongoing work, it is pointless to try to disguise these. The Stewpot is unique in Dallas, and would be recognizable no matter what name I assigned it. While it may make sense to disguise place names and institutions when the focus is on homeless persons themselves, when the research focus *is* the city and its institutions as they respond to homelessness, then it can often be counterproductive *not* to identify them. Personal names given to all staff and volunteers, however, are pseudonyms. They would be recognizable to other Stewpot insiders, but likely to no one else.

4. However, during the time period of my research, the Stewpot moved its meal service location from the its own site to the new city-owned shelter located about four blocks to the south, and expanded from serving weekday lunches only to three meals a day, seven days a week.

5. In creating the SPSS worksheet/database to track clients' needs along with basic demographic information, I found that I needed more than sixty different "values" to account for the different tasks and/or information that a front desk staff person or volunteer must master in order to do the job effectively. For example, it is not sufficient simply to say, "The Stewpot cannot help you get a Social Security card." Staff are expected to know where the client *can* get that card, and to provide directions.

6. Though it is unusual to find client-staff power imbalances as a major topic of analysis, the following have interesting depictions and discussions of shelter staff power and control over residents: Desjarlais 1997; Dordick 1997; Hopper 2003; Marvasti 2003; Wagner 1993.

7. Without such a basic form of identification, the homeless are often caught in a Catch-22 when they try to obtain more official, government-issued forms of ID. In order to get a copy of one's birth certificate—at least, in the state of Texas—one must present a photo ID at the Bureau of Vital Statistics. But, in order to get a state photo ID card or driver's license as proof of identity, a birth certificate is one of the forms of ID that is most commonly utilized because it is (relatively) easily obtained.

8. IDs are also available for persons without Social Security numbers, such as undocumented immigrants; these will include the photo, name, and birth date. Obviously these are of limited use for legal and bureaucratic purposes, but they are recognized for such needs as admittance to a shelter.

Part Three
Research and Transformation

Throughout this volume, the authors have explored critical themes of advocacy, relationships, motivations, and ethics in the context of personal narratives and professional research on the issue of homelessness. Implicit in all of this work, and explicit in much of it, has been an impetus to promote positive change in society around matters as profound as sociopolitical marginalization and what it means to be fully human in a rapidly dehumanizing world. The notion of "making a difference" is palpable, admirable, and in many instances desirable. But the question remains as to how exactly one is to best accomplish this, and moreover what ethical concerns arise in the process of actively seeking to foster transformation under the auspices of conducting research. Do our personal predilections and connections to the issues we are exploring serve to help or hinder these potential outcomes? How do we reconcile the institutional ethics of academia and other professional settings with the larger humanistic ethics of doing "no harm" and in fact actively promoting our versions of what constitutes "the good" in society?

These are among the most germane and (increasingly) pressing issues in the contemporary social science milieu, and the chapters presented in this ultimate section convey a sense of the range of possible responses. Vin Lyon-Callo begins by "throwing down the gauntlet" in evocative and provocative language, arguing forcefully that under present conditions of expanding hegemony and creeping fascism, any research that does not strive to directly transform society for the better is not only unethical, but is not even worth conducting in the first place. Taking up this call, Randall Amster delivers an analysis of a "new paradigm" of homelessness based on "internal displacement" on a citywide scale as evidenced in post-Katrina New Orleans, unabashedly connecting the dots of personal struggle and political activism in order to empower those seeking change and encourage others to pick up the thread themselves. David Cook likewise enters the field with a "social justice" lens tuned to the authentic experiences of the people in his community, coming to learn in the process that it is oftentimes our own complicity with the very forces we are seeking to expose that most directly keeps us from achieving truly transformative outcomes with our work as researchers and scholars. Bringing these issues to a head, Don Mitchell and Lynn Staeheli wade into the myriad intersections between ethics and politics in research around issues such as homelessness, asking us to consider even more deeply how (and whether) we might "use" homeless people for transformative ends in a manner that is consonant with our multiple roles as scholar-advocates.

Taken together, these chapters produce an emergent framework for engaging both the micro-ethics of research (e.g., institutional review requirements, duty of care to participants, accuracy of presentation) and the equally compelling macro-ethical concerns for deploying our privileges to positive effect and on behalf of those less situated than ourselves. More broadly, and perhaps more to the point, these questions are raised in the context of a world order that increasingly appears unstable, unsustainable, and untenable in many of its baseline assumptions and bedrock practices alike. Shall we simply collect royalty checks, seek professional advancement, and pad our résumés while a teetering economy disproportionately impacts those already in its margins? Should we bog down in the incessantly bureaucratized details of the research enterprise while the life-supporting capacities of the planet—again, to the disadvantage of those already disadvantaged—are increasingly impinged? Such emotive queries may inform our work while also being indicative of our desire to be effective in how we undertake it. This yields an understanding of the transformative potential of research as an enterprise that is equally informed by the heart and mind all at once.

Chapter 9
Do We Really Need More Research on Homelessness? An Autoethnographic Exploration of Ethics, Advocacy, and Exasperation
Vin Lyon-Callo

Abstract. As homelessness has become commonplace throughout the landscape of the United States, much significant research has been produced. We now have a wealth of analytical studies offering insights into almost all facets of homelessness. Yet, despite the range of academic research, homelessness continues largely unabated, organized social movements aimed at altering the structures of inequality producing homeless people are still difficult to locate, public policy largely continues to ignore the systemic conditions producing increasing inequalities and poverty, popular imaginings about homeless people remain largely unchanged, and helping practices continue to focus on treating perceived pathologies within the perceived individualized and pathologized bodies of homeless people. In short, the work done thus far has done a nice job of describing and analyzing homelessness, yet falls far short of contributing to transforming the social processes producing widespread homelessness. How is it that our well-designed research has done so little to transform common sense? This paper builds upon insights from feminist, public, and decolonized ethnography to offer an autoethnographic analysis that challenges the ethical value of continued scientific research on homelessness in light of these concerns. As someone with almost two decades of work on homelessness as a staff member and manager in homeless shelters, as an anthropologist who has done over ten years of ethnographic research on poverty and neoliberal restructuring and governance, and as an activist working to build collaborative resistance against the discursive production of systemic inequities, I suggest that research on homelessness that does not connect homelessness to broader issues of economic and political restructuring, involve working in collaboration with the subjects of the research, and resonate emotionally with a broader public is not only ethically lacking, but is just not worth doing any longer.

One beautiful early summer evening in June 2005, I was sitting outside a café in Amherst, Massachusetts drinking a lousy three-dollar iced tea with one of my former graduate students, when I heard a voice from the past call out my name. Jim, a talented artist and pianist, whom I had known very well almost a decade before, stopped his unpaid labor of picking up trash and trimming the surrounding shrubs to join us at my table. After asking about my family and my academic career, Jim proceeded to update me on dozens of fellow former guests of the shelter where I had worked and he had lived for most of the mid-1990s. Jim, like most of the people he told me about, had remained homeless or near homeless for most of the years since I had moved.

A few minutes after Jim went back to "work," Raymond, another very intelligent, articulate, and caring man I had been close with while he lived (and I worked) in homeless shelters came by the café. He was traveling the street, singing songs while playing drums on an empty five-gallon paint bucket asking for donations. We too caught up on the years since we had last seen each other, with him explaining how his wife was still in a nursing home and he was still on and off the streets. Raymond updated me on more people I had known quite well prior to moving to Michigan in 1998. Again, most were still struggling with poverty and homelessness.

It was pleasant talking with Raymond and Jim again, but more than a bit discouraging, too. Not only have they remained in poverty as I have analyzed and written about their stories to obtain tenure and an upper middle-class lifestyle, but they have been joined by increasing numbers of homeless people every year. This sense of discouragement was only heightened later in my visit when I discovered that virtually all of the efforts we (along with dozens of other housed and homeless people) had made in the late 1990s to link responses to homelessness with poverty and inequality in the region had been undone. Once again, the regional shelters and advocacy efforts now overwhelmingly embraced a clinical approach to treating homelessness, while they had largely given up the struggle of working to end or prevent widespread homelessness.

A few months later, I attended a fascinating public meeting in Kalamazoo, Michigan. Activists and advocates lined up to give testimony in an effort to influence a consolidated plan for the city of Kalamazoo. This plan was represented as a blueprint for how Community Development Block Grant (CDBG) money from the U.S. Department of Housing and Urban Development (HUD) would be prioritized within the city for the next four years.

As has occurred regularly in the city—on issues ranging from police harassment of African-American youth and the need for a living wage and affordable housing, to demands that the police put more efforts into stopping a pattern of seemingly organized, routine violence against homeless people—at this meeting, advocates, service providers, and activists from two local community-organizing efforts appeared at the meeting to speak and attempt to influence public policy through their testimony. Person after person described the very important work they were involved with and how much more funding was necessary to, for example, continue to document housing discrimination in the city and region, continue to provide assistance for elderly residents to remain in their homes through a program offering help with home repair, continue to provide disabled residents with accessible housing options, begin to provide affordable housing opportunities for people unable to secure such housing currently, avoid clustering all low-income housing on the predominately poor and African-American north side of the city, and provide funds for homeless people to obtain secure housing. The meeting ended, and those testifying filed out—once again hoping that their testimony would be influential with the "decision makers."

There was, of course, some reason to doubt that it would be influential, despite the city's 2000–2004 Consolidated Plan listing "assistance to extremely low income and low income renter households" and "assistance to the homeless" as the top two priorities, since the city had failed to follow up in practice and most of those funds were targeted at programs for homeowners. And, in fact, when the Kalamazoo City Commission eventually voted to allocate CDBG funds for the coming year, no money was allocated to what participants in the hearing identified as the most important goal: that of establishing an affordable-housing trust fund. Instead, almost all funded programs again were aimed at middle-class homeowners. The City Commission did later vote to allocate $400,000 toward a housing trust fund, but only if the County Commission would match the money. Of course, knowing that there was no way that the overwhelmingly conservative county commissioners would go against their faith in allowing the market to determine pricing, this was largely an empty promise.

The city manager argued that with the current budget crisis facing all cities in Michigan, they could not afford to commit more funds to public housing. Somehow, though, the city did find $1.4 million the next winter to allocate in a plan for road alterations to accommodate private development plans for the downtown area. Of course, within dominant current political sensibilities of deregulation, privatization, and marketization, governmental support for private industry makes much more sense than helping to provide a social safety net.

Yet, most people I spoke with who attended the meeting and/or work on housing and homelessness issues in the city, expressed a sense of satisfaction with the process. Several people articulated that they were able to get the "commitments" from the city because the community organizing groups had stopped being disruptive and instead had worked with the city in a reasonable manner. Some local anti-poverty activists who spoke at the meeting expressed to me a continuing belief that somehow that was a victory and the county commission just needed to be "educated" to get them to provide the funds. And, in fact, after a few more years of effort, the county and city commissions did agree to a very short-term program of providing much less funding for affordable housing units, but with a caveat that the people living in the units would be selected based upon their agreeing to a contract regarding how they would work with service providers in curing what *they had been doing wrong to make themselves homeless.* It was the same sort of "responding to homelessness by governing the behaviors of homeless people" that I had described earlier regarding my work in Massachusetts (Lyon-Callo 2004).

To be fair, at least advocates in Western Massachusetts have recently embraced efforts toward a "housing first" approach to homelessness—something that many activists I work with in Kalamazoo have been suggesting, but to little positive reception. Of course, housing first would be an improvement upon a medicalized approach to treating perceived individual pathological homeless people, but what it does not challenge are the systemic processes producing widespread poverty and inequality. Even that marginal approach has not been widely accepted, despite the decades of research and advocacy suggesting that to resolve homelessness it would be most useful to address providing housing for people who lack it.

Unlike many of my fellow participants at the Kalamazoo meeting, I went home with a feeling of regret that I could not quite articulate, but a deep sense that I had witnessed a great deal of well-intended, well-meaning efforts that had the actual effect of being complicit in maintaining inequality and homelessness.

A partial explanation for my feeling began to become clearer to me two days later. Arriving at my office at the university, I noticed a catalog of children's games in my mailbox. Upon closer inspection, the catalog was about 40 pages of games designed to help children "control their emotions," "conquer their anger," "get along with others," and similar themes. Of course, those all seem like laudable goals at first glance. However, later in the day, as my ethnography class discussed the possibility of knowing through emotions and I brought up bell hooks' (1996) article "Killing Rage" for discussion, something began to click for me.

Like hooks, I understand the squelching of justifiable rage as not only unhealthy on an individual level, but also as functioning to constrain the possibilities of resistance and thus to maintain the structures of racism and the patriarchal and capitalist exploitation and oppression rampant in the city, the nation, and the world. We are living and working in a society with vast class and racial inequalities that are only getting worse. National and global trends are even more frightening to anyone concerned with equity, justice, and freedom. Those trends are easy to document, but if we want to really understand such exploitation, we need to also examine how and why people respond to it in particular ways.

Many people feel frustrated, angry, hopeless, and upset, but what are they to do with those feelings? How are they to act? There are all sorts of pressures placed on people to remain "reasonable" and "realistic" and to learn to control their passions as they compete within the "free" market. Hooks suggests that what is needed instead is to embrace your anger so that you can begin to understand the causes of it and how to act to counter those forces. Instead, though, many people attempt to respond to anger through therapy, substance use, exercise, medication, hopelessness, conspicuous consumption, or similar types of coping efforts. As I have argued elsewhere (Lyon-Callo 2008), all of those make sense when there is no Left suggesting how to embrace anger to work against white, capitalist privilege in practice. Most of us want to be liked and not be the subject of ridicule and scorn. So, we try to get along, to be "embraceable" as best we can. Yet while such efforts like those dominant in Kalamazoo County certainly represent reasonable responses, they cannot end the conditions they remain enmeshed within and thus work to reinforce those very structures of inequality.

A few weeks after the meeting regarding CDBG funding priorities, I attended a forum at my university for a "homeless awareness week." This forum, like the dozen or so previous ones I have attended or participated in, had a room full of earnest students listening to service providers and faculty explain how many people were homeless, why people were homeless, and what their programs were doing about it. As usual, one of the providers made the claim that they had the programs in place to solve the problem; they just needed more money to expand their efforts.

I sat there listening until almost the very end, becoming more and more frustrated, but not really wanting to ask the scores of questions going through my mind. I knew the speakers and many of the students there. They are all well-meaning people doing their best, and I really had to force myself to risk asking a question. Finally, though, I posed a multiple-part question, asking if they had any data on the racial breakdown of homelessness in the city and what their programs were doing to counter the structures of racism operating in the city and throughout the nation, especially the impacts of the war on urban black men under the guise of the "War on Drugs" that contributed to the overwhelming disproportionate number of African-Americans who are homeless in the United States. I asked if, for example, they were working in collaboration with the activists challenging the local police force's embodiment of the war on young black men. And, since there is a direct correlation between the routinization of homelessness in Michigan (and the United States) and the profound socioeconomic restructuring of "the social" toward a system that is beginning to more closely resemble a fascist merging of state and corporate interests under the guise of neoliberal globalization, what practices were being undertaken within their programs to challenge that contribution to homelessness? And, finally, since there are dozens of studies that have demonstrated a clear link between domestic violence and homeless women, what practices did their programs engage in that would work to decrease the incidents and the gendered impacts of domestic violence?

The reaction was what I expected; they were clearly flustered and upset. But upset at me, not at the conditions I was describing, and they gave a vague answer admitting they did not address structures of inequality in their work. Then, they ended the program. Of course, service providers do not address such issues. Granting agencies certainly do not provide funds for doing so. More distressingly, though, the vast majority of research on homelessness never even considers such links—never mind works to actively forge the possible coalitions needed to alter those conditions. But why not, and at what cost? By not adequately addressing these links, aren't we as researchers also complicit in maintaining homelessness and the structures of inequality unfolding across the globe?

One of the few speakers at the Kalamazoo public hearing who did show any emotion was a homeless man, who articulated the beginnings of an interesting set of responses for people who begin to embrace anger. In closing his presentation, he stated, "if you don't want to support housing for the working poor, then I don't want to clean your house, cook your meals, or provide all of the other services that low waged workers provide throughout the city (and world) today." You could just dismiss his talk as being "emotional" and "unreasonable," but what if working people began to see the power that withholding their labor, not as individuals, but as a collective force, holds? What new forms of resistance might emerge if exploited and oppressed people, and the activist and advocacy groups working on poverty, homelessness, housing, and other issues of inequality, began to see the possibilities for working together to challenge the discursive renderings of inequality in which they are situated?

In Kalamazoo County, at least, such collaborative practices are difficult to locate. There are at least five anti-poverty organizations, two more dedicated to assisting the "Hispanic community," seven homeless shelters, and several groups working on various facets of racial inequality. Yet these groups almost always try to be reasonable and embraceable and rarely collaborate on any effort. For example, representatives from the largely African-American north side of the city spoke out in opposition to spending CDBG funds on affordable housing at city meetings while several social service organizations worked to defeat a living wage ordinance a few years earlier.

The one effort that gained a bit of broad attention was when the Kalamazoo Homeless Action Network publicized a complaint about discriminatory treatment of homeless people at the McDonald's located near downtown Kalamazoo. It was nice that people supported this effort to be treated with dignity, but I really wonder if already existing anti-McDonald's sentiment may have made that easier to build upon. More importantly, the broader support for the complaint eroded after the activists rallied outside the home of the manager of the McDonald's. That was seen as being too disruptive and "personal."

Keep in mind that those responses happened in Michigan, with some of the highest rates of poverty and unemployment in the nation during those years. Kalamazoo is a city that lost four percent of its population in the 1990s along with over four thousand good-paying jobs in manufacturing, banking, and pharmaceuticals due to corporate mergers and the global transfer of jobs out of the higher-waged and more unionized Midwest—only to see those jobs replaced by low-waged, non-union food service and retail trade employment. By 2005, over 32 percent of city residents and more than one half of children lived beneath the poverty line as Kalamazoo broke into the top ten poorest cities in the nation. And, of course, that was prior to the housing and financial crises of 2008 and 2009 that made hunger, poverty, and homelessness in the region even more pronounced. Yet letting homeless people sit in McDonald's without buying anything was seemingly the only issue that could bring advocacy groups together—but only if the demands remained reasonable and the actions remained embraceable. Why is that? What are the social forces that restrict the possibilities of these people and groups from building on the commonality of their struggles to develop collaborative and effective resistance movements?

In my current research, looking at how a broad array of community members are responding to the profound social and economic restructuring occurring in Kalamazoo County, Michigan, I have identified a number of contributing factors thus far. Certainly, global neoliberal restructuring's transformation of communities and the production of job insecurity everywhere for almost everyone has had emotional as well as economic consequences, and thus has contributed to people adopting new subject positions where they are less likely to take a chance on a practice or public policy that they believe may jeopardize employment. Likewise, the ascendancy of a neoliberal celebration of the individual and the market has concrete ramifications in terms of human agency. Issues of longstanding racial segregation and distrust, social distancing by class, changes and stresses being brought with the arrival of a fast-growing population of workers from Central America, increased geographic mobility altering people's sense of community and belonging, and gender dynamics within and between organizations of course also play important roles. Finally, the desire to be embraceable and squelch or medicate rage, as described above, further contribute to preventing broad-based coalitions from working for change. But what are the other complexities to consider and how can they be articulated and then challenged?

I do not intend these questions in a rhetorical way. I ask them because I really think those are the questions we need to be answering. I believe those are the heart of where our work should be headed at this point and, although I am studying this in one setting currently, I certainly do not have all of the answers.

I have been working on homelessness for almost two decades now. Other contributors to this volume have been doing this work much longer than I have. Of course, obviously we are not the only ones who have been doing this important work. Martha Burt for the Urban Institute, the National Coalition for the Homeless, the Economic Policy Institute, the U.S. Conference of Mayors, the National Alliance to End Homelessness, and the National Law Center on Homelessness & Poverty put out reports, press releases, and studies documenting homelessness and homeless policies in much complexity on a routine basis. Scholars such as Kim Hopper (2003) have been documenting the medical, policy, political, and economic dimensions of homelessness for decades. Others explore the psychological implications of the issue. We have largely done the research, written articles and books and policy reports, investigated just about every aspect of homelessness, and offered well-reasoned arguments and analyses. Concurrently, hundreds of millions of dollars are spent on a wide range of homeless prevention and treatment programs. Still, inequality and homelessness had continued to grow. The last years of the Bush Administration saw increased overall homelessness despite the federal government's claims about less "chronic homelessness" and their focus on the "moral" response to homelessness touted by homeless czar Phillip Mangano. As the 2007 National Alliance to End Homelessness report documented, homelessness has continued to steadily increase across the nation. Of course, this is accompanied by increasing numbers of people living in poverty and record numbers of people living in what is described as "severe" poverty (Pugh 2007). Of course, 2009–2012 have seen even more people suffering in poverty and homeless with the severe economic downturn accompanied by further cutbacks in state and federal spending on a social safety net. Some communities have experimented with various incarnations of a "housing first" approach to homelessness during these years, but that has done little to slow the increasing numbers of poor and/or homeless people in the nation. And yet academics working on homelessness continue to do the same type of work in the same ways.

To me, that is not a very satisfactory equation. There certainly appears to be an ethical consideration in continuing to do what has been shown not to work over and over again. Honestly, I do not really care to read one more article or book on "homeless people." As the theme of this volume is ethical issues involved in research on homelessness, I want to suggest that there are several ethical implications to how research on homelessness has been conducted.

On the most basic level, it does remain a problem that there are aspects of homelessness that the vast amount of research on homelessness that has been done have not adequately explored. For example, it is hard to imagine that anyone working on homelessness can fail to see the racial dimensions of the issue. And yet, with the exception of the work of Joanne Passaro (1996) and a few others, most studies continue to fail to explore how systemic racial inequalities contribute to producing homelessness as it exists. I suggest that not naming or working against such obvious racism is an ethical concern.

The same can certainly be said for issues of sexuality and sexual violence. The National Coalition for the Homeless identified sexual violence as a major contributor to homelessness of women and children over a decade ago. But, while there have certainly been some very good explorations of the gendered components of homelessness produced since then (for example, Connolly 2002;

Rivera 2003), most ethnographic works, public policies, and helping practices have continued to fail to explore how violent relationships impact homelessness.

Likewise, two recent studies have suggested that issues around how people respond to sexuality may play a significant role for many homeless young people, with claims that as many as 40 percent of homeless youths may identify as gay, lesbian, or transgendered (Byrne et al. 2005; Ray 2007). When one of my undergraduate students attempted to research programs in Michigan addressing this aspect of homelessness in the spring of 2006, he (perhaps unsurprisingly, as most shelters and social services in the state continue to be religious-based) found it impossible to find a program even willing to discuss the issue. It is nearly as difficult to find policy or academic literature that accounts for this aspect of life.

Finally, there is a question about where our research is focused. Although the poverty rate in large cities remains significantly higher than in suburbs, more than one million more poor people lived in suburbs in the United States by 2005 than in cities (Berube and Kneebone 2006). And yet, there remains very little detailed, analytical work exploring the multifaceted dimensions of suburban poverty or the possibilities for building collective mobilizations toward decreasing the structured violence of suburban poverty. Of course, embedded within that same study is a discussion of how poverty rates across the United States, but primarily and most significantly in the Midwest where I work, rose steadily during the first half-decade of the twenty-first century. Kalamazoo in fact reached the top ten of the poorest cities of over 50,000 people in the nation in 2006. But poverty is not confined to Michigan. Poverty and the gap between the extremely wealthy and the rest of the population has been expanding rapidly across the country, leading to record numbers of Americans living in "severe poverty" by 2005 (Pugh 2007), and what has by now appeared to some commentators as the end of the illusion of middle-class status for tens of millions of Americans (Dobbs 2007).

So, despite the wealth of very good work that has been done on homelessness, there certainly are issues that have been underexplored. That is ethically problematic, but at the same time I doubt that it would make much difference even if the research was done to more adequately address issues such as the roles that racism or sexuality play in homelessness. Of what value is all the knowledge produced in our studies and reports if it does not actually alter the social processes producing homelessness? The evidence is clearly in by now. Twenty years of data demonstrates that scientifically documenting homelessness does not sway social policies or build the needed social movements. Thus, the work would still be problematic if it addressed those concerns but was done in the same tried and failed manner in which we have been working. But I also want to suggest that there are other at least equally important ethical considerations to consider in how we go about doing our work.

As Loic Wacquant (2002) argued in his scathing review of the works of Katherine Newman, Elijah Anderson, and Mitch Duneier, much of the ethnographic work on urban poverty avoids situating poverty within an analysis of contemporary global capitalism and neoliberal restructurings while, instead, offering descriptions of the worth or value of hard-working poor people. Much the same is the case with the preponderance of ethnographic work on homelessness, with a rare exception such as (contributor to this volume) Talmadge Wright's work (1997). From earlier works like Jennifer Toth's (1995) study of "the mole people" living in subway tunnels or Elliot Liebow's (1995) moving portraits of homeless women, to more recent efforts (Duneier 2000; Geliebter 2007; Morrell 2007; Yankoski 2005), much of the ethnographic work has focused on describing—in emotional, moving terms—the moral worth of homeless people. Homelessness gets treated as an isolated cultural issue rather than as part of a broader set of social processes unfolding over the last three decades. As Wacquant nicely demonstrates, such works contribute to framing poverty and homelessness within a moralistic framework, simultaneously contributing to the further marginalization of conceptualizing the role that class-based processes play.

Of course, a major problem with such emotionally moving, moralistic arguments is what the reader is supposed to do with the new knowledge gained from reading the work. When it is framed as a moral argument, the obvious answer is, for example, to forego paying off some of your growing personal debt to make a donation to a homeless shelter to care for these deserving poor people. Of course, nearly three decades of empirical data now clearly demonstrates that better-funded homeless shelters are not a solution to homelessness. Is it any wonder then, as Anthony Marcus (2005) argues, that despite all of the research and writing on homeless people, homelessness appears to have ceased being a major concern of mainstream media, political actors, and much of the public?

What these efforts fail to adequately challenge is a system of social and economic restructuring that has created much less social cohesion, the transformation of public space, communities that are disrupted as individual mobility becomes paramount, much more severe poverty, economic and emotional instability for a much larger segment of the population, and an embracing of private sector, market-based solutions to just about every issue. Indeed, the devastating impacts of globalizing capital coupled with neoliberal social and economic policies on working people across the globe by now have been well documented (see, e.g., Davis and Monk 2007; Navarro 2007; Wacquant 2001).

The continued tendency to act as if homelessness was somehow completely separate from poverty and inequality—and thus can be studied and responded to in isolation from an analysis of neoliberalism—is perhaps the paramount tendency needing to be altered if we hope to eradicate homelessness. It is in this light that I feel that Wacquant's critique perhaps does not go quite far enough. We know that most of what has been tried thus far does not work very well—but absent a large-scale, collective, mobilized effort to transform the social, economic, and ideological underpinnings of the current systemic conditions (i.e., increasing rates of exploitation coupled with increased authoritarianism, which are producing greater homelessness, poverty, and inequality), we are not going to see a program that works. Simply adding an analysis of class processes into our existing research models seems unlikely to contribute to producing the movements needed to challenge the recent consolidation of wealth and power of which homelessness is one part.

To me, conducting more scholarly work focused only on homeless people or even the social processes producing homelessness is ethically problematic. Such scholarship does not help us to both understand and overcome barriers to collaborative resistance movements toward ending the almost three decade long erosion of the lives of working class people and people's sense of belonging and community produced by the discursive merging of corporate, elite, and governmental interests. What I would urge, instead, is for applied scholars to work within communities analyzing and uncovering the barriers to cooperative, broad-based movements against the impacts of neoliberal social and economic restructuring that are so profoundly impacting the lives of so many people in communities across the globe—and, in the process, help facilitate the development of new imaginings about how to respond together to local manifestations of neoliberal policies and practices, as well as emergent fascism. And, to do that work effectively, we must return to the idea of emotions. Human beings are not just political or economic actors. If we hope to transform current conditions, we must consider the multiplicity of subject positions people operate within, much of which is influenced by emotions. While I might not go so far as Ruth Behar (1997) in asserting that the only work worth doing today is that which breaks one's heart, I certainly agree that any analysis of inequality that does not account for the roles that emotions play in both the subjects of the research and those whom one hopes to influence through the work is not of much value.

The world has changed in profound ways in recent years. We cannot afford to be doing work looking at issues like homelessness as though they occur in isolation, nor can we be content with simply producing and disseminating even the most critical and well-informed knowledge. I am certain that many people researching homelessness are also active in their communities. Perhaps developing new activist research strategies that explicitly engage social actors in dialogue and debates with the aims of expanding the range of ways in which responses to homelessness and inequality are crafted might prove more effective. Similarly, by focusing our research efforts while working on the grassroots level to build collaborative movements more broadly aimed at neoliberal restructuring and capitalist exploitation, we might contribute in new ways. Obviously, these alone are not the ultimate solutions, but, through critically exploring the impacts of our existing practices and thinking about new ways to act, it may be possible for new, more transformative efforts to emerge.

Conclusion

In short, the research and scholarship thus far has done a nice job of describing and analyzing homelessness, yet falls far short of contributing to a transformation of the social processes producing widespread homelessness. How is it that our well-designed research has done so little to transform common sense? I suggest that research on homelessness that does not connect homelessness to broader issues of economic and political restructuring, involve working in collaboration with the subjects of the research, and resonate emotionally with a broader public, is not only ethically lacking, but is just not worth doing any longer.

Perhaps, instead, we could engage in research that might play some small role in producing another possible world, one in which homelessness and extreme poverty and inequalities are eradicated; one in which people like Raymond and Jim do not have to live the next decade in poverty. Space for such a world is still possible, but to move toward that would demand a different type of conceptualizing of homelessness, scholarship, and how to engage with each other and the world around us. To me, that is the paramount ethical question those of us concerned with erasing homelessness, poverty, authoritarianism, and inequality—while working toward a world with more freedom and democracy—should embrace.

Chapter 10
Homelessness as "Internal Displacement": Scholarship and Activism in Post-Katrina New Orleans
Randall Amster

Abstract. Events following the aftermath of Hurricane Katrina have raised the specter of a troubling evolution of the concept of homelessness, namely an *internal displacement* on a city-wide scale resulting in multitudes left without homes and in a perpetual state of diaspora. While many view this as the result of a "natural disaster," others very clearly see it as a thoroughly manmade disaster, with familiar overtones of racial stratification, urban gentrification, collapse of social services, removal of public housing, and a resulting sharp rise in homelessness. Still, there has been a groundswell of local efforts to champion the *right of return* to New Orleans for the "victims," even as they increasingly become coded as the "homeless." What ethical considerations arise when taking a stance of advocacy under such conditions? How might scholarship, advocacy, and activism intertwine to help illuminate these issues and foster the creation of positive alternatives? This essay analyzes a troubling new paradigm of homelessness, including the challenges and transformational possibilities that it presents both personally and politically.

Where were you when Hurricane Katrina was making its way toward the Gulf Coast states? I was living my life in the late-summer comfort of northern Arizona, vaguely aware that something monumentally significant was in the offing, but unsure quite how to articulate it. Despite doing extensive research into phenomena such as homelessness, gentrification, and displacement, my thinking had not yet led me to the realization that this would be the inevitable widespread outcome of the impending storm. When it hit, I quickly began working with

131

others in my community to raise money and collect needed supplies. A week later, I was in an old school bus literally filled with tons of food and gear, heading toward the disaster zone on some still-fuzzy errand of mercy with a preponderance of good intentions but a dearth of critical analysis. By the time we landed in New Orleans, however, I had realized, almost intuitively, the full implicaimplications of this "perfect storm"—and my life has never been quite the same since. This is my attempt to connect the dots of a personal and political journey that combines the essence of my scholarship and activism alike.

New Paradigms in Homelessness

Hurricane Katrina revealed more about American society than just its utter lack of preparedness for dealing with region-wide disasters. It also made evident the baseline racism and classism that is prevalent in the United States yet rarely dealt with in the public dialogue in a meaningful way. While some critical light has been shed on these issues in the post-Katrina aftermath, another set of related concerns that were exposed by the storm received far less attention—namely the patterns of homelessness and displacement that have been engendered in the years following the hurricane that devastated much of the Gulf Coast and the city of New Orleans in particular. Despite media pronouncements at the outset that "the United States is facing a massive homelessness crisis in the wake of Hurricane Katrina" and dire warnings that people would not be able to return to their homes for a significant period of time, if at all (SkyNewsHD 2005), such patterns continue to be in evidence years later. In fact, the unresolved homelessness crisis in New Orleans may have helped set the tone for a general hardening of perspectives on these issues, as reflected in a recent statement by police after Occupy activists sought to "draw attention to homelessness" by taking over an abandoned building: "The city of Oakland welcomes peaceful forms of assembly and freedom of speech but acts of violence, property destruction and overnight lodging will not be tolerated" (Harrison and Burg 2012). The casual equation of violence with the attempt to secure housing is quite illustrative in its inverted logic.

There is a simple (yet oft-unspoken) truism about homelessness: it is largely and ultimately a product of "people being displaced from homes" (Huus 2009). In the years immediately preceding the current and euphemistic cycle of "economic downturn," and following on the heels of the prior one, there was an intervening event that triggered a crisis in homelessness, one that remains unresolved and that forces us to rethink our preconceptions about what causes homelessness and what is to be done about it. This seminal event in recent American history—essentially comprising the wholesale destruction of an entire city and the diaspora of a large percentage of its population—weaves together in a web of crisis and despair many complex issues of race, displacement, official neglect, housing affordability, public infrastructure, and gentrification. Yet it also raises equally important questions of advocacy and action, of risk and reward, of engagement and solidarity. In short, Hurricane Katrina yields new ways of thinking about the politics of homelessness and the ethics of redressing it through positive transformation.

News from NOLA: Race, Class, and Catastrophe

New Orleans is a unique and singular city in terms of its politics and culture (Colten 2006; Haletky 2006; Masquelier 2006). In addition to being widely known as a "party town" and the site of Mardi Gras, it is also home to the first free black community in the United States, and is the place where Homer Plessey advanced the arguments that eventually found resonance in *Brown vs. Board of Education* decades later and that were so integral to the civil rights movement as a whole—i.e., that segregation is inherently untenable. Pre-Katrina New Orleans was possessed of an impressive public infrastructure that included stable and decent public housing as well as a public health care option administered through Charity Hospital; it also had one of the highest rates of black home ownership in the United States. Politically speaking, it was known as a liberal city in the otherwise conservative south, and that sensibility also informed the music and art that helped to define the city in the public imagination. While some of this survived Katrina, much did not, leaving the city a shell of its former self and thus ripe for the eminently color-coded processes of "renewal" and "redevelopment."

Developers and gentrifiers had long coveted New Orleans before the hurricane hit. Plans had been floated for waterfront condominiums, office parks, and even casinos. Many public housing projects in the city had already been demolished in favor of tony townhouses and big-box retailers, with the former inhabitants essentially relocated to sea-level shanties on the east side of town—places that would devastatingly flood when Katrina hit. Like many cities in America, New Orleans was racially stratified despite its progressive past; efforts to push impoverished people "out of sight" were well under way; and there was already a demonstrable homeless population in the city (see, e.g., Wright and Devine 1995). If Katrina had spared the city in 2005 rather than striking it, it is entirely possible that the same sort of outcomes eventually would have been reached incrementally and (to some extent) invisibly as in many other locales, with certain segments of the population (oftentimes poor people of color) being displaced in favor of upscale development and infill urbanization (generally for wealthier and whiter people). Katrina essentially accelerated the timetable for these processes (Hetzler et al. 2007; Kates et al. 2006, 14658), and the results were dramatic and disturbing—yielding, as Mike Davis (2005) has observed, "a partial ethnic cleansing of New Orleans" impelled largely at the behest of "the local gentrifying class."

If you are after a neutral rendering of the entire episode, you won't find it in this chapter. From my perspective, what Katrina was allowed to do to New Orleans was emblematic of the Bush Administration's overall policies and practices. Plaintive warnings were ignored, resources were intentionally squandered, nonwhite people were sacrificed, and the military was called upon to "restore order" to a place where disorder had been hand-delivered. What transpired in New Orleans was reminiscent in many ways of the perpetual wars in Iraq and Afghanistan, including the creation of untold thousands of refugees and a decimated landscape that would become fodder for corporate entities after a quick buck. It was not mere coincidence that led then-President Bush to promptly announce his plan for a "Gulf Opportunity Zone," or that both Halliburton and Blackwater soon appeared in the city after being awarded reconstruction-related contracts. Many of the tropes deployed by the mainstream media in the aftermath of the storm—including descriptions of "looting," "anarchy," and a "war zone"—likewise fed into this mindset of militarism as the only viable response (cf. Stock 2007, 709).

It might be said that Katrina was effectively a "natural" version of WMD ("weapons of mass destruction"), although like its analog it too was manmade to a large extent (Haletky 2006; Waugh 2006), comprising at root "a scandalous political disaster" that left hundreds dead and upwards of a million people in the region homeless (Rothschild 2005). The crisis was palpable, mind-boggling, and historic in its scope and breadth (see Masquelier 2006, 737; Popkin et al. 2006, 5), as described by Nigg, et al. (2006): "Hurricane Katrina resulted in the largest relocation of citizens within the United States since the Dust Bowl of the 1930s. However, the Dust Bowl migration of 300,000 to 400,000 people from the southern plains states to California took place over several years, in comparison to an estimated 1.2 million people who left their homes and communities within hours or days before Hurricane Katrina's landfall along the Gulf Coast on August 29, 2005. . . . Due to the subsequent flooding of New Orleans, the 100,000 to 120,000 residents who remained in the city were rapidly transformed into a second wave of evacuees, greatly intensifying the need for shelter and housing."

Unquestionably, the storm's impact was not equally distributed among the city's residents. "The African American majority of New Orleans was disproportionately affected by the hurricane and the events that transpired in the wake of the flood that displaced hundreds of thousands" (Miron and Ward 2007, 163). In 2008, a United Nations committee found that Katrina "had a greater negative impact on displaced black residents," and that this "disparate impact" continued to be felt years later (Hammer 2008). Data from the 2010 census revealed that New Orleans lost approximately 118,000 black residents, lowering the percentage of African-Americans in the city to less than 60 percent, down from more than two-thirds before Katrina (Robertson 2011). Indeed, following the storm there was a demonstrable "facilitated exodus of African Americans from the drowning city" that has resulted in a "new African American Diaspora" (Miron and Ward 2007, 164). As Malik Rahim, founder of Common Ground, bluntly told Greg Palast (2007), "they wanted them poor niggers out of there." Many residents echoed these suspicions, openly wondering whether this was "an excuse to clean out this poor, overwhelmingly African American community so that rich white developers could start anew?" (Landphair 2007, 844). Seemingly in direct response, Congressman Richard Baker (R–LA) was quoted in the *Wall Street Journal* on September 9, 2005: "We finally cleaned up public housing in New Orleans. We couldn't do it, but God did" (quoted in Davis 2005; Arena 2007).

As it turned out, plans were unfurled to essentially create a "*New* New Orleans . . . with the vast majority of native African Americans permanently removed from the city" (Marable 2006, 158). "With the largest and poorest section[s] of the city removed . . . New Orleans's single largest economic draw will be stronger than ever—tourism" (Miron and Ward 2007, 166). As Palast (2007) observed, what has been created is "a new city: a tourist town with a French Quarter, loose-spending drunks, hot-sheets hotels, and a few Black people to perform the modern version of minstrel shows," a sentiment confirmed to him by Rahim: "It's two cities. . . . There's the city for the white and the rich. And there's another city for the poor and the Black. You know, the city that's for the white and rich has recovered." Jay Arena (2007, 369) likewise concluded that "the ruling elites in New Orleans . . . have seized upon the hurricane . . . to ensure that the black working-class majority does not return." This notion was seemingly affirmed (and subsequently borne out by the census data) in the 2010 elections, which "marked the consolidation of a change in the city's political power structure. For more than three decades, most elected positions in the city were in Black hands. But now, in the context of mass displacement after Katrina . . . that has changed. For the first time in more than 30 years, New Orleans will have a white mayor and a 5-2 majority-white city council" (Flaherty 2010).

The largest part of the city, the part reserved for "the poor and the Black" as Rahim describes it, remains plagued by "a justice system in tatters" (Templeton 2007) and a significant health care crisis (Patchan 2009) that includes great burdens on the mental health systems in the region (Levin 2007). Beyond the estimated quarter-million residents displaced by Katrina, most of whom have not returned (Arena 2007, 369; Miron and Ward 2007, 165), there remain thousands of workers, mostly African-Americans, who have either lost their jobs or been forced into untenable positions of employment: "Since the storm, these workers have faced tremendous structural barriers to returning home and to finding the employment necessary to rebuild their lives. Without housing, they cannot work; without work, they cannot afford housing. . . . These workers and former residents, mostly people of color, recognize that New Orleans is being rebuilt *by* them, but not *for* them" (Browne-Dianis et al. 2006, 5).

Bill Quigley (2008), a local human rights lawyer and professor, further notes that "half of the working poor, elderly and disabled who lived in New Orleans before Katrina have not returned," and the rebuilding of the city, with all of the concomitant changes in demographics, politics, and economics, "has gone as many planned"; in the final analysis, "one of the major casualties of Katrina will be the permanent displacement of tens of thousands of African Americans, the working poor, their children, the elderly, and the disabled." This has led Quigley (2008) and others to demand a "right of return" (e.g., Briggs 2006; Haletky 2006; Marable 2006) for displaced peoples, and to argue forcefully that any meaningful recovery "requires supporting thousands of displaced residents in their desire to return home" (Landphair 2007, 845). To date, these sentiments have gone largely unheard in official quarters, and in fact "those who wanted a different New Orleans rebuilt probably see the concentrated displacement as a success" (Quigley 2008). Unfortunately, whatever "window of opportunity" to restore the city and return its residents that might have existed "will begin to close as the memories of the disasters fade" (Waugh 2006, 23), leaving not only thousands of people displaced *from* the city but also many more displaced *within* the city, as its complexion and landscape will have been forever altered.

A case study of redevelopment in New Orleans addressed this sense of ongoing crisis and opportunity lost (Hetzler et al. 2007): "Initially, we had high hopes for the prospects of redevelopment in New Orleans. The devastation created by this disaster opened many discussions of racial and class inequalities and it gave New Orleans the opportunity to take serious steps toward redressing this long-standing inequity. Instead, developers, policymakers, and corporations alike have taken this opportunity to thinly veil racist and classist New Urbanism in the name of development [that] is rife with squandered opportunities." It thus has been observed that "the devastation produced by the hurricane could have brought attention to the social roots of violence and poverty," but instead "the public was presented with labels and images that often criminalized the poverty of the victims" and "surreptitiously excluded poor New Orleans residents from its public" (Masquelier 2006, 236–37). Palast (2007) cogently summarized the unfortunate reality: "Hurricane recovery is class war by other means."

The Ethics of Engagement:
On Whether to Return and Rebuild

Like most major U.S. cities, pre-Katrina New Orleans already had a sizable and largely underserved homeless population (cf. Wright and Devine 1995) as well as an affordable housing crisis (Popkin et al. 2006). When the storm hit the city, the "mandatory evacuation called on August 28 [2005] made no provision to evacuate homeless or low-income" people (Takeda and Helms 2006, 404). Of the nearly 1,500 killed and thousands more listed as "missing" in the aftermath

(Takeda and Helms 2006, 397), it is unknown how many were homeless people. Social services and health care practitioners faced many ethical dilemmas following Katrina, as scarce resources needed to be administered effectively under extremely trying conditions. An interview with a local doctor, Benjamin Springgate, addressed some of these issues, connecting the dots to the question of homelessness (in Patchan 2009):

> One has to adopt a somewhat different lens when, instead of facing the challenges of a homeless individual or family, or the collective needs entrenched in a given homeless shelter, one faces the challenges of a community that has lost 100,000 housing units, the homeless population has doubled, and, at least initially, half of the population is at risk of becoming homeless. This prompted many questions. What should my priority as a doctor be? . . . Should I try to help an individual stabilize his or her housing situation, knowing that housing stability plays a major role in determining how successfully one can manage health conditions? Given the breadth of the needs and the limits of resources, prioritizing interventions raises a host of ethical issues.

People interested in the rebuilding effort in New Orleans likewise face certain ethical concerns, including how to reduce future catastrophic potential; how to preserve public safety in the city; what to do about public and/or affordable housing options; and how to create a more equitable city overall (see Kates et al. 2006). Others have considered questions of whether displaced persons would do better to "return or move on;" whether upon return they would find a city created by virtue of "urban renewal on steroids" in which they would be "sidelined and forgotten;" whether substandard and "distressed public housing projects" ought to be re-created at all; and indeed, whether to even rebuild the city in the first instance (see Briggs 2006, 119–22). While some of these sentiments may seem fairly hardhearted, there is an important point here, namely that the advocacy aimed at rebuilding the city and returning its residents need not seek to *literally* rebuild with the same pre-Katrina patterns and practices entirely intact, but rather might also strive to alleviate some of the issues that had previously plagued the city in the process.

As Popkin et al. (2006, 2–3) have opined, "the challenge going forward is even greater if New Orleans is to avoid old patterns of concentrating assisted housing and poor families in a few isolated communities. If assisted housing . . . is systematically excluded from the city's better-off neighborhoods, New Orleans will simply reproduce the severe neighborhood distress and hardship that prevailed before the storm." Similarly, others have noted that "those who do return could find themselves confined—as many were before the storm—to high-poverty neighborhoods that may have high rates of crime, few jobs, and poor schools," and likewise that "the pattern of concentrated poverty that existed on Katrina's eve could well reassert itself in a rebuilt New Orleans" (Fischer and Sard 2005). Consequently, it has been asserted that "rebuilding must take historical social inequalities into account when forming reactivation plans for essential social services," utilizing post-disaster reconstruction as an "opportunity to correct stubborn patterns of structural discrimination," and in the end not to "return to the *status quo ante* but rather to ensure better access to critical social services in the rebuilding of a better society" (Stout and Dello Buono 2008).

These sentiments raise familiar sorts of ethical conundrums faced by homeless rights advocates in general, creating a sphere in which we are oftentimes constrained to argue for the mere right to occupy unsafe dwellings or marginal spaces rather than wider ameliorations of the structural issues that initially created the hardship (Amster 2008). This is why some have argued that the "direct participation of the residents and the displaced is vital" in any reconstruction efforts (Stout and Dello Buono 2008). Whatever happens in post-Katrina New Orleans, it must be led by those with a direct stake in the matter, and debates about the future should necessarily "include evacuated residents in decision making on reconstruction and other pressing issues;" naturally, "dispersal has made this difficult," and "public meetings and discussions on rebuilding are not as easily handled when those involved are scattered over many states" (Weiss 2006, 7). Still, there is something of a self-fulfilling prophecy to all of this, in the common logic that displaced or marginalized people cannot be included in discussions about how to alleviate displacement or marginalization because they are unavailable and/or difficult to locate. Essentially they are being doubly punished for their (oftentimes involuntary) vulnerable status.

A more constructive scenario—one that is more ethical and that many advocates in fact have been arguing for—would be to simply create initial conditions favorable to bringing people back to the city *en masse*, and then to have the larger dialogue about how to plan the future. This would ensure fuller participation of all voices in the rebuilding process, and while it perhaps carries a risk of reifying prior unsatisfactory conditions, displaced people will at least then get to make the decision about whether to "return or move on" on their own terms and not at someone else's behest. Moreover, there is no guarantee whatsoever that the places to which Katrina evacuees have been dispersed will be any better than what they would return to in New Orleans, even one that is a shadow of its former self in terms of public infrastructure and historical legacy. Sensibly, to fulfill this promise, many argue that "rebuilding should be carried out in a manner that ensures that the region's poorest residents have the same opportunities as more affluent families to return home if they choose to do so"—including in this framework that pre-Katrina housing subsidies be restored; rebuilding monies be partly utilized to create additional affordable housing for the poorest residents; and housing aid be administered at the regional level in accordance with federal standards (Fischer and Sard 2005).

Grassroots activist organizations such as Common Ground have practiced a similar philosophy of assisted self-help to positive effect (Haletky 2006, 96): "Without input from the community, decisions lack the element of justice needed to create healthy neighborhoods and cities. . . . Long-term goals are not just to supply people with relief but to supply them with a solid foundation for the future in which community strength, political awareness, and subsequent action become a way of life for New Orleans residents." The ethical stance fostered by this sort of advocacy is palpable and inspired: "New Orleans has a unique opportunity to recreate itself as an economically diverse, inclusive city that offers its low-income residents authentic opportunities. With careful planning by and for all, New Orleans can bring back its families and offer them homes in vibrant mixed-income communities" (Popkin et al. 2006, 12). Unfortunately, as yet "there are few indications that officials are working together toward a systematic and open process; indeed, there are legitimate concerns that many residents may never be able to return, and that New Orleans will be a significantly smaller city with a much smaller African American population" (Popkin et al. 2006, 12). The full cultural and economic implications of this eventuality are sobering, and most likely will negatively impact the entire region, as Fischer and Sard (2005) observe: "New Orleans and other damaged areas on the Gulf Coast also will be worse off if large numbers of low-income people are unable to return. In many cases, the families involved may have lived in the region for generations. . . . Losing large numbers of low-income households could have harmful economic implications as well, since these households provide many of the janitors, waiters, nurse's aides, laborers, hotel clerks and other workers who play a significant role in the region's economy."

Promisingly, many "scholar-advocates" working in the post-Katrina era have taken up the call to produce not merely "relevant knowledge" but to make it "actionable" as well, recognizing that "most useful knowledge about the storm's effects and the pain and promise of rebuilding will not emerge from a timid or hyper-specialized science. . . . We should take risks and think outside of narrow specialties" (Briggs 2006, 125–26). This may well be the primary ethical consideration when confronting a problematic and potentially devastating situation: taking the risk of imperfect knowledge and multi-disciplinary exploration in the service of action aimed at improving the lives of people and communities. It is not an exact science, to be sure, and is fraught with its own dangers of speaking *for* rather than *with*, as well as the professional pitfalls of striving to nudge academics toward advocacy. Still, the risks pale in comparison to those taken by vulnerable and marginalized people every day, and if scholar-advocates can subsume even part of these risks, it is worth the effort to help foster "an historic opportunity to lift thousands of the nation's most vulnerable families out of ghetto poverty and the associated physical and social risks that Katrina has so vividly illustrated. . . . [We can] seize this extraordinary opportunity to rebuild lives, not just the physical infrastructure. Thousands of families can come back stronger than before" (Briggs 2006, 128). Perhaps so—but only if they have a home to which they can return.

Homeless Again (and Again) in New Orleans

Undoubtedly, the need to create and maintain suitable living spaces for hurricane victims has been paramount in the minds of many people working to foster a sense of justice and equity in the city. One of the initial challenges has been the stigmatization—both linguistic and legalistic—suffered by those who once had stable domains but suddenly found themselves "hapless and homeless" in the aftermath (Masquelier 2006, 736). This re-coding of people's status from "flood victims" to "refugees" or "evacuees" and ultimately to "the homeless" has served primarily to strip them of their situatedness in "culture, place, and history" (cf. Masquelier 2006, 737). Similarly, black victims were ostensibly framed as *looters*, "whereas their white counterparts were simply survivors looking for food" (Masquelier 2006, 740). Some have considered adopting the United Nations moniker of "internally displaced persons" (IDPs) to describe those "who have sought refuge without crossing borders" (Arena 2007, 369; Masquelier 2006, 738), but at the end of the day it is apparent that the final nomenclatural destination for many of Katrina's victims is simply that they will be subsumed into the realm of *homelessness*.

A sample of media representations culled over a three-year period (from early 2006 to 2009) starkly indicates the magnitude of the "homeless problem" in post-Katrina New Orleans, as well as the subtle mechanisms by which people are moved into ever-increasing positions of vulnerability and disempowerment. Sifting through the articles and essays written in this time period, one immediately sees strands of the major themes and issues outlined above, weaving a complex narrative of devastation, desperation, and determination. Indeed, the sense of human tragedy comes through strongly in many of these reports, casting the experiences of individuals and communities in the context of larger forces of displacement and subjugation. The voices of advocates and activists are likewise reflected here, as are the ethical and political issues that serve as their driving force. Ultimately, these articles comprise a coherent narrative and a nascent "living history" of unique individuals, their besieged communities, and the macroscopic (and frequently violent) structures of our society. These accounts—and the people whose views and stories they encapsulate and represent—deserve a modicum of space to speak for themselves:

> Although famous restaurants are reopening in the French Quarter, and a trickle of tourists has returned, much of New Orleans remains apocalyptic. . . . Officials say New Orleans can't handle an influx of traumatized, homeless families, but that may be what it is about to get. Five months after Hurricane Katrina, many of the storm's victims are facing a second crisis. The Federal Emergency Management Agency is ending its hotel subsidy program despite the fact that thousands of Katrina victims have nowhere else to go, [and] advocates for the homeless are bracing for disaster. "The tidal wave is about to happen," says Michael Stoops, acting executive director of the National

Coalition for the Homeless. "The homeless shelters in this country for the 'regular' homeless are already full. and they can't accommodate many more people. They will have to turn people away. Before Katrina." he adds. "I always believed that the victims of natural disasters were treated better and differently than the regular homeless population. When Katrina happened, I realized that the victims of natural disasters are not treated any better than the old and regular homeless" (Goldberg 2006).

The deepening housing crisis in storm-battered New Orleans is putting the lives of the city's poorest and most vulnerable residents at risk—and officials so far have failed to take adequate action. . . . Executive Director Martha Kegel with UNITY of Greater New Orleans, the lead agency for the local network of homeless service organizations, says adults and children are now living in cars, ungutted houses and abandoned buildings throughout the city: "I don't know that people are aware of the homeless crisis we are experiencing in New Orleans post-Katrina. It's grown tremendously. and it's getting worse every day." At the same time, the federal government is moving ahead with plans to tear down four of the city's biggest low-income housing developments—even though they did not suffer extensive storm-related damage. The demolitions are part of a rebuilding effort that *New York Times* architecture critic Nicolai Ouroussoff calls "one of the most aggressive works of social engineering in America since the postwar boom of the 1950s" (Sturgis 2006).

Hurricane-ravaged New Orleans faces a major crisis with homelessness.... Facing a severe shortage of affordable housing, displaced residents returning to the city along with an influx of construction trade workers are being forced to sleep in everything from cars to flooded-out houses to long-abandoned motels, as Katrina relief workers from across the country still struggle to fill gaping holes in the city's social services. . . . While New Orleans has long struggled with poverty, the face of homelessness has changed since Katrina, Ms. Kegel and other advocates say. The population now includes the chronically homeless who never left the city or have returned; residents who lost their homes to the flood and have run out of federal assistance—or may have never received assistance—and cannot afford higher rents. . . . On any given night, more than 12,000 homeless men, women, and children need shelter in New Orleans, Kegel estimates. Before Katrina it was 6,000 a night; just a year ago it was 2,000. . . . According to homeless advocates, the city has no effectively functioning social-services agency offering case management to the homeless (Sasser 2007a).

As she pushed a shopping cart of belongings through the still-life of the Lower 9th Ward. Tamara Martin knew only one source of shelter for this city's burgeoning homeless population: the thousands of buildings left vacant and rotting nearly two years after Hurricane Katrina. . . . Because she's homeless. she said. "I can't get right. you know . . . I'm striving hard. I'm striving hard. I'm losing so much weight I'm striving so much." Across New Orleans . . . a homeless population that has nearly doubled since Hurricane Katrina is squatting in the ruins of the storm. Through pried-open doors of some of the city's estimated

80,000 vacant dwellings, the poor, mentally ill and drug-addicted have carved out living conditions like those of the Third World. "These are abandoned people, living in abandoned housing, in a city which in many ways has itself been abandoned," said Martha Kegel (Gonzalez 2007).

A long-time resident of the Lafitte public housing apartments, since Katrina [Odessa Lewis] has been locked out of her apartment and forced to live in a 240 square foot FEMA trailer. Ms. Lewis has asked repeatedly to be allowed to return to her apartment to clean and fix it up so she can move back in. She even offered to do all the work herself and with friends at no cost. The government continually refused to allow her to return. Now she is being evicted from her trailer and fears she will become homeless because there is no place for working people, especially African American working and poor people, to live in New Orleans. . . . Renting is so hard in part because there is a noose closing around the housing opportunities of New Orleans African American renters displaced by Katrina. They have been openly and directly targeted by public and private actions designed to keep them away. The U.S. Department of Housing and Urban Development (HUD) just added their weight to the attack by approving the demolition of 2966 apartments in New Orleans . . . HUD and the Housing Authority of New Orleans [HANO] argued passionately that residents displaced from public housing . . . are financially "better off" than they were before. This echoes the infamous Barbara Bush comment of September 5, 2005 when, after viewing the overwhelmingly African American crowd of thousands of people living on cots in the Astrodome, she said: "And so many of the people in the arena here, you know, were underprivileged anyway, so this—(she chuckles slightly) this is working very well for them" (Quigley 2007).

Over the past 10 months, Steven Gioustover has slept on the floor of a friend's federally provided trailer, in a shuttered elementary school, and on a cot at the Ozmann Inn, one of only two operating homeless shelters for men in New Orleans. With just over 200 beds available in a city with more than 10,000 homeless, he's fortunate to have a roof over his head. . . . An ongoing housing shortage, high rents, rising costs of living, and a dearth of federal and state housing assistance have made it difficult for many of the city's lower-income returnees to find affordable rental housing. . . . "I had never been homeless in my life before now," said Mr. Gioustover, who owned a car, earned a decent living as a carpenter, and lived in a two-bedroom apartment in New Orleans East, a suburb devastated by Katrina, before losing it all to 15 feet of floodwater. "If I had family here like I did before Katrina, I'd be staying with them. But all of my family lost their houses in the flood, and they're still in Texas and Georgia. I'm the only one back" (Sasser 2007b).

Low-income residents of New Orleans are frantically struggling to secure the right to return to their homes before [HUD] begins demolishing thousands of public housing units next week. . . . This overhaul would eliminate 82 percent of the city's public housing, thereby excluding 3,800 families, according to the Peoples' Hurricane Relief Fund and Oversight Coalition. . . . Displaced residents of public housing and their activist supporters have raised an outcry about the housing demolition, which many fear will result in a widespread reconfiguration of the city's demographic makeup. "This is massive-scale, en masse gentrification." said Rev. Jeff Connor. . . . "What's at stake is the very essence of New Orleans." . . . Among the reasons offered by HUD and HANO . . . for the destruction of public housing developments is that these complexes encourage a problematic "concentration of poverty." But some experts question this reasoning, and point out that most of the units were untouched by the storm and didn't suffer any significant damage. . . . "[People are] going to come back home. And when they get back home, they will not have houses. And we will have a problem of even more homeless people. And we will have created it because we didn't stop this demolition." [Connor] said (Pollock 2007).

While it may be Christmas time in the city, the City That Care Forgot's homeless citizens and displaced residents are feeling anything but warm and fuzzy. With the city's ever-expanding homeless population scrambling to find a place to lie down safely when the sun goes down and former public housing residents facing an uphill battle to prevent the demolition of their former homes, it's crystal clear that there's little room in post-Katrina New Orleans for compassion or anything that even vaguely resembles genuine concern for those who are less fortunate. . . . What we're seeing is a piece-by-piece dismantling of Black New Orleans followed by a white-led re-organization of the city and its living arrangements. . . . Former public housing residents find themselves in a similar predicament to the homeless. . . . Whether we agree or not with the decision to demolish the city's housing developments and City Hall's clumsy handling of the homeless problem, we need to make it clear to all of the city's elected officials that we will not stand idly by and watch silently as people's constitutional rights are being kicked around (Lewis 2007).

Mayor Ray Nagin's administration appears to be preparing to move the city's biggest homeless colony, a highly visible collection of people and bedrolls just off Canal Street, to a Central City emergency shelter. . . . Calling the scene "a mess." Nagin said that . . . the city will begin enforcing its "habitation laws." . . . While Nagin did not specify which local habitation law he was referring to, the most often-used ordinance was found unconstitutional by the courts more than two decades ago and stricken from the municipal code six years ago. But in past years it still has been seen as a tool by local officials who wring their hands at the homeless people who linger in public spaces. [Martha Kegel] told the council that homeless people are suffering. . . . "We still have a humanitarian crisis." she said. . . . "We're already on the streets, where else are we supposed to go?" asked Sara Brown. 40, who before Hurricane Katrina rented an apartment Uptown and worked as a dishwasher in the French Quarter. Like many others interviewed beneath the expressway, Brown is a native New Orleanian who was displaced by the storm and returned to the city to find rents sharply raised (Reckdahl 2008).

Debra Reed, 54, used to rent a house in the Seventh Ward for $375 a month while earning $10 an hour at a drycleaner. She took home $400 a week, more than enough to pay her rent with enough left over to live comfortably. And then

Hurricane Katrina took it all away. The storm destroyed Reed's home and workplace. She spent four days on the roof of her house before being evacuated to Houston. The native New Orleanian came home nine months ago to a city where homes that once rented for $375 are now going for $800. With no job, no place to stay and no assistance from [FEMA]. Reed became one of the city's estimated 12,000 homeless. She is now living in a tent under the Interstate 10 overpass at Claiborne Avenue and Canal Street. . . . "How do they expect people to survive?" Reed asked. "A lot of people here want to work. I want my own place but none of us who grew up here can afford to live in New Orleans no more." Reed said she has few options and will remain in her tent under the bridge (Webster 2008).

Salvador is part of the growing ranks of homeless men, women and children struggling to survive in New Orleans. . . . [M]any are native New Orleanians who returned to their city only to find that rents had soared and the city's already meager safety net had been shredded. With nowhere to sleep and few social services, they have resorted to whatever makeshift shelter they can find: abandoned houses stalked by rats, park benches patrolled by police, bushes, underpasses, cars and, until recently, a sprawling tent city that sprang up in July in front of City Hall. . . . In post-Katrina New Orleans, in which every opportunity has been taken to pulverize—and then privatize—New Deal legacies like public housing and government-run social services, homelessness is the inevitable endpoint for thousands. . . . "Poor people just have not been the priority in this recovery." said Martha Kegel. . . . "And I think the fact that this situation hasn't been treated with the urgency it deserves is exactly why we're seeing these huge homeless camps in New Orleans, why so many people are living in abandoned buildings and why so many people are suffering in Third World conditions in the United States of America two and a half years after Katrina" (Ratner 2008).

The homeless population of New Orleans since Hurricane Katrina has reached unprecedented levels for a U.S. city: one in 25 residents. An estimated 12,000 homeless accounts for 4% of New Orleans' estimated population of 302,000, according to the homeless advocacy group UNITY. . . . New Orleans' rate is more than four times that of most U.S. cities, which have homeless populations of under 1%, said Michael Stoops. . . . The percentage of New Orleans' homeless is one of the highest recorded since U.S. housing officials began tracking homelessness in the mid-1980s, said Dennis Culhane, a University of Pennsylvania professor who has studied homeless trends for more than 20 years. "In a modern urban U.S. city. we've never seen it." he said. . . . Many of the homeless are Katrina evacuees who returned to unaffordable rents or who slipped through the cracks of the federal system designed to provide temporary housing after the storm, said Mike Miller [of] UNITY. . . . [Mayor] Nagin has suggested reinstating a city ordinance that would make it illegal to sleep in public places. Homeless advocates say the law would just crowd the jails. "It just shows a real disconnect" between the city and the problem." said James Perry, head of the Greater New Orleans Fair Housing Action Center. "The answer is not going to be jails" (Jervis 2008).

[Mayor Nagin] recently suggested a way to reduce this city's post-Katrina homeless population: give them one-way bus tickets out of town. Mr. Nagin later insisted the off-the-cuff proposal was just a joke. But he has portrayed the dozens of people camped in a tent city under a freeway overpass near Canal Street as recalcitrant drug and alcohol abusers who refuse shelter, give passers-by the finger and, worst of all, hail from somewhere else. While many of the homeless do have addiction problems or mental illness, a survey by advocacy groups in February showed that 86 percent were from the New Orleans area (Dewan 2008).

New Orleans is struggling with a growing number of sick and disabled people who have become homeless since the hurricane. This crisis will only get worse until local, state and federal officials come together behind a plan that finds short-term housing for them immediately, and permanent affordable housing for them quickly. . . . In what could be a harbinger of things to come, 30 percent of the people surveyed in one homeless encampment reported that they had moved onto the streets after being cut off from [FEMA] housing assistance or while living in a household that had lost the benefit. . . . This would be a terrible place to economize. The dollar amount is small, and the lives of some of this country's most vulnerable citizens—who were already abandoned once by their government—are at stake (Editorial 2008).

Some three and a half years after Hurricanes Katrina and Rita hit the city known as "The Big Easy," it has been anything but easy for thousands of displaced New Orleans-area residents to find housing. Many have been forced onto the streets or into temporary and long-term shelters, largely due to bureaucratic delays and inadequate government-assistance programs. . . . Thousands of others are living elsewhere, unable to return due to high rents, housing shortages, and delays in funding for rebuilding. Many who have made it back languish in substandard, crowded conditions. "Families are doubled up and tripled up in houses and apartments, trying to pay rent and utilities, unable to meet basic needs," says Ayesha Buckner, homeless liaison for the Orleans Parish School Board. "All of the shelters are filled to capacity. The media portrays that [New Orleans] is back, but we're not back. Every week we get new homeless children." . . . According to Mike Miller, "We have the perfect storm of homelessness in New Orleans—a natural disaster and no real infrastructure in place to handle the amount of need. We get the results of all of the failed systems: failed mental-health, housing, drug-treatment, and criminal systems. These people have nowhere to go" (Thomas 2009).

[Michael] Palmer is one of thousands of homeless people living in New Orleans' storm damaged and abandoned homes and buildings. Four years after Katrina, recovery and rebuilding has come slow to this city, and there are many boarded-up homes to choose from. The Greater New Orleans Community Data Center counts 65,888 abandoned residential addresses in New Orleans, and this number doesn't include any of the many non-residential buildings. . . . Overall, about a third of the addresses in the city are vacant or abandoned, the highest rate in the nation. UNITY for the Homeless is the only organization surveying these spaces. . . . They have surveyed 1,330 buildings—a small fraction of the total number of empty structures. Of those, 564 were unsecured. Nearly 40% of them showed signs of use, including a total of 270 bedrolls or mattresses. Using conservative estimates, UNITY estimates at least 6,000 squatters, and a total of about 11,000 homeless individuals in the city (Flaherty 2009).

The combined effect of these reports—which read like a "social autopsy" of humanitarianism in America—reveals themes familiar to homeless advocates: displacement, demonization, criminalization, desperation. These patterns are evident in cities across the United States and around the world (Amster 2008), but the New Orleans case adds troubling new layers to the mix, raising myriad ethical issues for researchers, advocates, and policymakers. Post-Katrina homelessness in New Orleans reached levels not seen before in a modern U.S. city, and these figures included a preponderance of internally displaced people who had no prior experience of homelessness before the storm. The concerted efforts of elected officials and government agencies seemed to be aimed more toward exacerbating the problem then remedying it, with the destruction of public housing and the evisceration of social services in the city. In June 2011, UNITY issued a report finding homelessness still at levels double that before Katrina, attributing this persistence to factors including escalating rents and the "devastation of rental stock," untreated trauma and the absence of healthcare, and the loss of neighborhood and family support systems; the report also found that 75 percent of those sleeping in abandoned buildings were "Katrina survivors" (UNITY 2011). Shortly after this report was issued—and more than six years after Katrina—current New Orleans Mayor Mitch Landrieu announced a ten-year plan to "end homelessness" in the city, calling it "an urgent issue that demands immediate action. After Hurricane Katrina, many who never thought they would ever be homeless were suddenly left with nothing," he said (Associated Press 2011). Nothing but trouble, it would appear. . . .

Conclusion

I truly wish this article did not have to be written, so many years now since Hurricane Katrina made its way through the Gulf Coast region. Shortly after the storm hit, I traveled to New Orleans with an ad hoc grassroots group to help provide food and support for the "holdouts" trying to sustain themselves in the city, some of whom had been "threatened with eviction at gunpoint" (see Arena 2007; Harnden 2005). The city itself was an apocalyptic tangle of wires and debris; fires burned unchecked, the air was fetid, and the place reeked of chemicals and death. Locals were conspicuously denied assistance from established relief agencies, while tens of thousands of armed troops and law enforcement officers turned the city into a perverse sort of American Baghdad. Still, the people trying to hold onto their homes displayed incredible dignity and solidarity in the face of long odds and relentless harassment. It was one of the most powerful and poignant moments of my life to be in the midst of this scene (see Martin 2005), and I have been forever altered in my personal, professional, and political bearings ever since. Compared to the people of New Orleans, however, my world has remained rock solid.

Writing this chapter has brought back many of the faces and places from those weeks in the fall of 2005. The unresolved emotions and open wounds still haunt me whenever more (often bad) news emanates from the city. Activists have been murdered and historical neighborhoods left to rot. Scandals and informants have shaken grassroots groups and undermined their efforts. "Disaster tours" sprang up and millions of dollars in relief were squandered—or worse. In 2009, the region sported an absurd rate of homelessness among children at just under 19 percent, almost four times the rate of the next closest state on the list (WDSU.com 2009). This statistic is doubly disconcerting for me, since one of the personal alterations I experienced on the heels of Katrina was meeting a local activist-holdout-evacuee and having two children together in the ensuing years. When we emerged from New Orleans, my partner and I gave a number of talks on topics such as "The Iraqification of New Orleans," having seen and experienced the complex interconnections among militarization, gentrification, homelessness, displacement, and resistance. In many ways, these same forces continue unabated today.

In my view, once this knowledge is given, one cannot remain silent nor refrain from using the resources of advocacy and dissemination at one's disposal in an attempt to shine a light and help right these wrongs. Sometimes this is referred to as a form of "public sociology" that "grounds itself within, and speaks to, the social struggles for fundamental and systemic change" (Arena 2007, 373). We can extend the concept further to envision a "sociology of liberation" in which we "immerse [our]selves in grassroots struggles" and, concomitantly, wind up as a matter of course "confronting the controls of the academy" as well (Arena 2007, 382–83). Whatever path we choose, and wherever we find ourselves located geographically and socioeconomically, it is incumbent upon us simply in our capacity as *human beings* to strive for a more just world.

Tell people about the situation in New Orleans—and about the next disaster, and the ones after that. Contact the people and organizations mentioned in this chapter, and offer to assist them. Look for similar regimes of displacement and control in your region, and take action to undo them. Don't let the memory of New Orleans fall gently into the dustbin of history, lest more such examples proliferate in other cities—or perhaps even at the level of entire countries, such as in post-earthquake Haiti. Write about these episodes of personal and political upheaval, talk about them, and refer back to them in your work. Seek evacuees and affected persons wherever you are, and forge a connection with them. Contribute your time, energy, resources, and expertise to alleviate suffering and confront the edifice of poverty and structural violence that pervades our society. In short, use the tools at your disposal to promote positive transformation and make a difference in whatever manner you are able to do so.

We can call this a principle of *ethics* if we like, but perhaps even more to the point is that it is simply what one must do in order to be able sleep at night. My profound wish is that the displaced people of New Orleans, and elsewhere, can find a place to do the same.

Chapter 11
Do (No) Harm: Homelessness Research as Personal Transformation
David Cook

Abstract. For an extended period in 2007, the author collected, conducted, and retold life story interviews with homeless men and women in and around Chattanooga, Tennessee. Utilizing the methodology of the life story interview as a way to re-humanize the homeless poor, the author also published the life stories within a public venue as a way of counteracting the dehumanizing policies, stereotypes, behaviors, and beliefs that oftentimes are violent in nature, uninformed in logic, and deficient in outcome. By doing so, the author himself was transformed by the process, realizing that the homeless poor contain a power that the non-homeless do not, and that his own advocacy and lifestyle may indeed be a hindrance to the creation of a just society in which poverty does not exist.

"Sincerely, to all that read this, stop and think, have a different outlook towards your fellow homeless man out there. Most all ain't what you think. But some of them are little bit rotten. They [my fellow citizens with homes] need to hear straight from one who has lived it, walked it, and talked it. Hear the real truth out there."—Billy Walker, homeless man in Chattanooga, TN

During the greater part of 2007, I asked homeless individuals living in Chattanooga, Tennessee, to tell me their life stories. Using clear standards endorsed and accepted by the journalism community—of which I have been a professional member for seven years—I documented the life history of homeless men and women in my community. Additionally, I conducted an extensive life story interview with one homeless man—a Gregorian monk—and transformed it into a chapter-length biography. Obtaining his or her permission and then allowing each individual the opportunity to change their name, I published their words in a series of essays for an online news source, *The Chattanoogan*. Each life story was published in narrative form, and only slightly edited for the sake of grammar, and never for content.

The life story interview is a research method rooted in intimacy. There is nothing more personal than our own life story, and asking the homeless poor in Chattanooga—already living in vulnerability and insecurity—to freely publicize the story of their lives meant they had to trust me as a researcher to do no harm. Participation in this life story interview could never have as its consequence the addition of even more suffering into their already marginalized lives. As an anti-poverty activist, and as a researcher-journalist committed to accuracy and professionalism, this was in fact my overarching ethic: "Do no harm."

The United Nations' Universal Declaration of Human Rights (UDHR) is widely considered the pioneering vision for how humans should treat one another within frameworks of democracy, peace, justice, and equality. In order for all of us to live fully human lives, certain parameters must be acknowledged and upheld. In 1948, the international community signed onto the UDHR, agreeing that the thirty listed human rights contained within it are to be the measure and international standard for how humans should treat one another. Four of these rights are categorized as economic: the right to shelter and housing, health care, a living wage, and an education. These economic human rights are the lens and foundation through which a concrete and organized movement may be able to restore dignity—in the form of shelter, living wages, health care, and education—to homeless and poor people in the world around us who are victims of human rights violations. We can surmise that nearly every homeless person in the United States is lacking in one or more of these fundamental categories. Therefore, the very existence of homeless persons is an indication that our system—i.e., the basic way we have arranged our lives—violates the humanity of others. And homeless research must have at its core the belief that homelessness is an economic crime. We may disagree about the cause or the criminals, but if we are doing research and are not applying it in a way that seeks to end that crime, then we are on the side of the criminals. Neutrality does not exist. Thus, this also was part of my ethic: to work to restore human rights to the homeless poor.

The life story interview was my bridge, my way of connecting these two aspects of my life—as a researcher-journalist and an activist—in order to help give voice to this voiceless population. The life story interview is an effective research method for three reasons. First, it empowers the storyteller. By asking a homeless woman to tell me her story, I am honoring her, acknowledging that her life has value, and this validation is one rarely heard by the homeless poor. As Atkinson (1998, 7) observes:

> We become fully aware, fully conscious, of our own lives through the process of putting them together in story form. It is through story that we gain context and recognize meaning. Reclaiming story is part of our birthright. Telling our story enables us to be heard, recognized, and acknowledged by others. Story makes the implicit explicit, the hidden seen, the unformed formed, and the confusing clear.

Second, the life story helps to rehumanize this group of dehumanized people by revealing their humanity to those who are not homeless. In certain fundamental ways, their lives are not unlike ours, and publicizing the life story interview of a homeless child is a vehicle by which the non-homeless population may realize this and thus re-organize their own lives so that they may be of benefit and do less harm to their homeless neighbors. Of course, the danger here involves the exploitation of an already victimized community. Homeless folks are not billboards, purposed solely to awaken the better angels of middle- and upper-class communities. Preventing this, I confirmed with each interviewee multiple times their desire to have their life story published. Those that agreed did so, by their own volition and testimony, because something transforming exists within the process of telling your own story:

> Life stories told seriously and consciously, in the voices of the persons telling them, are timeless; settings and circumstances change, but motifs and the meanings they represent remain constant across lives and time. Life stories instruct by making the connections from our own, or someone else's, past to our future clearer than they were before. They renew by illustrating how things can and will be different than they once were. They carry the wisdom of lived experience. They show us the direction of human development and the possible paths through life. Maybe most important, they lead us to the human spirit, to our deepest feelings, the values we live by, and the eternal meaning of life (Atkinson 1998, 76).

Third, the life story interview transformed me. By conducting this research, by receiving and transmitting the life stories of others, my own life was changed. The homeless poor became my teacher, and all I did was sit down and listen to them talk about their lives as, again, Atkinson (1998, 70–71) likewise found:

> We are each other's teachers. Like a novel or a poem, the life story has something to say to us about life—and about our life in particular. We often learn something from the stories we hear or read. They teach us something about life, they validate our own experience, or point out a contrast to our own experience. The person sharing his or her life story is the teacher. The person receiving another's life story is the student.

During my research, I began to see the homeless individual as mythological, a symbol of universal humanity. In looking at the homeless I began to see myself and all people. While the homeless individuals I interviewed could in no way represent the complete portrait of universal homelessness, they do, at the same time, represent parts of that universality and of our universal humanity as well. Their stories are also our stories. "Although their problems are more severe, however, destitute people living on the streets and in homeless shelters are not so different from the rest of us. They never have been. Any genuine effort to end homelessness must begin with recognition of that essential truth," writes Kenneth Kusmer (2002, 247). My research emerged out of the belief that the life story could make public Kusmer's well-articulated point, placing it solely and unapologetically within my bias: inequality, discrimination, and violence occur on a regular and systemic basis for homeless citizens in Chattanooga (and every other city in the United States), and this violence represents a violence against all homeless persons throughout the world. I believe that the dignity and rights of all humans should not rest on economic or property-owning status, nor should attempts at achieving democracy and equality in all its forms be hindered, resisted, subverted, or denied. My work was a social, political, academic, and personal act designed out of this bias.

Therefore, on some level, my ethic was also to *do* harm—to harm our system that allows and even encourages homelessness, along with the apathy, ignorance, subtle and overt violence existing within the non-homeless communities towards the homeless poor. To those structures, I wanted to do harm.

But in the end, I do not know if I accomplished anything. In the end, I was also left wondering: what if I was the criminal? What if I was the person who needed to be harmed?

A Crisis of Identity

The homeless constitute poverty made visible, and this public poverty represents a threat to tourism and economic activity, especially when the poor are made visible right in the heart of downtown urban life. Their visibility is problematic to the city's economic and tourist progress, and historically the homeless are seen and treated as "urban graffiti"; for the mainstream public, an encounter with the visible poor "disrupts the ordinary rhythms of public life" (Blau 1992, 3–4). This encounter is a disruption, one that most non-homeless citizens wish they could avoid. It is this disruption that also explains the efforts, broad and wide, of many U.S. cities to criminalize their homeless population, rendering them invisible to the public at large. Thus, their very presence becomes a form of resistance and contestation. Not only, then, is their suffering a material one, but the homeless also suffer from a crisis of identity that is equal to if not greater than their crisis of economics and space. It is their crisis of identity—an inability to belong—that pushes this struggle; for if our nation and its powers would begin a transformation of perception and view the homeless differently, then the issues of economics and space would in turn follow.

The general stereotype of the homeless individual involves the following: he or she is addicted to drugs or alcohol or both; he or she is mentally ill; he or she is lazy; he or she is a product of his or her own decisions and circumstances. The general stereotype of the solution for the homeless individual is even more simplistic: take a shower and get a job. In a response to a column I (2007) wrote in our city's online newspaper, published in an attempt to encourage a transformation of public perception, one response said that the solution to homelessness was simple: "Here's a much easier and less expensive, 3 step method for any urban outdoorsman to pull himself up out of the streets: (1) Take a bath. (2) Get a shave and a haircut. (3) Get a job." Included later in this response was an excerpt from the "Ballad of the Lone Ranger," apparently written to encourage these "urban outdoorsmen" to pull themselves up by their cowboy bootstraps. To evoke the story of the Lone Ranger—whose ballad sings of the glories of self-reliance and cowboy independence—in a discussion on homelessness is both humorous and tremendously sad, and further it allows a fine example of what much of our research has documented as a typical response to homelessness.

"If work was one's salvation and idleness a vice, it is no wonder that the tramp was portrayed as he was. In a nation comprised, ideally, of sturdy yeomen, small capitalists, and upwardly mobile working men, he seemed a footloose, goalless wanderer, living not by his hands but by his wits and—worst of all—in the dissipation of idleness," writes Kusmer (2002, 47). In our nation's psyche, work is the ladder that reaches the American dream, and anyone who does not work, who is idle, is deserving of the condemnation of a life on Skid Row, or under a bridge, or in jail. As history tells us, idleness has been a crime since at least the colonial times, and it is this scarlet badge the homeless individual wears, placing him outside the fruits of labor that all working people deserve. "They make it their own choice for staying out there," President Reagan once remarked (in Miller 1991, 161).

Reagan, whose own policies helped dismantle many of the support systems and safety nets for poor and homeless people in the United States, deploys a logic suggesting that if homelessness is a choice, then so is its solution: *get a job*. And what of those who choose not to work, as Hopper (2003, 26) inquires?

A deep-seated ambivalence toward dependency, anxiety about the shaky purchase of the work ethic among unsettled men, fears of mobility itself, resentment by ordinary working people of their own ordinary working lot, the deep distrust shown by organized charity toward those of its charges who prove uncooperative or indifferent. All were variations of a theme: These men are "not like us." This insistence makes the annals of US homelessness a tangled tale of contempt, pity, and, curiously, blank disregard.

This dehumanizing belief—that they are not like us—is again at the core of our efforts in defining this crisis of identity. The homeless, as explained earlier, suffer from a crisis of space, and also inhabit the same streets that millions use for their daily economic routines. If, then, homelessness is seen as a product of the refusal to work, then finding the homeless within the urban streets—where so much work takes place—only furthers this hostility, resentment, and resignation. As Blau (1992, 4) writes: "If an event draws both tourists and media, the poverty that is public is the poverty that is sure to be concealed." Why? Because the homeless exist as a symbol that the system is not working. The homeless shatter the American Dream, as they stand outside, knocking at the door yet unable to find entrance. The homeless individual symbolizes a wrecking ball to the belief that work is salvation, and that U.S. capitalism provides for all, or rather, for all who are willing to work. This is not a realization that many want to face, and thus concealing the homeless is perhaps, superficially, a much easier prospect to endorse.

Therefore, in my research I have sought to reveal that the common myth was a fallacy, and using the life story method I allowed those who knew the most about poverty (the poor themselves) to tell their own stories to the larger working world. One man I interviewed explained clearly his crisis and its accompanying despair: "I'm just existing. . . . I ain't got no influence. You can't hardly get a job without knowing somebody . . . There ain't nothing to do. I'm just bored. Bored to death. No finances, and nothing you can do" (Bubba, Personal Interview, May 1, 2007). Bubba—his given name—had seen his life unravel after he wrote a bad check. After months on the streets, his troubles accumulated, as did his despair. Publishing his life story was an attempt to counteract the generalization that homelessness is solved through quick fixes and immediate steps such as "take a bath, and get a job."

Yet in my attempt to counter their crisis of identity, I realized that another crisis of identity that was equally problematic was my own: my identity was hindering the abolition of homelessness and poverty, and this crisis-making realization only came about through my research and direct contact with the homeless poor.

The Leper Within

Each day in the United States, millions of non-homeless citizens encounter homeless and visible poor citizens, and this encounter is rife with emotional and psychological underpinnings. The encounter between the non-homeless and the homeless is an exchange that travels in both directions; seen as a message— either spoken or unspoken, said or left unsaid—this exchange contains meaning for both parties involved. The homeless receive a message, ranging from subtle to blatant, as they are ignored and devalued by those, for example, on the sidewalk going to work. The nonhomeless also receive a message from the homeless, who represent poverty and despair and the idea that something somewhere is malfunctioning in our society. In both cases, these messages carry emotional, psychological and even spiritual impact and residue. Through this lens I see the homeless as representing our modern-day lepers, and it is within this context that I can explain the rashness of criminal legislation and widespread punitive reaction to their presence. They represent something we do not wish to see. They remind us of something we do not wish to know.

As others have done before him, psychologist James Hollis attempts to uncover the unconscious aspect of human existence in his book *Why Good People Do Bad Things*. Calling this unconscious aspect "the Shadow," Hollis states that it is "composed of all those aspects of ourselves that have a tendency to make us uncomfortable with ourselves. The Shadow is not just the unconscious, it is what discomforts the sense of self we wish to have" (2007, 9). In our urban setting, the homeless individual represents this discomfort; he or she provokes frustration, outrage, and blind contempt simply by what he or she is not: a well-dressed, forty-hour-a-week working homeowner. The response is often punitive, harsh, and punishing—and Hollis says these are the hallmarks of the Shadow at work, for whomever we project such vitriol upon only reminds us of something in ourselves. Our enemies "are the carrier of our secret life, and for this we shall hate them, revile them and destroy them for they have committed the most heinous of offenses. They remind us of some aspect of ourselves that we cannot bear to see" (Hollis 2007, 18). The homeless, in all their downtrodden existence, represent our own inability to accept our brokenness, our frailty in the face of the human condition. The homeless become the literal manifestation of the "poor human," which is a symbol that runs counterintuitive to our Manifest Destiny narrative and our American Dream culture. The American culture is one of pop-success, three-car garages, beach homes, and tanning beds. The homeless are countercultural, a roadblock, both literally and figuratively, to such pursuits.

Therefore, no solution to homelessness will exist without some complete acceptance of their humanity, and this type of acceptance will only occur with an acceptance of our own personal, cultural, economic, and national Shadow. In *A Monk in the World*, Wayne Teasdale equates modern homelessness with ancient leprosy, confessing his own inability to accept the homeless as long as he viewed them as different than himself. "I had to face my own inner leper, my own fear of the vulnerability I saw in these souls" (Teasdale 2002, 122). The homeless, Teasdale (2002, 130) says, remind us of things we wish to ignore:

> We have so much, and when confronted with people who have nothing—who are vulnerable, helpless and destitute—we receive their help in overcoming fear and insecurity. The poor hold this power—the power of truth itself. When we respond in love instead of fear, when we don't ignore them but instead see them and consider their condition, are we not reminded of our own ultimate fragility and tentativeness as beings in this world.

And we want them to vanish for this. This is why they are hated. The burden of the crisis of identity is not theirs, but ours—or more to the point: mine. *I am the one causing the problem.*

"The Poor Teach Us"

The foregoing ideas are not provable; they confound quantitative research methodologies. But it was my own personal experience—aided by the methodology of heuristic research—that allows and even encourages me to speak about this as clearly as I would with measurable research results. Conducting, collecting, and re-telling the life stories of homeless individuals has had a transforming effect on many aspects of my life. It fueled my activism, informed my politics, softened my anger towards other people around me, and shook my patterns of consumption and affluence. Most importantly, I became less afraid.

Fear is a vast emotion within the realm of homelessness. For the homeless poor, fear of not being able to survive is common, and for the non-homeless, fear is a driving emotion behind reactionary and violent policies and behaviors. I have not always been a homeless activist, and at some point in my journey, I had to descend from my position of privilege and enter a world where I was uncomfortable, and not in control, and surrounded by people living markedly different types of lives, where wealth and comfort were not the common, shared experience. In this world, I was the outsider. Yet through this process, the homeless became demystified and my fear of them gradually vanished. And this influenced other areas of my life, where traces of xenophobia—conscious or not—had been wedged into my thinking and attitudes.

The poor save us from ourselves by reminding us of the essential truths in life. One man in Chattanooga wrote me of his neighbor who woke up on a regular basis to find a man digging through his trash each morning. Understandably, the homeowner angrily wished the trash-digger to be gone, to vanish. It is out of this spirit that much criminalizing legislation is passed, and much work done to remove such a sight from the public eye. Yet within this moment, there is a lesson. The trash-digger exists as a reminder to the homeowner for how the other half lives. The trash-digger is a symbol, a messenger, reminding the world that all is not well, that poverty exists, that humans suffer. To acknowledge the trash-digger requires a profound shift in the homeowner, and this is the descent that is demanded in order to reshape society so poverty no longer exists. Gary Smith (2002, 57), a priest who made such a descent into a life of voluntary poverty, confesses that it was the trash-digger who saved his life:

> The poor teach us to be truth tellers: to speak to what must be done to transform oppressive structures even as we are meeting individual needs. The poor teach us of compassion: to feel another's heartache even as we are creating concrete

practices of relief. The poor teach us to embark on the sacred search for indignation: to discover our anger in the face of the greed, malice, and human indif-
ference that give birth to suffering and to speak to it. No, we must yell about it.

Present within discussions on homelessness must be our own experience as
the non-homeless. We must understand both sides of the tension. The middle-
and upper-class non-homeless are able to live comfortable lives, making it easy
to forget those that are quite uncomfortable. Therefore our encounters with them
awaken us to the very basics of our existence—food, shelter, work, meaning,
dignity, love—and help to prevent us from blinding ourselves with unnecessary
and even destructive tendencies and priorities. Soon, though, we may find ourselves asking the nagging question of the ethical non-homeless: how do we continue to live in a way that uplifts and honors those who are homeless?

One common thread in most spiritual traditions is that materialism is counterintuitive to our work as humans in finding meaning and love in life. Materialism is a roadblock to the spirit, and it is no accident that the downtown urban
environment is the site of this tension between capital gains and the homeless
poor, between materialism and humanity. Alan, a day laborer I interviewed
whose back was broken and job lost after a New Year's Eve car crash, understood this dynamic quite clearly. I spoke to him while he was in a wheelchair.
His girlfriend was pushing him. As he described his plight (Alan, Personal Interview, April 16, 2007):

> One day I had to go to Wal-Mart to get a prescription. I got there, and they told
> me it was at the Walgreens. The doctor had told us the wrong place. We had to
> turn around and go back. It took us four or five hours for her to wheel me there
> and back. We were on the side of the road. Somebody threw a bottle and almost
> hit (my girlfriend). They drive by and laugh at you. One guy in a convertible
> slowed down, waved and took off laughing. Some of them don't care I guess.
> People cuss at us. Ninety percent of the time, poor people will pick you up in-
> stead of rich people. People that pick me up say, "I've been there." Rich people
> won't even stop to look at you. That don't make any sense to me. The more
> money you have, the more you want to help people, right?

It became clear to me that my research with the homeless poor was countercultural, and their role in my life encouraged proper prioritization of my own
affairs. I realized that ending poverty requires a move toward voluntary poverty;
I must learn to live with less and practice resisting my impulsivity and greed. I
must sacrifice my social standing by naming the social structures that enable and
encourage poverty, in many of which I am a complicit member. And oftentimes,
I am unwilling to do this.

It was not until late in my research that I realized the full extent of the limitations of my work. I own a home, have a job and extended education, and am
surrounded by a large support network of family and friends existing in middle-
to upper-class lives. Homelessness had become like a zoo: it was a place I visit-

ed and then, after taking some notes, I left to return to my own home. Doing so smacked a bit of imperialism, of hegemony cloaked as research, as even one more example where the privileged take from the poor.

And publishing life stories was not enough to tip the balance to its proper equilibrium. I am still responsible. I have not done enough to support those who are poor and those who are working to end poverty with their time, funds, and energy. I still spend my money on items and experiences that have no lasting impact, knowing that this same money could instead be spent on saving lives. So ending poverty requires an end to various aspects of my own life. Sometimes it feels as if ending homelessness requires more of me than I am willing to give.

Conclusion

In writing this chapter, I came to a sobering conclusion: I do not know if one single individual has found an end to his or her homeless life because of my research and activism. Life stories will not transform our society into one where the Universal Declaration of Human Rights is fully realized. Life stories may not even pay the heating bills at the soup kitchen in town. Life stories were a form of easy research. I was comfortable. I still am comfortable, and millions of people in the United States are not.

What do I owe them? What do I owe the homeless in my own community? These are questions that are ethical ones that I must ask myself every day. In the relationships I have described—between myself and the homeless citizens I interviewed and hopefully advocated for—it is quite clear to me that the scales tipped in their balance, that they have done more for me than I have for them. My life has been transformed to a greater degree because of their presence. Their influence has been longer-lasting, yet I am the one using words like "activist" and "ethical researcher." I have no conclusions for this tension except to state that it is simply what transpired. Perhaps that is something to build upon.

A few years ago, I began to investigate—from a spiritual perspective—the New Testament claim that Christ makes when he declares the poor to be blessed. How could this be? Liberation theologian Gustavo Gutierrez (1970, 9) demands that we understand that "poverty is death," and in light of this, how then could poor people be blessed? This question was ancillary to my research using the life story methodology; it was always lurking in my consciousness. This is not the space to explore all the manifestations of this question, and the religious and theological implications it carries—but from a secular level, I do wish to include it in my concluding words.

There was a power I found within the homeless community that was unlike any power I found elsewhere. Paradoxically, this power was coupled with the overarching powerlessness that their very existence entails, but somehow through this lost sense of life, a new sense was discovered. Again, I do not mean to imply a romanticism, but consistent in my research was this theme of resilience and resistance, and while I would wish upon no one a life in poverty, I found that there is great poverty caused by wealth. There is a great inadequacy that overabundance causes, and I was transformed by the understanding that poverty is not exclusive to the lower classes of society. Poverty of the upper echelons may take a different form, but it is a poverty nonetheless.

"Blessed are the poor. They are blessed because poor people are strong," said Alan (2007). "They know they can go through anything. Rich people, if their money got taken away, they wouldn't know how to go on in society. Take everything we have, beat the shit out of us, and we can still go on. It can't get no worse for poor people. We're at the bottom. I guess we're blessed, because when little things happen, it's a blessing. On the way over here, I got happy to find a dollar and half a cigarette in the parking lot. Rich people would look at that and throw their head up and say who cares."

The ethical work of the homeless activist-researcher is perhaps, in large part, to make sure that they—that we—*do* in fact care.

Chapter 12
On the Politics and Ethics of "Using" "the Homeless" in Social Justice Research
Don Mitchell and Lynn A. Staeheli

Abstract: We do not do research with, or even about homeless people. We do not do research on the lives and experiences of homeless people, on the quality of being homeless, on who the homeless are, on what they may desire and want, or on such things as pathways into or out of homelessness. We do not do (much) research with or on advocacy groups working with the homeless. Instead, we do research on homeless*ness*, not as a condition of individuals but as a product of, and a problem for, society. We seek to understand how homelessness is indicative of how contemporary society structures the spaces of its cities; how local and global capitalism constructs a set of social possibilities, within which homelessness is both a solution and a problem; and what the rise of homelessness in contemporary cities means for what citizenship actually is. We do this, usually, through a close analysis of (a) the structural transformations of urban capitalism; (b) laws governing homeless and other marginalized people's behavior; and (c) the changing forms and meanings of public space. This research is highly politicized, treading the line between polemic and analytical: the goal is always to hold a mirror up to a society that pretends to be just and show it what it is really up to. In this project, we tend, in essence, to *use* homelessness, and therefore homeless people, as something of an "indicator species"—seeing homelessness and homeless people as something of a bellwether for all manner of processes and trends. We do not spend time speaking with homeless people to see how they see themselves or to test our interpretations against their realities. What are the politics and ethics of this sort of work? What issues of ethical responsibility are traded for political efficacy? What value obtains in politicized research on homelessness that in effect ignores flesh-and-blood homeless people? These are not easy questions. For many scholar-activists, the answer would be none: that it is irresponsible to conduct research that in effect *uses* homeless people—or at least the figure of homeless people—for political ends in which they have no say. In this chapter we argue otherwise. While examining the real ethical dilemmas that arise in work such as that which we conduct, we will defend such an arms-length approach as necessary precisely because the target of our research is not homelessness *per se*, or homeless people, but instead the structural conditions of a society that produce homelessness in specific forms and specific places. Such research is no replacement for research directly with homeless people, but it is, we will suggest, a necessary addition, especially for those of us who wish to attack and transform the structural determinants of contemporary homelessness.

Ethics—or Politics?

A couple of years ago, when one of us (Don) was chair of the Geography Department at Syracuse University, a quite talented, politically committed student defended her Master's degree thesis. Researching the politics and geography of abortion, this student had conducted in-depth interviews with abortion providers, support personnel, and others deeply knowledgeable about the geography of abortion in a particular city and region. Following a protocol laid out in her "human subjects" review, and which was approved by the University's Institutional Review Board (IRB),[1] the student gave each interviewee a written release form, on which they could declare whether they wished their names to remain confidential or waive their right to confidentiality. Each of the interviewees was interviewed in the context of her or his professional capacity (e.g., clinic director, doctor, abortion rights activist). All the interviewees save one waived their right to confidentiality for themselves and their organizations. Moreover, several told the student that they wanted their names used because they thought it important to resist the politics of cloaking that shrouds so much debate in the United States on abortion. Since they regarded abortion as a legitimate medical procedure, they thought the light of publicity was a crucial ingredient in maintaining it as such.

The student wrote what her committee agrees is an excellent and important thesis. But none of the names and affiliations of the interviewees appear in it, despite their wish to be publicly named. At the defense, the student's advisor, who was an untenured assistant professor, objected to the inclusion of names. The professor thought it put the informants unnecessarily at risk, should the thesis, or an article derived from it, come to the attention of violent anti-abortionists. The professor further argued that, as the official signatory of the human subjects protocol, she was ethically responsible for the safety of the informants in the study: she had an obligation to protect them, and indeed the student, as much as possible. The student was adamant about her own ethical and political responsibility to name names. She thought it was vital to give her informants what she thought of as the right to their political voice. Don agreed with the student (though not vocally during the defense itself). The other member of the committee (a tenured full professor) agreed with the advisor. During the committee's in-camera discussions at the end of the defense, the three committee members agreed that the student should strip all identifying materials out of her thesis. Don supported the decision—despite his own personal views—not only because he was on the losing side (as it were), but also because he was aware of the power relations at stake. Don was the chair of the department and a tenured professor. The advisor was untenured. It was vital that the assistant professor's authority with the student, the student's peers, and the advisors own faculty colleagues not be undermined.

These are the sorts of ethical dilemmas with which anyone who does social research is familiar. Raised during this defense, and in the course of doing the research on the thesis, were thorny questions of power (between student and advisor, advisor and department chair, among committee members, researcher and researched); of professional position and responsibility (the director of a clinic speaking "for" the clinic, informants using their official positions to promote particular political agendas, researchers having to determine whether and how to relay those agendas, advisors and committee members deciding whether and how a student-researcher's own politics can or should be relayed); and of personal danger (the possibility, however remote, that information in a research project could be used to endanger the informants or those to whom they have a professional responsibility). These are the sorts of issues that review processes and IRBs—however flawed—are designed to address. Informed consent forms, data protection procedures, and all the rest, as cumbersome as they often are, are designed to anticipate many of the issues that arose in this defense. They are meant to both protect human research subjects,[2] and to hand at least some degree of power over to them so they may help determine how the information derived from their participation is and is not used. Interestingly, in this regard, at Syracuse University, as at many other institutions, "public" individuals speaking in their official capacity are not considered "human subjects." While the IRB still insists on vetting all research projects,[3] most of the informants in our student's research were not, in fact, covered by IRB rules. The advisor, however, felt that it was important to provide maximum protection for all those involved in this research.

What the IRB process was not equipped to deal with, and indeed is not designed to deal with, is exactly the *political* issue—which is also an ethical issue—that arose in the defense: to what degree does protecting the "safety" of informants trump their own political desire to be heard and to be identified? The advisor's overall position is that in ethnographic research, informants should never be identified. The student's argument is that sometimes they must be in order that *their* political interests ought to prevail. But what if you do not know their political interests? Or what if they are not consonant with your own? This is an issue that the IRB process does not address well.

This is a question we face frequently in our research on homelessness and other topics. For example, several years ago we conducted research in San Diego on changing urban property regimes and their effects on homeless people's spaces in the city (Mitchell and Staeheli 2006; Staeheli and Mitchell 2008, chapter 3). We had the occasion to speak with (among many others) a public relations person employed by an association of property owners in what had recently been renamed "East Village"—a gentrifying area to the east of downtown. Over an expensive lunch in the long-since gentrified Gaslamp Quarter, this representative commented, on tape, that the large St. Vincent de Paul campus and other surrounding services for homeless and street people had to be pushed entirely out of downtown if its redevelopment was ever going to be successful. Defending this position, the representative commented that while such a move might mean that some homeless people would die, that was not an overriding concern as "they are going to die anyway." We always gave our interviewees the option of signing the consent form before or after the interview; if they signed before and waived their right to confidentiality for themselves and the organizations they represented, we gave them the option of changing their mind after the interview. This respondent signed after the interview, with the comment that nothing was said that would be a problem for the property owners in the area. Later, as was our practice, we sent transcripts of the interview to each of our interviewees. We asked them to make any corrections they wished and to strike anything they wanted excised, and we invited them to revisit their consent and decide whether they wanted to change their waiver of confidentiality (or vice versa). The respondent never returned the transcript and never indicated that we should maintain confidentiality. By the rules of the IRB, and we would argue by any ethical standard, it would be perfectly reasonable for us to name this individual, identify the organization, and use the words from the interview to represent a particular view of homelessness in the city.[4]

But, in our published accounts of San Diego's property and homeless geographies, we have not done so. We have downplayed the consultant's comments. This has been a political decision as well as an ethical one. Politically, the point the public relations (PR) person was making—that homeless people just need to be disappeared out of downtown to make room for redevelopment and gentrification—is not the most effective way to highlight the effects of redevelopment on homeless people; they were the crude, and we believed easily dismissed, comments of a PR consultant. Rather, the effect of redevelopment practices is more compellingly made by specific actions at work in the city. These actions included legal struggles over conditional use permits for shelters, the creation of an army of "Clean and Safe Ambassadors" (who, as the director of the program told us, "get in the face" of the homeless), and the monetary donations from property and business owners to build shelters and provide services—as long as they are located in another part of town. Ethically, we judged that no matter the interviewee's naïveté in both making the comments and waiving confidentiality, those who were being represented *would* object to the comments. While they may have reflected a real truth about the desire on the part of some powerful interests to rid the city of homeless people, the businesses and property owners who hired the consultant would perhaps be quite appalled by the mode of representation.

In essence, on a combination of political and ethical grounds, we made a judgment about the interests of one of our interviewees that was substantively no different than that made by the assistant professor in her dispute with the student over naming names in a thesis. We *assumed* that our interviewee was naïve (as we just put it above) and that the comments did not necessarily represent the opinions of those who were being spoken for. In many ways, therefore, we silenced our respondents, and we did so in *our* interests, in terms of our own politics. Admittedly, the respondent was not as upfront about political interests as were the informants of the student in the abortion study. But what right do we have to *not* give the respondent's stated position its due? Similarly, what right did Don's colleague have to insist that all names be removed from her student's thesis, thereby undermining the stated political aims of the informants?

Ethics—of Politics

To phrase the question that way is, perhaps, to phrase it wrongly. It is not simply a question of what right we—as researchers, writers, and teachers—have to undertake such political interventions; rather such political interventions are unavoidable. We have no choice but to make them, for that is the nature of doing socially relevant research or research rooted in *advocacy*.

This is a volume about the ethics of advocacy as it relates to homeless people. To raise the issue of advocacy is already to stake out a political position. It is already to assume a goal, whether that goal is to find a way for homeless people's own voices and desires to be better heard, or whether the goal is some form of direct action or intervention.[5] Other chapters in this book delve into the knotty ethical issues at stake in such interventions in giving voice to homeless people and sparking direct action. Our goal is something different. In this chapter we will examine the ethical-political issues in research and writing that advocates a certain political position. We want to be clear: our research is motivated by concerns over the kind of public sphere that is created through urban redevelopment, raising questions about who belongs in a place and under what terms. We are thus motivated by political and ethical commitments to social justice. Our focus on homelessness reflects our belief that the treatment of homeless people is a particularly clear indication of the kind of public sphere that is constructed in a place. This is a rather different sense of ethical commitment, raising different concerns about ethical practice, than those involved in ethics procedures or the practical dilemmas that are confronted in research that advocates *for* homeless people.

That is to say, our political position does not necessarily begin from the interests of homeless people; nor does it begin from a direct interest in homeless people's modes of survival in urban space; nor does it begin *directly* from an argument that homelessness must be abolished if we are to construct a more truly just society. We do, of course, think all of these issues are important and are relevant to our task. We also share the same normative commitment to addressing injustice. But our research begins from a concern with how the rights to urban space—the "right to the city"—are structured and how the rights of some people are thwarted (Lefebvre 1996). Though our San Diego research is certainly concerned with the fate of homeless people in the redeveloped city, it is even more concerned with using the fate of homeless people to assess the role of the transformation of public space in the construction of public spheres. Homeless people, to be as honest as we can, are something we *use* to push forward our own arguments about the contemporary city, to shape political agendas, to advocate for particular ways of reshaping urban space and urban life. Neither of us works directly with homeless people. Neither of us works directly with providers of services to homeless people.[6] Neither of us works directly to advance homeless people's own political aims. We do not advocate on their behalf—at least not directly.

In this regard, we tend to treat homeless people as an "indicator" in a way quite homologous with the way those we politically disagree with treat them. For many on the urban right, the homeless are diagnostic of the ill health of the city—not of the political economy, but of the spaces of the city itself. Like an invasive weed or a broken window, they indicate the need for cleaning out and cleaning up, the need to rationalize and order public space so that the health of the city may be restored. In an analysis of this discourse, Don once wrote:

> In such a discourse, "the homeless" are presented as a homogenous mass, with few if any characteristics to distinguish them—in essence denying homeless people's individuality and humanity. This discourse operates simultaneously with another that seeks to particularize the homeless, showing that this one is an alcoholic, that one a drug addict, still another is mentally ill, and a fourth is all three. The strategy here is to particularize the homeless so as to deny what is common among them: namely, that they are without personal shelter of their own. I take on this latter discourse [in my work]; but . . . I also engage in my own essentialization of "the homeless." This is purely a political choice on my part: it is a means to focus on the political processes and struggles that shape and define the homeless as a class with a set of common interests rather than as pathological individuals needing treatment or other forms of paternalistic intervention (Mitchell 2003, 158, note 21).

While recognizing—and in some ways *appreciating*—the logic, Lynn in fact disagrees with this tactic. Thus our joint writing always involves a negotiation of the different political stances we take and the implications—political and ethical—of representational tactics.

Politics matter in many ways. And in Don's writing homeless people remain indicators of something else just as they do in so much political academic debate; they stand for some other political, social, or economic imperative. Homeless people are dehumanized; they are denied their "individuality and humanity." Homeless people are a means to an end. They become *the* homeless, an undifferentiated mass. Research along these lines (from either the right or the left) does not speak with or for homeless people or homeless individuals so much as it draws on the figure of "the homeless" so that a position may be advocated. In some cases, this might not be a problem. In a methodological discussion on studying homeless people, Cloke et al. (2000, 140) write that "our experience was that many of the homeless people we met were, in fact less troubled by the idea of one-sided contact than we were: it was enough that their story might contribute something towards somebody, somewhere, sometime."[7]

Ethics—and Politics

We argue, however, that pragmatics aside, there *are* ethical issues in such an approach; they are simply not the ethical issues raised by proponents of more participatory forms of research. In the process of abstracting from their lives, homeless *people* are only present by their absence; *their* interests are rarely to be found, except insofar as they may incidentally or accidentally be incorporated into the political projects of the advocates. In most respects, our projects are in accordance with geographer Paul Cloke's (2002, 597–98) call for an "ethical" study of homelessness and other issues that "sponsor[s] imaginations of power that recognize 'evil' in various forms." By this, he intends both the malevolent evil of intentional harm and what he calls the "ordinary evil" of "the lack of thought about the unanticipated/invisible/distant effects our actions may have on others, just because our actions are simply fitting in with the prevailing norms of socio-economic life." But we want to do more than just imagine power and recognize evil. We want to *name* that power and its associated practices, and we want to *analyze* it so that it can be acted upon. Our research nevertheless also goes against a growing ethos in geographical research on marginalized populations that seeks to put "empowering research strategies into practice" (Valentine 2003, 375) and to make the practices of research directly affect reality *through* the research process itself (Pain and Francis 2003).

As Gill Valentine (2003, 376) writes in a review of recent work on the geography of disability (which is closely aligned with, although not identical to, research on homelessness), many geographers argue that "it is not enough for researchers to disseminate this knowledge through academic publications and conference papers. Rather, they argue that researchers also have a moral responsibility to contribute to the political struggles of disabled people against social injustice outside the academy." Brendon Gleeson (2000) calls such work "enabling geography" since it seeks to enable people to work and struggle in their own interests. Valentine (2003, 377) thus comments that "researchers committed to an 'enabling geography' approach have sought to define new ways of establishing genuinely collaborative research partnerships with disabled people." The point can be extended, of course, to other forms of marginalization.

It is a point that is—or ought to be—deeply familiar. The calls to committed, activist research are rooted in now two generations of feminist activism, theorizing, and research practice, and they are tethered to emancipatory pedagogic practices such as those developed by Paulo Freire and his followers. They have been codified in many fields as participatory action research with an explicit goal of "democratizing" knowledge by altering the relations of knowledge production and distribution such that people who might have once been termed "research subjects" become co-producers of knowledge and the primary (if not the only) beneficiaries of the work done. The range of ethical considerations operating at a lower level of abstraction than the primary one of a political commitment to a certain kind of enabling practice are, of course, immense.

But at both levels of abstraction—the level of political commitment and the level of research practice—"enabling" research carries with it a double, and too often unexamined, assumption: first, that such enabling research is necessarily good, and second, that it is politically efficacious. Whether or not either assumption is true (and in many circumstances, they may be), they do point to certain limits and problems with such research. In our research in San Diego, we interviewed a range of actors involved in addressing and regulating homelessness: social service providers, the director of the Property-based Business Improvement District that ran the "Clean and Safe" private policing program, a public defender, a representative of the Chamber of Commerce, and more. While our political commitment was certainly to understanding how homeless lives were structured in the city, and thus how they could be made better, we did not conceive this as an "enabling" project. Rather, we wanted to understand the production of particular social relations and structures of social life and governance that condition the quality of democracy and the public sphere. For that aim, a participatory action project would have been unsuitable. We needed to understand the actions and ideas not of the marginalized, but of the (more or less) powerful: redevelopment authorities, social service providers, police, and so forth. Many of those whom we interviewed expounded positions and engaged in activities that we politically opposed. We did *not* want to empower them, or enable them, or (further) emancipate them. Just the opposite. Indeed, while we endeavored at all times during the interviews and in our writing to treat our "subjects" with respect, we had no interest whatsoever in working with many of them to co-produce our knowledge. Rather, we have adopted, if implicitly, an adversarial relationship with some of our research subjects that comes through our writing, in our teaching, and in our discussions about redevelopment. This was, in fact, a *necessary* part of our research: we had to examine those *against* whom we hoped to make a difference, not only those *for* whom we hope to make a difference. Therefore, we thought it was more politically efficacious to expose how actions and ideologies—intended or not, malevolent or ordinary (to use Cloke's terms)—affected the life-chances of homeless people in the city than to understand in detail the actual nature of those life-chances.

When researching homelessness—as when researching disability, the geographies of sexual minorities, or the landscapes of immigrants—an ethical concern with empowerment and therefore a project oriented around that may open up certain political avenues, but it necessarily closes off others. If, as some writers on ethnographic research seem to imply, we *only* engage in research that is empowering or enabling, then we have no possibility of undertaking what can be politically powerful adversarial research. The very closeness and direct exchange between researcher and researched that empowering research requires may preclude the very distance that "speaking truth to power" demands. The powerful, too, are the subjects of our research—or at least they might be for those who are concerned with the plight of homeless people in the contemporary city.

Such an adversarial and distanced stance, which is a stance that we believe answers Cloke's (2002, 591) call for an ethical commitment "*for* the other,"[8] is every bit as vital to attacking contemporary homelessness as is participatory action research or directly relevant social research (on, say, appropriate sites for intervention into homeless people's lives). And it requires, for reasons of political effect, that homeless people are sometimes homogenized into "the homeless" and abstracted into a condition labeled "homelessness." It requires that the figure of the homeless be allowed to stand for the multiplicity of states that force people to live at least part of their lives on the streets, in shelters, in insecure housing, and so forth. It requires, sometimes, that we understand the homeless to be "something of an 'indicator species.'" Such a position can create real problems. It is in some ways an infantilizing tactic that demeans homeless people's capabilities, and in particular, their abilities to analyze and describe the structural reasons for their lack of shelter. By not listening to them, our analysis might be dreadfully—and fatefully—wrong. And we cannot control the way our argument is received or diffused. It is quite possible, for instance, that people might read our work and believe that it gives license to a range of actions to remove homeless people from the precincts of citizenship, the public, and urban space. At the same time, however, and for very similar reasons, it also licenses a set of actions that those of us who seek to advocate for the rights of homeless people to public space as part of the public (as well as to shelter, decent health care, bodily security, and so forth) might find quite progressive. That is to say, to maintain some distance from homeless people themselves (their concerns, their immediate needs, their views of the world and the forces that structure it), or to homogenize people experiencing homelessness as "the homeless" is not *necessarily* ethically bad. Whether it is good, bad, or a more complex mixture is not a question that is easily susceptible to abstract ethical reasoning and not at all capable of being assessed through institutionalized ethics review procedures. Rather, the moral value of such distancing is best addressed through ethical analysis that is also political.

Ethics—is Politics

Indeed, the ethical and the political cannot be easily separated, since ethics involves the assertion of moral values and orders. Using research about homelessness to better understand the structuring of urban social relations and spaces, and therefore perhaps to advocate for their radical transformation, sheds a rather different light on typical ethical questions and procedures. In anticipation of our research in San Diego (which was part of a larger project on public space in the United States), we had to complete IRB reviews at our respective universities.[9] The basic premise of such reviews is "do no harm," which, in some ways, is unassailable—but in other ways not. One of the goals of our research was to make it, at least in some way, harder for some people—for example, those who worked to make public space open only to those with money or standing—to do their work. Especially as we learned more about it, we wanted the designers of San Diego's Clean and Safe program to be troubled, not validated, by what we made of what they told us in interviews. We wanted—and have—stayed true to what they told us, but to do so posed a particular dilemma. We described the problem this way:

> In any given project, one is likely to come across people with whom one disagrees, but those people are still important to talk with and to engage. The difficulty is that they will often ask for—and sometimes expect—assistance with *their* political missions. In other instances, people are not so interested in mutuality in the research process and the democratization of knowledge production so much as they are in having their story told on their own terms. . . . Were we obliged to do this when we believed [an informant] was seriously distorting the situation? . . . In most projects, it is helpful and important to consider the arguments of people with whom one does not agree, to study the "opposition," as it were. If we have an obligation to the people we study, however, it is not clear what the nature of that obligation is, and whether it differs according to the degree of agreement with the political position a respondent takes (Staeheli and Mitchell 2008, 161).

A second premise of IRB reviews is that research subjects should not be exploited, which also seems unassailable, until we read that requirement in light of the above passage. Isn't taking the arguments of an individual, arguments made to us in good faith in the process of a research interview, and then turning those arguments against that person's own interests (or at least the interest of that person's role as, e.g., a director of a specific program or a Vice President of a Chamber of Commerce), the very definition of exploitation? Does it make it any less exploitative that the person occupies a position of relative power and influence?

The question is worth repeating: does our obligation to those we engage in our research change according to political orientation? This is a question that is not directly addressed in a wide-ranging, and very useful discussion of ethical issues that arise when conducting research with and on homeless people by a team of researchers in Britain (Cloke et al. 2000). They are concerned with that close, asymmetrical relationship that develops between researcher and marginalized other that is the focus of so much writing on ethics in the social sciences. But they make an argument that bears thinking about in the context we are raising here. "The practice of research can never be a neutral exercise," they write (Cloke et al. 2000, 151):

> For good or ill, the very act of entering the worlds of other people means that the research and the researcher become part co-constituents of that world. Therefore we cannot *but* have impact on those with whom we come in contact, and indeed on those with whom we have not had contact, but who belong in the social worlds of those we have talked to. Much of this impact is, frankly, unknown. For every visible occurrence of distress or other harm, there are hundreds of invisible impacts amongst networked actors. Ultimately, such matters are entwined with the need to avoid exploitation of research subjects, and to give something back to them through the research process.

What does "giving back" look like when the goal of the research might precisely be instead to take away—to take away, for example, the very taken-for-grantedness of the kind of "broken windows" ideology that governs Clean and Safe-like programs? What sort of "invisible" impacts and harms should we worry about? Should we care if our use of an interviewee's freely given comments, made in the context of her professional role, might conceivably imperil her job (as with our public relations representative in San Diego)?

Choosing sides is a *sine qua non* of socially engaged research, and yet discussions of the ethics of research often do not seem to recognize this. There are starting assumptions that research subjects are necessarily vulnerable, and rules are written in light of that assumption. This leads to counterintuitive results. In a footnote in the introduction to her book on the "myth of disposable women" in the global economy, a book that is very clear as to the author's political positions, Melissa Wright (2006, 171, note 9) writes, "In compliance with human subject review requirements, I use pseudonyms for all my informants and for all companies." Her informants are managers of assembly plants in northern Mexico and southern China. The companies are, apparently, both large multinationals and smaller subcontractors. The main argument of the book is that the myth of disposability licenses highly exploitative—and sometimes deadly—labor and social practices that differentially affect women workers. Such practices, she argues are integral to the global manufacturing economy as it is now structured; they are now a necessary part of capital accumulation. In compliance with the rules of her university's IRB, she does not name names—not even corporate ones. An argument can be made that the ethics review process led to an ethically compromised research. While naming names might mean that Wright would lose access to her research sites, it might also help expose, and put an end to, abusive and exploitative practices. The uproar that ensued when the labor practices of subcontractors making the Kathy Lee Gifford line of Wal-Mart clothing was exposed by the National Labor Committee was a function of being able to link particular manufacturers to a particular product (see Bowden 2003). Whatever their longstanding merits, the sorts of reforms that then followed—codes of conduct, for example—were likewise in part a function of naming names. The ethics regulations to which Wright is subject, however, seem to have no room for that kind of calculus, that kind of weighing political and ethical costs and benefits. For as Wright so clearly demonstrates, there are ethical costs associated with the practices of the manufacturing companies. Yet the ethics procedures protected the firms and managers, rather than the women who were exploited in the manufacturing process.

Similarly, rules of ethics that require blanket anonymity can have a scholarly cost—or more grandly, a cost to "truth"—as well. Using pseudonyms for companies, or as sociologists and anthropologists frequently do (and as geographers are increasingly doing), using pseudonyms for places as well, can in some circumstances make impossible a full analysis. It can close off, for example, access to key *public* data sources such as news reports, company filings, tax records, planning documents, and so forth, if there is a chance that these might identify the company or the place. In an intriguing and important book on community policing, for example, Steve Herbert's (2006) decision not to name the (relatively large) area of Seattle he was researching meant that the very political decisions and debates that he constantly reflected on in the book were never actually described. In the book, it is difficult to tell, for example, exactly *why* some community factions argued one way or another, because none of the contextual social history and geography is provided. Readers can only understand that they *did* argue in a particular way, not, exactly, why they argued that way, or what was at stake. There is only limited contextual discussion of the local issues driving how the subjects of the research were framing, for example, their understanding of homeless people, other "outsiders," and the fate of their neighborhoods. Such context was likely available in local newspaper articles and letters, planning and strategy documents, and through a historical geographic discussion of the neighborhoods themselves and their evolution as urban places. While making a research site anonymous may have certain benefits, it can also have costs.

In both of these examples, the procedures mandated through institutional review served to cloak the stakes involved in the research topic in ways that closed off some ways in which the research could be used *to the benefit* of socially, politically, and economically marginalized groups—groups that the authors had hoped would benefit from the research, thereby addressing the researcher's ethical obligations. This is an issue with which we also struggled in our research in San Diego. For Wright and Herbert, it is clear that their research has in fact raised awareness, and the discussion of the political and moral implications of the research has moved beyond the academy. We remain (somewhat) confident that we followed the correct strategy in not naming the consultant in San Diego. But a nagging question remains: What if, in the *political* judgment of the researcher, the best way to "contribute something"—to act ethically as a researcher—is by naming names?

Conclusion: Ethics/Politics/Policies?

The goal of this essay is modest in many ways. We have merely attempted to recognize some of the limits of contemporary debate and practice on ethics in homelessness research, advocacy, and beyond. But recognizing those limitations, we argue, leads us to address what we think are crucial questions—questions of ethico-political practice—that can be more fully examined. It might very well be the case that the advisor of the thesis on abortion access at Syracuse University was right in her judgment, but it was a judgment in which ethics and politics were fully conjoined, not at all somehow separate as current human subjects requirements seem to expect. It might be that our own ethical responsibility to those we interviewed in our research on homelessness in San Diego or in other work requires us to toe *their* political line (though we do not think so), but this too is something that neither current ethical discussions about advocacy nor contemporary rules of research practice has much debated. We think such debate is urgently needed, however. Since ethics and politics are fully conjoined and cannot be severed, it is important to expand the range of ethical considerations. We hope this essay is helpful in this regard. Even more, however, we hope that discussions over ethical practice embrace the ineluctably political nature of research. Indeed, we have argued that we need to move beyond discussions that seem to distinguish ethics and politics in research.

It is unlikely that the issues and questions we have raised will ever be "resolved" or "fixed." Decisions that make sense in one context are unlikely to make sense in other contexts. As we noted, we decided that not reporting a respondent's answer fed into our representational strategy and into our political goals. Yet we readily raised questions about similar decisions that other people have taken. Situationalism and relativism seem unavoidable in socially engaged research.

There is, however, a more intractable problem if we take seriously the tight, co-constitutive relationship between ethics and politics: institutional review procedures. As Blake (2007) has argued, the relationship between researcher and researched is, in the ideal, based on trust; ethics procedures are a poor substitute. But we have argued that there are situations—such as in research where there is an adversarial relationship or when researchers "use" their subjects—that building a relationship of trust would not be ethical. These are cases in which one might assume that ethics procedures might work well, or at least might be re-worked in order to do so. We do not believe that is the case, however, because such an assumption is based on a view that ethics can be separated from politics. We have argued against that view, and believe that the political-ethical relationship cannot be managed by fiddling with bureaucratic practices. The issues are simply not amenable to bureaucratic resolution. Or more accurately, perhaps, we do not believe that bureaucratic resolution is apt to be a resolution that adequately addresses the questions at stake. It seems, then, that research on homelessness is agonistic at several levels, reflecting the structures, practices, and power relationships that consistently leave some people without shelter as well as the complex interweaving of ethics and politics.

Notes

1. "Institutional Review Board" is a generic label for research ethics committees that operate at the university level in the United States. Almost all universities that received federal funds for research have them. In other countries, such as the United Kingdom, the procedures for ethics review are less institutionalized and are often devolved to Schools and Departments, rather than the University.

2. Universities also include review boards for treatment of animals. Less common are ethical procedures related to the environment, although these issues are incorporated into the ethics guidelines for many disciplines.

3. An IRB administrator at Syracuse University once tried to force Don to submit a human subjects application for historical, archival research. Neither the fact that he was using publicly available documents in libraries, nor that dead people cannot give consent seemed to mollify this administrator who felt that all research receiving federal funds had to be reviewed. The reason reflects the power of certain research funding organizations in the United States. The National Institutes of Health (the organization that funded the infamous study of syphilis in which African-American men at Tuskeegee University were infected with the disease as part of the study) now insists that a university's commitment to ethical research extends to *all* research. Universities must agree to review all research—from the smallest study by an undergraduate writing a senior thesis to archival

studies such as Don's to large-scale pharmaceutical trials—as the entry price for applications for National Institutes of Health (NIH) funds.

4. The somewhat tortured language in this discussion reflects our continuing unease about identifying the respondent. It would be so much easier to use personal pronouns that would identify the person as a man or a woman, but that would also make identification of the person much easier.

5. So too is it already a political intervention to conduct research to assess, say, the role of "civility" or "order" in creating a "successful" urban landscape or an enjoyable urban life (cf. Tier 1998); to conduct research on the siting of shelters or other services (cf. Dear and Wolch 1987); or to conduct research that seeks to understand the everyday lives and paths of homeless men and women (cf. Rowe and Wolch 1990)? These are already political because they require an answer to a previous, often unstated question: What is "success"? What are the contours of order and in whose interest are they shaped? For whom shall life be enjoyable? Are shelters necessary? Is there some reason one must know how those we deem homeless live their daily lives? Answers to such questions are sometimes explicit, but more frequently implicit, in the very establishment of a research project.

6. While Lynn has worked with a variety of social service organizations that assist homeless people, her goals have been to understand the ways in which these organizations help to structure the public sphere.

7. The part of the sentence after the colon is from a journal kept by a member of the research team.

8. Although it also pushes it in another direction than Cloke does. For him, such a commitment *for* the other demands a Christian attitude of love, charity, and faith. It can also demand a strongly developed sense of outrage and anger.

9. At the time, Lynn was a member of the Institute of Behavioral Science and the Department of Geography at the University of Colorado.

Conclusion
Synthesizing the Personal and Professional: A Systematic Consideration of Ethics and Advocacy in Social Science Research
Trenna Valado

The issues raised in this collection range from the most basic areas of self-presentation and the representation of research participants to ones that shake the very foundations of the research endeavor. Should we be doing this? Are we exploiting people for our own gain? If we realize that we cannot affect meaningful change in the structural factors that underlie homelessness, is it ethical to continue to do research on the topic? On the other hand, is it ethical to stop? Does research imply a promise of possible change to participants that we cannot fulfill? Should researchers become advocates, and if so, what should we advocate *for*?

We started this volume with broad questions about what the ethical issues were in research on homelessness and the role of advocacy in such research. It turns out that research is rife with ethical issues and that all of the contributors to this volume—from relative neophytes to those with decades of experience—continually struggle with how to handle these issues and what role advocacy should play in their work. The issues in this book are not unique to the study of homelessness. Just as the contributors represent a wide array of disciplines—anthropology, geography, political science, sociology, urban studies—their insights are applicable to various areas of inquiry, especially those that involve research with or about marginalized and vulnerable populations. The insights also span all stages of the research process, from conceptualization to implementation and dissemination.

Also notable are the myriad professional histories, methods, and research foci that the contributors bring to their work. Many worked in direct service provision before, during, or after their research. Most are currently involved in academia, while one currently works in the private sector evaluating social service programs. The contributors have conducted research in a range of settings (e.g., shelters, public parks, activist enclaves) and with varied groups (e.g., homeless individuals, social service workers, government employees, business people, advocacy groups). The topics they have explored include the transformation and use of public space, the effectiveness of specific service interventions, the relationships among and between social service workers and homeless people, and public perceptions of homelessness. Some of the contributors are actively engaged in advocacy and activism, whereas others question the utility of these practices.

Despite varied backgrounds and research agendas, the contributors to this volume are all unified by a common desire and willingness to write honestly about the ethical dilemmas they have faced in conducting research on homelessness. This is not an easy task, in part because this sort of self-reflexivity is often not encouraged or rewarded. Yet by discussing the varied professional and personal dilemmas confronted during the course of their research, the contributors highlight several themes that span academic disciplines and may inform the efforts of other scholars. These themes include such issues as the need to "study up," the balance between advocacy and efficacy, how to manage field relationships, and the underlying purpose of research on entrenched social problems. In reviewing these and other issues, it becomes apparent that researchers can strengthen their work by more openly discussing ethics and advocacy concerns and by systematically addressing these topics throughout the research process. The following section builds on the contributors' insights by providing a framework to encourage continued dialogue and to guide future researchers across disciplines in thinking more systematically about ethics and advocacy in their own work.

A Systematic Consideration of Ethics and Advocacy

Issues of ethics and advocacy are endemic to social science research, yet they are rarely discussed in much depth in the scholarly literature. This is somewhat ironic, because they are common topics of verbal discussion and debate among researchers. While such informal exchanges are undoubtedly useful in helping scholars sort through the dilemmas raised during their research, there is also a need for more formal guidance and a shared framework for bringing these issues to the fore. This section seeks to offer some guidance by presenting an operational framework that scholars can use to systematically consider issues of ethics and advocacy before, during, and after their research. To do this, we have divided the research process into three broad stages: conceptualization, implementation, and dissemination. For each stage, we pose a series of who, what, when, where, why, and how questions that may aid researchers in thinking through some of the issues they are likely to confront in their work.

The following questions are certainly not exhaustive or exclusive, and dividing them into stages is purely instrumental. In reality, there are no clear boundaries between the myriad issues raised, just as there are no clear boundaries between stages of the research process. Research is iterative and organic, with each aspect informing and shaping the others. The questions posed are not intended as an end point, but rather as the beginning to more in-depth consideration of ethics and advocacy issues. As such, each question will likely raise even more questions. Ultimately, the answers to all the questions are deeply personal; there is no definitive right or wrong, and each individual must reach his or her own decisions about how to conduct research. But thoughtfully and thoroughly answering these questions (and others that flow from them) may help researchers minimize unforeseen dilemmas and be better prepared for those that are unavoidable.

Conceptualization

The research process obviously begins long before scholars conduct interviews, make observations in the field, or even start combing through the existing literature on a subject. The first steps in any research endeavor are the identification of a topic of study and the determination of how best to go about exploring the chosen topic. This planning stage often includes the sometimes tedious activities of obtaining grant funding, applying for approval by an Institutional Review Board (IRB), and beginning to obtain various permissions to conduct research in certain locations. While this may not be the most glamorous part of the research process, it is one that is filled with ethical considerations that ultimately shape every facet of the ensuing work. As such, it is imperative to carefully consider the motivations underlying the proposed research as well as its potential impacts. Answering the following interrelated questions may help begin this process of deliberation.

Who should my research focus on? Although much research on homelessness involves direct study of homeless people in various contexts, several contributors question the efficacy and ethics of this approach. The underlying issue is largely one of whether to "study down" or "study up." Doing research on homeless people's lives and experiences may serve to give voice to a population that is highly marginalized, but studying other, more powerful groups that actually have the ability to shape policy may be more effective in bringing about changes in the structural causes of homelessness. Wright addresses this issue in his chapter, concluding that studying down is only ethically responsible if the resulting knowledge is used to try to improve the lives of those being studied. Thus, he suggests that researchers who study homeless people have an obligation to use their work for the purposes of advocacy. At the same time, Wright emphasizes that much more effort should be invested in studying up, particularly in terms of public attitudes toward poverty and the exercise of power. Many other contributors echo this sentiment, noting that the only way to effect meaningful change in the structural factors that produce and maintain homelessness is to study up.

What should I study? The issue of who to study is closely related to the issue of what to study. Despite the fact that homelessness is inextricably linked with numerous other economic and social issues (e.g., neoliberalism, poverty, housing, racism, sexism), much of the existing research examines homelessness in isolation, as if it were a phenomenon unto itself. This is especially true in research that involves direct interaction with homeless people; a search of the literature in this arena reveals a vast amount of information on individual traits of homeless people, most notably mental illness and substance use. Indeed, almost the entire social service system is oriented toward remedying such "pathologies" in order to "cure" homelessness. Both Rosenthal and Wright note that this tendency to attribute homelessness to individual-level characteristics ultimately deflects attention from underlying structural issues and, in so doing, limits possible responses and solutions. This is not to suggest that researchers should avoid these topics, and in fact, Rosenthal points out that doing so carries its own potential dangers. However, researchers do need to carefully consider how to connect their chosen topic of study to broader structural factors that create and perpetuate homelessness, as Amster strives to do in his investigation of homelessness in post-Katrina New Orleans.

When is IRB review insufficient? Perhaps simply posing this question already implies the answer. Although human subjects review by an IRB is a necessary component of most studies on homelessness, the process sometimes fails to adequately address certain issues that arise during research. One example, discussed by Mitchell and Staeheli, is research that involves studying up. They note that IRBs typically endorse the maxim of "do no harm" and require that research not exploit participants. But when studying powerful groups that have a stake in the issue of homelessness (e.g., policymakers, business coalitions), the ultimate intent of the research may be to "harm" the participants by critiquing and even actively working against their interests, which would appear in essence to be exploitive. Cook echoes this sentiment in his chapter by saying that despite his overarching ethic to "do no harm" to the homeless participants in his study, he did intend to do harm to the overall "system" that produces homelessness. Mitchell and Staeheli also point out that the IRB emphasis on anonymity as a method of protecting research participants is sometimes problematic. In particular, they indicate that "naming names" may actually be the ethical thing to do (a notion that Adkins grapples with in her chapter) in two types of circumstances: when participants want to be named; and when not doing so could result in the continuation of abuse or exploitation by powerful groups.

Where are the gaps in current knowledge? This is an important question to consider when conceptualizing any research project. Yet, as Lyon-Callo notes, much of the existing work on homelessness continues to focus on the same topics, namely describing homeless people's experiences and analyzing the social processes that produce homelessness. He suggests that research on homelessness tends to neglect several important topics: broader social issues, including racial inequality, sexuality and sexual violence; the widespread existence of suburban homelessness; and various social and economic transformations associated with neoliberalism. Lyon-Callo believes that continuing to conduct such anemic research is ethically problematic, because it has not proven effective in overcoming the barriers that impede collective action to challenge the underlying causes of homelessness. He, along with several other contributors, offer suggestions about potential avenues for future research that shift away from simply describing and analyzing homelessness toward producing practical, actionable knowledge to support resistance movements.

Why am I doing this research? The choice to focus on homelessness as a topic of research typically reflects a deeper motivation than fulfilling professional goals such as obtaining degrees or producing publications. Indeed, several of the contributors to this volume openly struggle with the ethical issue of profiting from the study of homelessness. All the contributors express hope that their work might positively impact the lives of homeless people. However, the types of impact that they hope to achieve can vary greatly, as reflected in Arnold's chapter—from giving voice to and empowering research participants, to improving service delivery, to transforming the systems that produce and maintain homelessness. The decision to pursue a particular impact has ethical implications, as does the related decision about whether to engage in advocacy during the course of research. While conducting research in a large service agency, Adkins wondered if making suggestions for policy changes might compromise her ability to do useful research. This reflects a tension felt by many of the contributors, who question whether making their biases known by advocating on behalf of homeless people could ultimately impact the validity and/or utility of their research, and thus undermine the effect it might have on the lives of those they hope to help.

How can I minimize potentially harmful impacts of my research? Although most scholars who work with homeless people aim to live up to the IRB tenet of "do no harm," there are sometimes unintended negative side effects of research. For example, Rowe notes that service interventions, and the accompanying research designed to assess their effectiveness, can simultaneously help and hurt people. Whereas a given intervention may result in positive outcomes for some participants, it may also leave many participants with "high hopes" that service providers and researchers are not equipped to meet. To borrow a phrase from Rowe, even research that does not involve direct service provision may carry "implied promises" to participants—promises that their voices might be heard, and promises that something might change in their lives as a result of the research. Borchard speaks to this issue when he refers to the "unspoken promise" he made to research participants to value the stories they shared and use those stories to inspire positive change, as does von Mahs in his analysis of being a "buddy researcher" and potentially creating expectations of assistance. These contributors encourage researchers to think hard about the possible negative impacts of their work and about ways to minimize those impacts. Importantly, this need to mitigate such impacts continues throughout the research process. In my chapter, I discuss some of the dilemmas I faced in writing up my study results, including how to talk about substance use and mental illness without reinforcing negative stereotypes, and how to examine the role of personal choice without downplaying the need for comprehensive social services.

Implementation

Although much planning and preparation precedes the implementation of a given study, this is the stage that many people in the general public identify as "research." It is often both the most rewarding and the most challenging portion of the research process. Anyone who has conducted research with or about marginalized populations knows that the knowledge gained from talking to study participants can be simultaneously invigorating, disturbing, confusing, and illuminating. Even the most well prepared scholars may find themselves questioning nearly every aspect of their research. Issues that may have seemed relatively straightforward in the abstract—self-presentation and disclosure, representation, boundary maintenance, intervention, etc.—become complicated when interacting with real people. The following questions highlight some of these issues and encourage further reflection on research design.

   Whose interests am I trying to represent? This question, of course, ties back to the issue of who to study. Many researchers who work directly with homeless people may, in part, be trying to give voice to the participants by reporting their experiences and perceptions of homelessness, as Cook explicitly seeks to do. However, this does not necessarily mean that the publications resulting from a study rely solely upon the participants' interpretations or understandings of their lives. In some cases, participants actually embrace the "individual pathologies" view of homelessness that dominates the social service system. Thus, their proposed "solutions" to their own problems follow the standard litany of more and better services. Yet these types of solutions are often unsatisfactory to researchers who may have a broader understanding of the social and economic forces that contribute to homelessness. Therefore, scholars sometimes end up using participants' stories in ways that do not represent their avowed interests. The issue of representation is particularly problematic when studying up, since researchers are often not trying to represent the interests of those they work with in this context. In fact, quite the opposite may be the case, as Mitchell and Staeheli note in their discussion of using information provided by research participants to work against their political agendas. I raise this issue in a different way in my own chapter, when I articulate the importance of incorporating the voices of seemingly powerful groups (e.g., service providers, government workers, law enforcement officials) in my own analyses despite my primary intention to represent the perspectives of homeless individuals. Ultimately, as Arnold observes, part of the purpose of good research should be to help empower marginalized people to represent themselves and advocate for their own interests.

What should I tell people about my research and its potential impacts? Although IRB rules require researchers to inform participants about their study and the possible benefits and risks of participation, there are no firm guidelines provided for doing either. Thus, scholars who study down often grapple with the issue of self-disclosure, specifically when and how to reveal their identity as researchers. Borchard discusses this topic, concluding that disclosing one's identity early on is essential given that homeless people are forced to carry out much of their private lives in public spaces. If the "when" seems relatively straightforward, the "how" certainly is not, in part because it involves some explanation of the purpose and possible impacts of the research. In terms of impacts on research participants, most proposals to study homelessness emerge from IRB review firmly in the "no benefit" category. Yet this seems contradictory to the experiences of many researchers, who find that homeless people often feel that being listened to and treated respectfully are significant personal benefits of participation. In addition, there may be myriad other possible benefits or risks of participation that are not captured in the IRB review process. This is equally true when researchers study up, since scholars like Mitchell and Staeheli are sometimes actively working against the agendas of participants, as we have seen. Overall, it is important to consider whether researchers have an ethical obligation to go "above and beyond" IRB requirements for informed consent and whether doing so might carry its own risks.

When should I intervene in the lives of people being studied? Researchers clearly span the spectrum between non-interference and active engagement in the lives of research participants. But one thing shared by all researchers who work with homeless people is the struggle to define their role. Von Mahs questions how his responsibility as a researcher dovetails with his personal obligation to help people. In particular, he felt conflicted about whether to share information on services with participants and thus possibly influence the results of his study. Borchard also expresses reluctance about becoming too involved in the lives of research participants but for a very different reason, namely because he did not have the resources to help them. Both von Mahs and Borchard address the issue of paying participants, again approaching the topic from different perspectives. Whereas von Mahs does not express much concern about providing payment, Borchard wonders whether doing so might negatively impact his research. This highlights that intervention in the lives of participants can take many forms—such as providing material assistance, sharing information, offering rides, advocating on their behalf—and that researchers do not necessarily agree on what constitutes intervention. Furthermore, decisions about whether and how to intervene may be dependent on the individual circumstances of each participant. For example, Borchard did end up paying participants but decided to withhold payment from one person due to concerns about his severe alcoholism. The issue of intervention is closely related to that of setting personal boundaries, and both are things that scholars who work with marginalized populations inevitably confront in their research.

Where do my loyalties lie? The answer to this question may at first appear straightforward, since many scholars express a sense of loyalty to their research participants. However, various features of the research context may complicate the issue. For example, Wright conducted some of his research under the auspices of a county organization, which left him questioning whether he answered to his employers, the county itself, or the homeless people who he talked with during his study. This can also be the case when doing services-based research such as that undertaken by Adkins, because it may seem inappropriate to criticize the agency and/or workers that helped facilitate a study, especially when the research reveals the challenges and constraints faced by these groups. In some studies, the researcher may even be employed by a service provider and thus under pressure to produce recommendations that mesh with the avowed goals and strategies of that agency. There are also situations in which scholars may not have an overarching sense of loyalty to the research participants, as demonstrated in the work done by Mitchell and Staeheli that explores the challenges of "adversarial research." Regardless of whether scholars study down or study up, it is important to remember that research participants often expect that the scholars conducting the work will support or even promote their political agendas.

Why should I continue this course of research? In the midst of implementing research on homelessness, it is easy to become overwhelmed by the complexities of the issue as well as the varied experiences and perspectives of the people who participate in a study. Many scholars may even come to question why they are focusing on a certain topic or whether the method they have chosen to do so is appropriate. At the same time, researchers may learn things during their study that seem to merit immediate action rather than ongoing documentation or observation. Adkins faced this dilemma in her research, prompting her to ask "which is the greater goal in the present moment: to increase useful knowledge over the long term, or to make an immediate impact on vulnerable lives?" When scholars experience such doubts, they essentially have three possible courses of action: forge ahead as planned; modify the research agenda to reflect new knowledge; or discontinue the work. Sometimes the simple act of revisiting the original motivation for and purpose of a study can help scholars refocus their attention on what is important to them, both professionally and personally. In many cases, this may mean that they continue on with the research project while remaining cognizant of the limitations of their work. Yet it is also essential to remain open to the possibility of changing the course of research if it seems ethically justified and is feasible given funding sources and other practical considerations.

How do I handle sensitive or potentially harmful information? When delving into the lives of marginalized or vulnerable individuals, researchers often hear information that is sensitive or could even bring harm to research participants if divulged. Scholars generally have a legal obligation to report any intent to harm oneself or others to the proper authorities, but there are many other types of information that fall outside this requirement. Von Mahs discusses some examples, including the prevalence of substance use and criminal behavior among the participants in his study. While he wanted to accurately report the activities that he witnessed, he was concerned that doing so might serve to further demonize homeless people and justify cuts of needed services. Rosenthal also addresses the issue of substance use, worrying that his desire to "de-demonize" homeless people and emphasize the structural contributors to homelessness may have led him to downplay the importance of the issue and thus contribute to avoidable alcohol- and drug-related deaths. Another potentially problematic situation occurs when researchers witness criminal behavior such as drug dealing, shoplifting, and trespassing. Although they may not have a legal obligation to report such activities, scholars should remember that their audio recordings, interview notes, and field notes are subject to subpoena. Thus, it is imperative to think carefully not just about what is reported in publications but also what is recorded during the course of a study. It may also be helpful to allow participants to review and censor research records, though this can be challenging with transitory individuals. The same precautions apply to geographic information—such as where people sleep, congregate, etc.—especially given the ongoing trend of criminalizing homeless people's use of public space.

Dissemination

Research projects typically culminate in sharing results through publications, lectures, and other media. This is the scholar's opportunity to foster discussion not only among colleagues but also with the wider public. Doing so requires researchers to make numerous decisions about how to frame their findings, what they hope to accomplish, and which audiences they are trying to reach. At the same time, researchers must consider how to proceed in their professional and personal lives in terms of future topics for study and ongoing involvement with the people who participated in the completed project. For many scholars, the culmination of one research endeavor is conceptually almost indistinguishable from the start of another. Thus, the following questions are intended to help researchers think through both the presentation of current findings and their plans for additional work.

Who am I writing for? Most researchers eventually produce scholarly publications to share their results with their colleagues. Although this is an important endeavor, and indeed one required for professional advancement, it may also be desirable to write for a wider audience. Borchard suggests that researchers should strive to "write about homelessness in *varied ways* and *for varied audiences*, or to at least work with others to disseminate their findings." He accomplished this in his own work by partnering with a local journalist to present some of his findings in a three-page newspaper article. Similarly, Amster has written extensively about his research in various non-academic venues including online and print op-ed columns, and Cook published the life story interviews he conducted in local media outlets. In my own work, I wrote "short reports" for various groups who participated in my research, including the city police department and a county coalition of service providers. In each case, the content was tailored to their interests and reflected the experiences and recommendations of local homeless people. This sort of wider dissemination is essential if researchers hope to have their work influence public attitudes or policy. At the same time, some scholars may feel a desire or obligation to share their research findings with homeless people. Articles in local newspapers or homeless newsletters are a good option for presenting summaries of key findings or issues, as Wright discusses, whereas lengthier publications can be donated to local libraries. Unfortunately, dissemination to wider audiences is not typically encouraged or rewarded in academia, so scholars must be motivated by their personal commitment to fostering positive social change rather than the promise of professional advancement.

What am I hoping to accomplish? The answer to this question affects not only whom scholars write for but also how they write. Various tones and styles may be required depending on whether researchers seek to illuminate a certain facet of homelessness, generate public indignation, reshape public attitudes, or influence policymakers. Many of the contributors to this volume believe that researchers should use their work to challenge the structures that produce and maintain homelessness. For example, Wright suggests that scholars have a moral imperative to use research for advocacy purposes. He is unwilling to settle for what he calls "social work 'solutions'" that center on providing more and better services; instead, he hopes to facilitate change in structural factors by drawing the attention of those who have the power to shape policy. Lyon-Callo also emphasizes importance of transforming the structures that underlie homelessness, in part by engaging in scholarship that can inform collective resistance movements. Whereas these high-level goals are essential for reducing homelessness in the long term, some researchers aim to use their findings to improve the conditions of homeless people in the short term. Thus, their work may be geared toward identifying potential improvements in service access and delivery. In essence, researchers may offer a variety of recommendations to combat homelessness, ranging from the transformative to the practical. At yet another level, some scholars may be interested in bringing public awareness to the issue of homelessness in hopes that this will foster positive change, as Cook sought to do in his community. These various goals are not mutually exclusive, of course, but each requires a different framing of the issues surrounding homelessness.

When should I become an advocate? As Adkins notes, researchers fall on various points of the spectrum between non-interference and advocacy. Given the focus of this volume, it is probably not surprising that most of contributors lean toward advocacy. Wright suggests that researchers have an ethical responsibility to advocate for those who cannot advocate for themselves. Amster refers to himself as a "scholar-advocate" and calls on researchers to engage in advocacy by producing and disseminating relevant, actionable knowledge. Yet amid these strong calls for advocacy, the contributors also recognize some of the possible pitfalls involved. Rowe voices concern that pushing services research too far into the realm of advocacy might obscure the fact that many homeless people do need the help offered through the social service system. Rosenthal worries that blatant advocacy could lead to research bias as well as dismissal by those with the power to affect change. Some of the contributors also debate what role scholars should play in advocacy work. Borchard proposes that researchers do not necessarily have to be organizers or activists but can instead inspire others to enact change, and Arnold believes that researchers should treat the homeless as political agents who are capable of advocating on their own behalf. Closely related to the issue of when (or if) to engage in advocacy is the issue of what to advocate *for*. I confronted this dilemma in my research, when I questioned whether I should advocate for the changes that homeless people wanted to see or for the structural changes that I believed were necessary to combat homelessness.

Where should I go from here? Although the majority of the contributors focused their research on homeless people, many emphasize that future efforts should instead concentrate on studying up. Arnold suggests that researchers need to spend less time "fixating on the homeless alone" and begin asking "how laws, shelter rules, interpersonal interactions and racism, sexism, and class bias lead to a distorted view of the very poor." Likewise, Wright highlights the need to examine the processes that shape public attitudes toward homelessness. Several other contributors offer suggestions for future research that also center on understanding the structural factors that contribute to homelessness and influencing the groups that have the power to enact meaningful policy changes. While it is important to ponder where one should go next in terms of professional work, the completion of a given research project can also raise issues of how to proceed in one's personal life. Cook reflects on how his life has been affected by working with homeless people, professing the belief that true solidarity and commitment to change would require him to make significant alterations in his own lifestyle. At a more general level, advocacy efforts often require time and energy that may be hard to come by amid a demanding work schedule. Similarly, scholars who wish to maintain some of the personal relationships established during their research might find it challenging to do so, particularly if their next endeavor involves working with a different population. Some researchers may feel an ethical obligation to remain engaged with participants, to not flee the field of battle, so to speak. But even for those who do not share this perspective, parting ways at the end of a project can be emotionally trying.

Why should I continue to study this topic? This question encapsulates two interrelated issues: whether to continue studying a specific topic such as homelessness and whether to do so in the same way. After many years of research and many different projects, Wright published an article that he believed offered practical ways to solve the problem of homelessness. His subsequent decision to shift the focus of his research is summed up in the following quotation: "For me to continue researching homelessness therefore implicated me in the reproduction of homelessness by simply continuing to use the poor as objects for my own advancement. Ethically, I just could not bring myself to continue this illusion that somehow my work could make a difference in the lives of those whose stories I had listened to." Yet Wright stops short of suggesting that scholars should not conduct further research on homelessness. Instead, he believes that future research should focus on the exercise of political power and ways to challenge it. Lyon-Callo makes a similar argument, saying that continuing to do the same type of research is no longer worthwhile and that the failure to examine structural issues makes researchers "complicit in maintaining homelessness." Like Wright, he urges scholars to conduct research that may help overcome existing "structures of inequality," a process he thinks will require collective resistance movements. Given these critiques, it seems fitting that the final chapter in this collection was penned by Mitchell and Staeheli, notably the only contributors whose work consisted primarily of studying up. Overall, the contributors argue that the topic of homelessness merits continued scholarly attention, but many believe that the form such research takes is a profoundly ethical issue.

How can I maximize the utility of my findings? While the various contributors do not all agree on the role that advocacy should play in their work, they are united by a desire to produce useful knowledge that can potentially lead to the betterment of homeless people's lives. This betterment can be very direct, such as the identification of effective service interventions, or indirect, through combating the structural forces that produce homelessness. One aspect of maximizing the utility of research findings is, of course, writing for and about the groups that have the power to shape policy, both of which have been discussed in prior sections. However, the tone and content of such writing are also important considerations. For example, Rosenthal suggests that an advocacy stance or the "appearance of subjectivity" may actually reduce the chances that research will influence public policy. As he puts it, "open declaration of support for a group . . . invites dismissal by opponents and those we seek to influence." Thus he suggests that explicit advocacy may not ultimately be beneficial to the people whose lives we hope to improve. I faced a similar concern in my own work, namely that voicing a radical critique of homelessness might lead policymakers to ignore any recommendations for change that I put forth. I therefore felt compelled to choose between two courses of action that should ideally be complimentary: offering practical recommendations that policymakers might actually be able to enact within the constraints they face, and providing transformative recommendations that address the root causes of homelessness but are extremely difficult to implement.

Navigating the Framework

Upon initial review, answering the guiding questions in the operational framework outlined above may seem like a daunting task. However, many of the issues of ethics and advocacy discussed inevitably arise during research, especially in studies of complex social problems like homelessness. Thus, thoughtfully and thoroughly answering these questions may help scholars more systematically prepare for, and write about, the challenges they are sure to face in their work. In combination, the guiding questions can help scholars reflect on the issues of ethics of advocacy throughout the research process. All the questions were drawn from or inspired by the chapters in this volume, but the chapters are so rich that the framework certainly does not capture everything; indeed, each chapter is uniquely instructive in itself.

One particularly strong theme that emerges in the chapters and, as a result, in the framework, is the fundamental issue of purpose. In one way or another, all of the contributors examine the purpose of their work and what they hope to accomplish through their research. The importance of this issue is captured in the framework by the "why" questions in each stage: "Why am I doing this research?" "Why should I continue this course of research?" "Why should I continue to study this topic?" Although this may at first seem redundant, the repetitiveness highlights the fact that it is imperative to revisit the question of "why" throughout the research process. This is not only because the resulting answers shape all aspects of research, from choice of topic to writing style, but also because the answers may change dramatically during the research process. Regardless of the varying inclinations that different scholars have toward advocacy, all suggest the need for expanded awareness and/or structural change simply by choosing to study an entrenched social problem such as homelessness. Perhaps a basic tenet of research with and about marginalized or vulnerable groups should be that *personal interest is necessary but not sufficient.* Continually answering the "why" questions reminds us of this and challenges us to identify the deeper purpose(s) of our work.

Moving Forward

While much of the content of this volume reflects back on questions of ethics and advocacy that the contributors confronted during their research, it also offers advice for moving forward. Most of the contributors are in agreement that there needs to be increased effort in understanding the broader context of homelessness. They recommend numerous topics for future study including: how homelessness is linked to issues of economics, social restructuring, poverty, racism, sexism, sexuality, and sexual violence; how stereotypes of homeless people are produced and maintained, and in turn how these images can be reshaped; how policy decisions are made and who has the power to alter policy; how service systems can function to either empower or humiliate their homeless clients; and how various social forces work to impede collective advocacy and activism. These and other issues are so fundamental that several of the contributors believe that research neglecting them is essentially unethical. Furthermore, many of the contributors do not wish to stop at understanding homelessness, but instead want to use that understanding to transform the structures of power that create and perpetuate homelessness.

Although future research on the broader context of homelessness can take many forms, most involve studying up. And this fact forces us to confront another question that is deeply ethical: why, despite all the collective knowledge and experience of those who research homelessness, is this upward gaze so rare? This is not a question we are presumptuous enough to try to answer here, but it is one that seems worthy of consideration in its own right. Perhaps in answering this question, we may come to better understand the forces that foster our own inaction despite "knowing better" and, in turn, help us to counter the societal inaction that allows homelessness to continue unabated and even expand.

In closing, we would like to return briefly to the theme of synthesizing the personal and the professional. Just as people who are homeless routinely blur the boundaries of the public and the private, this volume makes public some of the very private struggles that researchers face. Indeed, it is this synthesis of personal and professional life that defines the approach to ethical research that we believe constitutes an important form of social advocacy in its own right—namely the crucial goal of considering the purpose, values, and consequences of our research and our lives alike.

Bibliography

Adler, Patricia and Peter Adler. 1994. Observational techniques. In *Handbook of qualitative research*, ed. N. Denzin and Y. S. Lincoln, 377-92. Thousand Oaks: Sage Publications.

Agee, James, and Walker Evans. 2001 [1939]. *Let us now praise famous men.* Boston: Houghton-Mifflin.

Amster, Randall. 2004. *Street people and the contested realms of public space.* New York: LFB Scholarly Publishing.

———. 2008. *Lost in space: The criminalization, globalization, and urban ecology of homelessness.* New York: LFB Scholarly Publishing.

———. 2011. Welcome home: Building an inclusive movement for the 99 percent. *Truthout* (November 17), http://www.truth-out.org/welcome-home-building-inclusive-movement-99-percent/1321627883.

Arena, John. 2007. Whose city is it? Public housing, public sociology, and the struggle for social justice in New Orleans before and after Katrina. In *Through the eye of Katrina: Social justice in the United States*, ed. Kristin A. Bates and Richelle S. Swan, 367-86. Durham: Carolina Academic Press.

Armour, Stephanie. 2003. Homelessness grows as more live check-to-check. *USA Today*, August 11.

Associated Press. 2011. New Orleans lays out plan to end homelessness. *CBSNews.com* (November 29), http://www.cbsnews.com/8301-505245_162-57332905/new-orleans-lays-out-plan-to-end-homelessness/.

Atkinson, Robert. 1998. *The life story interview.* Thousand Oaks: Sage Publications.

Babbie, Earl. 1995. *The practice of social research.* Seventh edition. Belmont: Wadsworth Publishing Group.

Bauer, Rudolph. 1980. *Obdachlos in Marioth: Von der notunterkunft zum "modernen asyl"* [*Homeless in Marioth: From emergency shelter to the "modern asylum"*]. Weinheim and Basel: Belz Verlag.

Baxter, Ellen, and Kim Hopper. 1981. *Private lives, public spaces: Homeless adults on the streets of New York City.* New York: Community Service Society, Institute for Social Welfare Research.

Becker, Howard S. 2007. *Writing for social scientists: How to start and finish your thesis, book, or article.* Second edition. Chicago: University of Chicago Press.

Behar, Ruth. 1997. *The vulnerable observer: Anthropology that breaks your heart.* Boston: Beacon Press.

Behar, Ruth, and Deborah A. Gordon. 1995. *Women writing culture.* Berkeley: University of California Press.

Berube, Alan, and Elizabeth Kneebone. 2006. *Two steps back: City and suburban poverty trends 1999-2005.* Washington, DC: Brookings Institute.

Blake, Megan K. 2007. Formality and friendship: Research ethics review and participatory action research. *ACME: An International E-Journal for Critical Geographies* 6: 411-21.

Blau, Joseph. 1992. *The visible poor: Homelessness in the United States.* New York: Oxford University Press.

Borchard, Kurt. 2005. *The word on the street: Homeless men in Las Vegas.* Reno: University of Nevada Press.

———. 2011. *Homeless in Las Vegas: Stories from the street.* Reno: University of Nevada Press.

Bowden, Charles. 2003. Keeper of the fire: He made Kathy Lee Gifford cry and made the Gap treat its workers better. Now Charlie Kernaghan plans to put an end to sweatshop labor all together. *Mother Jones* (July/August), www.motherjones.com/news/feature/2003/07/ma_447_01.html.

Boyer, Paul. 1978. *Urban masses and moral order in America, 1820-1920.* Cambridge: Harvard University Press.

Bridgman, Rae. 2003. *Safe haven: The story of a shelter for homeless women.* Toronto: University of Toronto Press.

———. 2006. *StreetCities: Rehousing the homeless.* Toronto: Broadview Press.

Briggs, Xavier de Sousa. 2006. After Katrina: Rebuilding places and lives. *City & Community* 5: 119-28.

Browne-Dianis, Judith, Jennifer Lai, Marielena Hincapie, and Saket Soni. 2006. *And injustice for all: Workers' lives in the reconstruction of New Orleans.* Washington, DC: Advancement Project.

Buck, David S., Donna Rochon, Harriett Davidson, and Sheryl McCurdy. 2004. Involving homeless persons in the leadership of a health care organization. *Qualitative Health Research* 14: 513-25.

Buford, Bill. 1990. *Among the thugs.* New York: Vintage Books.

Butler, Judith. 1990. *Gender trouble: Feminism and the subversion of identity.* London: Routledge.

Byrne, Deirdre, Roy Grant, and Alan Shapiro. 2005. *Quality health care for homeless youth: Examining barriers to care.* New York: The Children's Health Fund.

Cassell, Joan. 2002. Perturbing the system: "Hard science," "soft science," and social science: The anxiety and madness of method. *Human Organization* 61: 177-85.

Clifford, James, and George E. Marcus, eds. 1986. *Writing culture: The poetics and politics of ethnography*. Berkeley: University of California Press.

Cloke, Paul. 2002. Deliver us from evil? Prospects for living ethically and acting politically in human geography. *Progress in Human Geography* 26: 587-604.

Cloke, Paul, Phil Cooke, Jenny Cursons, Paul Milbourne, and Rebekah Widdowfield. 2000. Ethics, reflexivity and research: Encounters with homeless people. *Ethics, Place and Environment* 3: 133-54.

Cohen, Carl I., and Kenneth S. Thompson. 1992. Homeless mentally ill or mentally ill homeless? *American Journal of Psychiatry* 149: 812-23.

Colten, Craig E. 2006. *An unnatural metropolis: Wresting New Orleans from nature*. Baton Rouge: Louisiana State University Press.

Connolly, Deborah. 2002. *Homeless mothers: Face to face with women and poverty*. Minneapolis: University of Minnesota Press.

Cook, David. 2007. An open letter, with three questions, to Mayor Littlefield. *The Chattanoogan* (October 18), http://www.chattanoogan.com/2007/10/18/115418/ David-Cook-An-Open-Letter-With-Three.aspx.

Cress, Dan. 1990. Look out world, the meek are getting it ready: Implications of mobilization among the homeless. Paper presented at the annual meeting of the American Sociological Association, August 13, in Washington, DC.

Davis, Mike. 2005. Catastrophic economics: The predators of New Orleans. *Le Monde Diplomatique*, October 1.

Davis, Mike, and Daniel Bertrand Monk. 2007. *Evil paradises: Dreamworlds of neoliberalism*. New York: New Press.

Dear, Michael J., and Jennifer Wolch. 1987. *Landscapes of despair: From deinstitutionalization to homelessness*. Princeton: Princeton University Press.

Dear, Michael, and Jürgen von Mahs. 1997. Housing for the homeless, by the homeless, and of the homeless. In *The architecture of fear*, ed. Nan Ellin, 187-200. Princeton: Princeton University Press.

Desjarlais, Robert. 1997. *Shelter blues: Sanity and selfhood among the homeless*. Philadelphia: University of Pennsylvania Press.

Dewan, Sheila. 2008. Resources scarce, homelessness persists in New Orleans. *New York Times*, May 28.

Dillman, Don. 1978. *Telephone and mail surveys: The total design method*. Hoboken: John Wiley & Sons Publishing.

Dobbs, Lou. 2007. *War on the middle class: How the government, big business, and special interests are waging war on the middle class and how to fight back*. New York: Penguin Books.

Dolgon, Corey. 2006. Review of *The word on the street: Homeless men in Las Vegas*, by Kurt Borchard. *Humanity & Society* 30: 116-17.

Dordick, Gwendolyn. 1997. *Something left to lose: Personal relations and survival among New York's homeless*. Philadelphia: Temple University Press.

Douglas, Mary. 1976. *Purity and danger: An analysis of concepts of pollution and taboo*. Boston: Routledge and Kegan Paul.

D'Souza, Dinesh. 1991. Illiberal education. *The Atlantic* 267: 51-79.

Duncan, James S. 1983. Men without property: The tramp's classification and use of urban space. In *Readings in urban analysis: Perspectives on urban form and structure*, ed. Robert W. Lake, 86-102. New Brunswick: Rutgers University Press.

Duneier, Mitchell. 2000. *Sidewalk*. New York: Farrar, Strauss, and Giroux.

Dylan, Bob. 1966. Absolutely sweet Marie. *Blonde on blonde*. New York: Columbia Records.

Editorial. 2008. Helping the Katrina homeless. *New York Times*, June 9.

Ellickson, Robert C. 1996. Controlling chronic misconduct in city spaces: Of panhandlers, Skid Rows, and public-space zoning. *Yale Law Journal* 105: 1165-248.

Emerson, Robert. 1983. *Contemporary field research: A collection of readings*. Prospect Heights: Waveland Press.

Evans, Michael. 2001. Bloomington is my home: The composite architecture of the homeless. *Folk Life* 40: 80-91.

Ferrell, Jeff, and Mark S. Hamm, eds. 1998. *Ethnography at the edge: Crime, deviance, and field research*. Boston: Northeastern University Press.

Fetterman, David M. 1989. *Ethnography: Step by step*. Beverly Hills: Sage Publications.

Fine, Gary Alan. 1993. Ten lies of ethnography. *Journal of Contemporary Ethnography* 22: 267-94.

Fischer, Will, and Barbara Sard. 2005. *Bringing Katrina's poorest victims home: Targeted federal assistance will be needed to give neediest evacuees option to return to their hometown*. Washington, DC: Center on Budget and Policy Priorities.

Flaherty, Jordan. 2009. Homeless and struggling in New Orleans. *Dissident Voice* (August 25), http://dissidentvoice.org/2009/08/homeless-and-struggling-in-new-orleans/.

———. 2010. A new day for New Orleans? *ZNet* (February 10), http://www.zcommunications.org/a-new-day-for-new-orleans-by-jordan-flaherty.

Foucault, Michel. 1984. *The Foucault reader*, ed. Paul Rabinow. New York: Pantheon Books.

Gans, Herbert. 1995. *The war against the poor: The underclass and antipoverty policy*. New York: Basic Books.

Geliebter, David Martin. 2007. *Underbelly: The Palm Beach no-one talks about*. Oregon: Meager Press.

Gibson, Timothy A. 2004. *Securing the spectacular city: The politics of revitalization and homelessness in downtown Seattle*. Lanham: Lexington Books.

Girtler, Roland. 1990. *Vagabunden in der großstadt: Teilnehmende beobachtung in der lebenswelt der sandler* [*Vagabond in the big city: Participant observation in the life world of homeless people*]. Vienna: Universität Wien.

Gleeson, Brendon. 2000. Enabling geography: Exploring a new political-ethical ideal. *Ethics, Place and Environment* 3: 65-70.

Goffman, Erving. 1959. *The presentation of self in everyday life.* Garden City: Doubleday Publishing.

Goldberg, Michelle. 2006. Homeless again in New Orleans. *Salon.com* (February 7), http://www.salon.com/news/feature/2006/02/07/hotels/index.html.

Gonzales, John Moreno. 2007. New Orleans homeless profess little hope. *Associated Press/MSNBC.com* (August 17), http://www.msnbc.msn.com/id/2032 4248/.

Gounis, Kostas. 1996. Urban marginality and ethnographic practice: On the ethics of research. *City & Society* 8: 108-18.

Graff, Harvey J. 2008. *The Dallas myth: The making and unmaking of a modern city.* Minneapolis: University of Minnesota Press.

Gutierrez, Gustavo. 1970. *We drink from our own wells: The spiritual journey of a people.* Maryknoll: Orbis.

Haletky, Nina. 2006. Rebuilding on common ground: Social and environmental justice in New Orleans. *Urban Action* 2006: 91-98.

Hammer, David. 2008. U.N. committee says poor, blacks harmed most by Katrina. *The Times-Picayune*, March 7.

Hanson, Royce. 2003. *Civic culture and urban change: Governing Dallas.* Detroit: Wayne State University Press.

Harnden, Toby. 2005. Threatened with eviction at gunpoint, Big Easy holdouts are now hailed as heroes. *London Telegraph*, September 18.

Harrison, Laird, and Emmett Burg. 2012. Police fire tear gas at Oakland protesters, 200 arrested. *Toronto Sun*, January 29.

Herbert, Steve. 2006. *Citizens, cops and power: Recognizing the limits of community.* Chicago: University of Chicago Press.

Hetzler, Olivia, Veronica E. Medina, and David Overfelt. 2007. Race, immigration and economic restructuring in new urbanism: New Orleans as a case study. *Sociation Today: The Official Journal of the North Carolina Sociological Association* 5.

Hill, Patricia Evridge. 1996. *Dallas: The making of a modern city.* Austin: University of Texas Press.

Hoch, Charles. 1990. The spatial organization of the urban homeless: A case study of Chicago. *Urban Geography* 12: 137-54.

Hollis, James. 2007. *Why good people do bad things.* London: Gotham Books.

hooks, bell. 1996. *Killing rage, ending racism.* New York: Henry Holt & Company.

Hopper, Kim. 2003. *Reckoning with homelessness.* Ithaca: Cornell University Press.

———. 2006. Redistribution and its discontents: On the prospects of committed work in public mental health and like settings. *Human Organization* 65: 218-26.

Hopper, Kim, and Ellen Baxter. 1982. *One year later: The homeless poor in New York City, 1982.* New York: Community Service Society, Institute for Social Welfare Research.

Huus, Kari. 2009. Homelessness surges as funding falters. *MSNBC* (January 30), http://www.commondreams.org/headline/2009/01/30-0.

Jervis, Rick. 2008. New Orleans' homeless rate swells to 1 in 25. *USA Today*, March 16.

Kates, R.W., C.E. Colten, S. Laska, and S.P. Leatherman. 2006. Reconstruction of New Orleans after Hurricane Katrina: A research perspective. *Proceedings of the National Academy of Sciences of the United States of America* 103: 14653-60.

Kerr, Daniel. 2011. *Derelict paradise.* Amherst: University of Massachusetts Press.

Koegel, Paul. 1988. *Understanding homelessness: An ethnographic approach.* Los Angeles: Los Angeles Homelessness Project, Working Paper 12.

———. 2004. The course of homelessness. In *Encyclopedia of homelessness,* ed. David Levinson, 247-63. Thousand Oaks: Sage Publications.

Koegel, Paul, M., Audrey Burnam, and Rodger K. Farr. 1990. Subsistence adaptation among homeless adults in the inner city of Los Angeles. *Journal of Social Issues* 46: 83-107.

Kusmer, Kenneth. 2002. *Down and out, on the road.* New York: Oxford University Press.

Landler, Mark. 2012. Obama proposes mortgage relief, with Romney in mind. *New York Times*, February 1.

Landphair, Juliette. 2007. "The forgotten people of New Orleans": Community, vulnerability, and the Lower Ninth Ward. *The Journal of American History* 94: 837-45.

Lawless, Martha, Michael Rowe, and Rebecca Miller. 2009. New visions of me: Finding joy in recovery with women who are homeless. *Journal of Dual Diagnosis* 5: 305-22.

Lefebvre, Henri. 1996. *Writings on cities.* Ed. and trans. E. Kofman and E. Lebas. Oxford: Blackwell Publishing.

Levin, Aaron. 2007. Region struggles to cope with Katrina evacuees. *Psychiatric News* 42: 1-3.

Lewis, Edmund W. 2007. Do they know it's Christmas? *The Louisiana Weekly*, December 17.

Liebow, Elliot. 1968. *Tally's corner: A study of Negro streetcorner men.* New York: Little, Brown, & Co.

———. 1995. *Tell them who I am: The lives of homeless women.* New York: Penguin Books.

Lipsky, Michael. 1980. *Street-level bureaucracy: Dilemmas of the individual in public services.* New York: Russell Sage Foundation.

Lyon-Callo, Vincent. 2004. *Inequality, poverty, and neoliberal governance: Activist ethnography in the homeless sheltering industry.* Toronto: Broadview Press.

———. 2008. Cool cities or class analysis: Exploring popular consent (?) to neoliberal domination and exploitation. *Rethinking Marxism* 20: 28-41.

Marable, Manning. 2006. Race, class, and the Katrina crisis. *WorkingUSA: The Journal of Labor and Society* 9: 155-60.

Marcus, Anthony. 2005. *Where have all the homeless gone: The making and unmaking of a crisis.* New York: Berghahn Books.

Marcus, George E., and Michael M.J. Fischer. 1986. *Anthropology as cultural critique: An experimental moment in the human sciences.* Chicago: University of Chicago Press.

Marcuse, Peter. 1988. Neutralizing homelessness. *Socialist Review* 18: 69-96.

Markee, Patrick, and Lizzy Ratner. 2009. Homelessness is at record highs: Let's show some real compassion. *The Nation*, February 3.

Martin, Alex. 2005. On a street named Desire. *Newsday*, September 26.

Marvasti, Amir B. 2003. *Being homeless: Textual and narrative constructions.* Lanham: Lexington Books.

Marx, Karl. 1968. Theses on Feuerbach. In *Karl Marx and Frederick Engels: Selected works.* New York: International Publishers.

Masquelier, Adeline. 2006. Why Katrina's victims aren't refugees: Musings on a "dirty" word. *American Anthropologist* 108: 735-43.

Miille, Margaret Ann. 2006. Homelessness in Las Vegas: Unconventional wisdom. *Las Vegas Review-Journal*, April 9.

Miller, Dana L., John W. Creswell, and Lisa Olander. 1998. Writing and retelling multiple ethnographic tales of a soup kitchen for the homeless. *Qualitative Inquiry* 4: 469-91.

Miller, Henry. 1991. *On the fringe: The dispossessed in America.* Lexington: Lexington Books.

Miron, Luis, and Robert Ward. 2007. Drowning the Crescent City: Told stories of Katrina. *Cultural Studies <=> Critical Methodologies* 7: 154-68.

Mitchell, Don. 2003. *The right to the city: Social justice and the fight for public space.* New York: Guilford Press.

Mitchell, Don, and Lynn A. Staeheli. 2006. Clean and safe? Property redevelopment, public space, and homelessness in downtown San Diego. In *The politics of public space*, ed. Neil Smith and Setha Low, 143-75. New York: Routledge.

Morrell, Jessica. 2007. *Voices from the street: Truths about homelessness from sisters of the road.* Vancouver: Gray Sunshine Publishing.

National Alliance to End Homelessness. 2007. *First nationwide estimate of homeless population in a decade announced.* Washington, DC: National Alliance to End Homelessness.

Navarro, Vicente. 2007. *Neoliberalism, globalization, and inequalities: Consequences of health and quality of life.* Amityville: Baywood Publishing.

Neuman, William Lawrence. 2002. *Social research methods: Qualitative and quantitative approaches.* Fifth edition. Boston: Allyn & Bacon.

Nigg, Joanne M., John Barshaw, and Manuel R. Torres. 2006. Hurricane Katrina and the flooding of New Orleans: Emergent issues in sheltering and temporary housing. *The Annals of the American Academy* 604: 113-28.

O'Flaherty, Brendan. 1996. *Making room: The economics of homelessness.* Cambridge: Harvard University Press.

Office of the Federal Register, National Archives and Records Administration. 2011. Homeless emergency assistance and rapid transition to housing: Defining "homeless." *Federal Register* 76: 75995. Washington, DC: U.S. Government Printing Office.

Pain, Rachel. 2003. Social geography: On action-oriented research. *Progress in Human Geography* 27: 649-57.

Pain, Rachel, and Peter Francis. 2003. Reflections on participatory research. *Area* 35: 46-54.

Palast, Greg. 2007. New Orleans two years after. *ZNet* (September 6), http://www.zcommunications .org/new-orleans-two-years-after-by-greg-palast.

Paradis, Emily K. 2000. Feminist and community psychology ethics in research with homeless women. *American Journal of Community Psychology* 28: 839-58.

Passaro, Joanne. 1996. *The unequal homeless: Men on the street, women in their place.* New York: Routledge.

Patchan, Kathleen M. 2009. When half a city's residents may be homeless: New Orleans after Katrina. *Virtual Mentor: American Medical Association Journal of Ethics* 11: 72-77.

Payne, Darwin. 1994. *Big D: Triumphs and troubles of an American supercity in the 20th century.* Dallas: Three Forks Press.

Piven, Francis Fox, and Richard A. Cloward. 1997. *Poor people's movements: Why they succeed, how they fail.* New York: Vintage Books.

Podschus, Jan, and Peter Dufeu. 1995. Alcohol dependence among homeless men in Berlin. *Sucht* 41: 348-54.

Pollock, Abra. 2007. Made homeless by Katrina, now government bulldozers. *Inter Press Service* (December 8), http://ipsnews.net/news.asp?idnews=403 91.

Popkin, Susan J., Margery A. Turner, and Martha Burt. 2006. *Rebuilding affordable housing in New Orleans: The challenge of creating inclusive communities.* Washington, DC: The Urban Institute.

Pugh, Tony. 2007. US economy leaving record numbers in severe poverty. *McClatchy Newspapers.* February 23.

Quigley, Bill. 2007. HUD demolitions draw noose tighter around New Orleans. *The Louisiana Weekly*, October 1.

———. 2008. Half New Orleans poor permanently displaced: Failure or success? *The Louisiana Weekly*, March 6.

Rahimian, A., J.R. Wolch, and P. Koegel. 1992. A model of homeless migration: Homeless men in Skid Row, Los Angeles. *Environment and Planning A* 24: 1317-36.

Ratner, Lizzy. 2008. Homeless in New Orleans. *The Nation*, February 25.

Ray, Nicholas. 2007. *Lesbian, gay, and transgender youth: An epidemic of homelessness*. New York: National Gay and Lesbian Task Force and National Coalition for the Homeless.

Reckdahl, Katy. 2008. City may move homeless from underpass to shelter. *The Times-Picayune*, February 9.

Rivera, Lorna. 2003. Changing women: An ethnographic study of homeless mothers and popular education. *Journal of Sociology and Social Welfare* 30: 31-51.

Robertson, Campbell. 2011. Smaller New Orleans after Katrina, census shows. *New York Times*, February 3.

Rosenthal, Rob. 1994. *Homeless in paradise: A map of the terrain*. Philadelphia: Temple University Press.

———. 1996. Dilemmas of local antihomelessness movements. In *Homelessness in America*, ed. Jim Baumohl, 201-12, Phoenix: Oryx.

Rothschild, Matthew. 2005. Katrina compounded. *The Progressive* (September 8), http://progressive.org/?q=node/2377.

Rowe, Michael. 1999. *Crossing the border: Encounters between homeless people and outreach workers*. Berkeley: University of California Press.

Rowe, Michael, and Madelon Baranoski. 2011. Citizenship, mental illness, and the criminal justice system. *International Journal of Law and Psychiatry* 34: 303-08.

Rowe, Michael, Ashley Clayton, Patricia Benedict, Chyrell Bellamy, Kimberly Antunes, Rebecca Miller, Jean-Francois Pelletier, Erica Stern, and Maria O'Connell. In press. Going to the source: Citizenship outcome measure development. *Psychiatric Services*.

Rowe, Michael, Bret Kloos, Matt Chinman, Larry Davidson, and Anne B. Cross. 2001. Homelessness, mental illness, and citizenship. *Social Policy and Administration* 35: 14-31.

Rowe, Michael, Chyrell Bellamy, Madelon Baranoski, Melissa Wieland, Maria J. O'Connell, Patricia Benedict, Larry Davidson, Josephine Buchanan, and Dave Sells. 2007. Reducing alcohol use, drug use, and criminality among persons with severe mental illness: Outcomes of a group- and peer-based intervention. *Psychiatric Services* 58: 955-61.

Rowe, Michael, M. Hodge, and D. Fisk. 1996. Critical issues in serving people who are homeless and mentally ill. *Administration and Policy in Mental Health* 23: 555-65.

Rowe, Michael, Patricia Benedict, and Paul Falzer. 2003. Consent of the governed: An experiment in leadership building for homeless persons with behavioral health disorders. *Psychiatric Rehabilitation Journal* 26: 240-48.

Rowe, Stacy, and Jennifer Wolch. 1989. *A proposed methodology for assessing social networks of the homeless in a sample of Los Angeles communities*. Los Angeles: Los Angeles Homelessness Project, Working Paper 24.

———. 1990. Social networks in time and space: Homeless women in Skid Row, Los Angeles. *Annals of the Association of American Geographers* 80: 184-204.

Ruddick, Susan. 1996. *Young and homeless in Hollywood: Mapping social identities*. New York: Routledge.

Sahlins, Marshall D. 1972. *Stone age economics*. Chicago: Aldine-Atherton.

Sasser, Bill. 2007a. Surge in homeless hits New Orleans. *Christian Science Monitor*, March 28.

———. 2007b. Back to New Orleans, but no home. *Christian Science Monitor*, December 5.

Schneider, Stefan. 1998. *Wohnungslosigkeit und subjektentwicklung: Biographien, lebenslagen und perspektiven wohnungsloser in Berlin* [*Homelessness and subjectification: Biographies, life circumstances, and perspectives of homeless people in Berlin*]. PhD diss., Free University Berlin, Germany.

Scott, James. 1985. *Weapons of the weak: Everyday forms of peasant resistance*. New Haven: Yale University Press.

Sells, Dave, Larry Davidson, Chris Jewell, Paul Falzer, and Michael Rowe. 2006. The treatment relationship in peer-based and regular case management services for clients with severe mental illness. *Psychiatric Services* 57: 1179-84.

Sells, Dave, Ryun Black, Larry Davidson, and Michael Rowe. 2008. Beyond generic support: The incidence and impact of invalidation within peer-based and traditional treatment for clients with severe mental illness. *Psychiatric Services* 59: 1322-27.

SkyNewsHD. 2005. Hurricane Katrina creates homeless crisis. *Sky.com* (September 5), http://news.sky.com/home/article/13430205.

Smith, Dorothy. 1987. *The everyday world as problematic: A feminist sociology*. Toronto: University of Toronto Press.

Smith, Gary. 2002. *Radical compassion: Finding Christ in the heart of the poor*. Chicago: Loyola University Press.

Snow, David A., and Leon Anderson. 1993. *Down on their luck: A study of homeless street people*. Berkeley: University of California Press.

Snow, David A., and Michael Mulcahy. 2001. Space, politics, and the survival strategies of the homeless. *American Behavioral Scientist* 45: 149-69.

Staeheli, Lynn A., and Don Mitchell. 2008. *The people's property? Power, politics, and the public*. New York: Routledge.

Stephenson, Svetlana. 2006. *Crossing the line: Vagrancy, homelessness and social displacement in Russia*. London: Ashgate Publishing.

Stock, Paul V. 2007. Katrina and anarchy: A content analysis of a new disaster myth. *Sociological Spectrum* 27: 705-26.

Stout, A. Kathryn, and Richard A. Dello Buono. 2008. "Natural" disasters are social problems: Learning from Katrina. In *Agenda for social justice: Solutions 2008*, ed. Robert Perrucci, Kathleen Ferraro, JoAnn Miller, and Glenn W. Muschert, 23-27. Knoxville: Society for the Study of Social Problems.

Sturgis, Sue. 2006. Lack of shelter imperils New Orleans' homeless. *Facing South Magazine* (November 20), http://southernstudies.org/2006/11/lack-of-shelter-imperils-new-orleans-homeless.html.

Szep, Jason. 2008. Homelessness rising as economy slides. *Reuters*, December 13.

Takeda, Margaret B., and Marilyn M. Helms. 2006. "Bureaucracy, meet catastrophe": Analysis of Hurricane Katrina relief efforts and their implications for emergency response governance. *International Journal of Public Sector Management* 19: 397-411.

Teasdale, Wayne. 2002. *A monk in the world: Cultivating a spiritual life*. Novato: New World Publishing.

Templeton, Robin. 2007. Deadly lockdown in New Orleans. *Salon.com* (August 23), http://www.salon.com/news/feature/2007/08/23/nola_prisons/index.html.

Thomas, Chandra R. 2009. Housing New Orleans: Still a work in progress. *The American Prospect* (February 23), http://prospect.org/article/housing-new-orleans-still-work-progress.

Tier, Robert. 1998. Restoring order in public spaces. *University of Texas Review of Law and Politics* 2. 256-91.

Toth, Jennifer. 1995. *The mole people: Life in the tunnels beneath New York City*. Chicago: Chicago Review Press.

Underwood, Jackson. 1993. *The bridge people: Daily life in a camp of the homeless*. Lanham: University Press of America.

UNITY. 2011. *Homelessness in New Orleans: The big picture*. UNITY of Greater New Orleans (June 30), http://unitygno.org/wp-content/uploads/2011/07/6.30.11-Presentation-to-the-Mayors-10-Year-Plan-to-End-Homelessness-Working-Group.pdf.

Valado, Martha Trenna. 2006. *Factors influencing homeless people's perception and use of urban space*. PhD diss., University of Arizona.

Valentine, Gill. 2003. Geography and ethics: In pursuit of social justice—ethics and emotions in geographies of health and disability research. *Progress in Human Geography* 27: 375-80.

Van Maanen, John. 1988. *Tales of the field: On writing ethnography*. Chicago: University of Chicago Press.

von Mahs, Jürgen. 2005. The sociospatial exclusion of single homeless people in Berlin and Los Angeles. *American Behavioral Scientist* 48: 928-60.

———. 2011a. Homelessness in Berlin: Between Americanization and path dependence. *Urban Geography* 32: 1023–42.

———. 2011b. Introduction: An Americanization of homelessness in post-industrial societies. *Urban Geography* 32: 923–32.

———. Forthcoming. *Out of sight, out of mind? The impact of public policy on homeless people in Berlin and Los Angeles*. Philadelphia: Temple University Press.

Wacquant, Loic. 2001. The penalization of poverty and the rise of neoliberalism. *European Journal on Criminal Policy and Research* 9: 401-12.

———. 2002. Scrutinizing the street: Poverty, morality, and the pitfalls of urban ethnography. *American Journal of Sociology* 107: 1468-1532.

Wagner, David. 1993. *Checkerboard Square: Culture and resistance in a homeless community.* Boulder: Westview Press.

Warren, Carol A., and Tracy X. Karner. 2005. *Discovering qualitative methods: Field research, interviews, and analysis.* Los Angeles: Roxbury Publishing Company.

Wasserman, Jason Adam, and Jeffrey Michael Clair. 2010. *At home on the street: People, poverty, and a hidden culture of homelessness.* Boulder: Lynne Rienner Publishers.

Waugh, William L., Jr. 2006. The political costs of failure in the Katrina and Rita disasters. *The Annals of the American Academy of Political and Social Science* 604: 10-25.

WDSU.com. 2009. Study: Louisiana has most homeless children. *WDSU.com* (March 10), http://www.wdsu.com/news/18897939/detail.html.

Weber, Max. 1958. Science as a vocation. In *From Max Weber: Essays in sociology,* ed. H.H. Gerth and C. Wright Mills, 129-58. New York: Oxford University Press.

Webster, Richard A. 2008. N.O. homeless policy on shaky legal ground. *New Orleans CityBusiness,* February 19.

Weinstein, Bernard L., and Terry L. Clower. 2000. *The cost of homelessness in Dallas: An economic and fiscal perspective.* Report prepared for the Central Citizens Association. Denton: Center for Economic Development and Research, University of North Texas.

———. 2006. *Improving services to Dallas' homeless: A key to downtown revitalization.* Report prepared for the Central Citizens Association. Denton: Center for Economic Development and Research, University of North Texas.

Weiss, N. Eric. 2006. Rebuilding housing after Hurricane Katrina: Lessons learned and unresolved issues. *Congressional Research Service,* RL33761, December 19.

Williams, Jean Calterone. 1996. Geography of the homeless shelter: Staff surveillance and resident resistance. *Urban Anthropology* 25: 75-113.

———. 2003. *A roof over my head: Homeless women and the shelter industry.* Boulder: University Press of Colorado.

Wolch, Jennifer R., Afsaneh Rahimian, and Paul Koegel. 1993. Daily and periodic mobility patterns of the urban homeless. *Professional Geographer* 45: 159-69.

Wolch, Jennifer R., and Stacy Rowe. 1992. On the streets: Mobility paths of the urban homeless. *City & Society* 6: 115-40.

Wong, Irene. 1997. Patterns of homelessness: A review of longitudinal studies. In *Understanding homelessness: New policy and research perspectives,* ed. Dennis Culhane and Steven Hornburg, 135-64. Washington, DC: Fannie Mae Foundation.

Wright, Bradley R.E. 1996. Pathways off the streets: Homeless people and their use of resources. *Dissertation Abstracts International, A: The Humanities and Social Sciences* 57: 5317-18-A.

Wright, James D., and Joel A. Devine. 1995. Housing dynamics of the homeless: Implications for a count. *American Journal of Orthopsychiatry* 65: 320-29.

Wright, Melissa. 2006. *Disposable women and other myths of global capitalism.* New York: Routledge.

Wright, Talmadge. 1995. Tranquility City: Self-organization, protest, and collective gains within a Chicago homeless encampment. In *Marginal spaces: Comparative urban and community research, Volume 5,* ed. Michael Peter Smith, 37-68. New Brunswick: Transaction Publishers.

———. 1997. *Out of place: Homeless mobilizations, subcities, and contested landscapes.* Albany: State University of New York Press.

———. 2000. Resisting homelessness: Global, national, and local solutions. *Contemporary Sociology* 29: 27-43.

Wright, Talmadge, and Anita Vermund. 1996. Suburban homelessness and social space: Strategies of authority and local resistances. In *There's no place like home: The anthropology of housing and homelessness in the United States,* ed. Anna Lou Dehavenon, 121-43. New York: Bergin & Garvey Publishers.

Wright, Talmadge, and Anne Roschelle. 2003. Gentrification and social exclusion: Spatial policing and homeless activist responses in the San Francisco Bay area. In *Urban futures,* ed. Malcom Miles and Tim Hall, 149-66. New York: Routledge.

Yankoski, Michael. 2005. *Under the overpass: A journey of faith on the streets of America.* Colorado Springs: Multnomah Publishing.

Index

About the Contributors

Julie Adkins, ABD, serves as an adjunct instructor in the department of sociology and anthropology at the University of Texas, Arlington. She is completing her PhD in cultural anthropology at Southern Methodist University (MA 2004), where she has also served as adjunct faculty in the department of anthropology and the Perkins School of Theology. She is also an ordained minister in the Presbyterian Church (USA), holding the MDiv from Princeton Theological Seminary (1985) and the DMin from McCormick Theological Seminary (1991). Her dissertation research focused on homelessness in the city of Dallas, Texas, and, more specifically, the city's response.

Randall Amster, JD, PhD, is a professor of Peace Studies and graduate chair of Humanities at Prescott College. He is the founder and editor of the online news and commentary site *New Clear Vision*, and is the executive director of the Peace and Justice Studies Association. Among his recent books are *Lost in Space: The Criminalization, Globalization, and Urban Ecology of Homelessness* (LFB Scholarly, 2008), and the co-edited volume *Building Cultures of Peace: Transdisciplinary Voices of Hope and Action* (Cambridge Scholars Publishing, 2009).

Kathleen Arnold, PhD, is a visiting professor in political theory at DePaul University. She is the author of *Homelessness, Citizenship and Identity* (SUNY Press, 2004), *America's New Working Class* (Penn State University Press, 2009), and *American Immigration After 1996: The Shifting Ground of Political Inclusion* (Penn State University Press, 2011). Her current work focuses on violence and gender.

Kurt Borchard, PhD, is a professor of sociology at the University of Nebraska at Kearney. He has published *Homeless in Las Vegas: Stories from the Street* (2011) and *The Word on the Street: Homeless Men in Las Vegas* (2005) with the

University of Nevada Press. He is also on the editorial board of *Humanity and Society*.

Vincent Lyon-Callo, PhD, is a professor of anthropology at Western Michigan University. He is the author of *Inequality, Poverty and Neoliberal Governance: An Activist Ethnography of the Homeless Sheltering Industry* (Broadview Press/University of Toronto Press, 2004) as well as numerous chapters exploring homelessness, neoliberal restructurings, and class processes within the United States He has worked in homeless shelters and been involved in anti-poverty, housing, and anti-homelessness activism and advocacy in Connecticut, Massachusetts, and Michigan.

David Cook, MA, is an educator at three academic levels: middle school, high school, and college. An adjunct professor in Peace Studies at the University of Chattanooga in Tennessee, he also teaches courses in democracy, civil rights, and American literature at the independent Girls Preparatory School. Receiving his Master's degree in peace and justice studies from Prescott College, Cook was named a Memorial Marshall Fellow in 2011 and publishes twice a week as a city columnist for the *Chattanooga Times Free Press*.

Jeff Ferrell, PhD, is a professor of sociology at Texas Christian University and a visiting professor of criminology at the University of Kent (UK). His books include *Crimes of Style, Tearing Down the Streets, Empire of Scrounge*, and, with Keith Hayward and Jock Young, *Cultural Criminology: An Invitation*, recipient of the 2009 Distinguished Book Award from the American Society of Criminology's Division of International Criminology. Ferrell is also the founding editor of the NYU Press book series *Alternative Criminology*, and one of the founding editors of the journal *Crime, Media, Culture*.

Jürgen von Mahs, PhD, is an assistant professor in urban studies at The New School in New York and holds a joint appointment in the Urban Studies Program at Eugene Lang College and the department of social sciences at the New School for Public Engagement. He received a PhD in sociology and social policy from the University of Southampton (UK). His research and teaching interests include poverty and homelessness, comparative social policy analyses, globalization processes, social control and the criminalization of the poor, social movements, as well as ethnographic and life course research.

Don Mitchell, PhD, is distinguished professor of geography in the Maxwell School at Syracuse University. His research focuses on homelessness, urban public space, and labor-capital relations in California agribusiness. He is the author of *The Right to the City: Social Justice and the Fight for Public Space* (Guilford Press, 2003) and, with Lynn Staeheli, *The People's Property? Power, Politics and the Public* (Routledge, 2007).

Rob Rosenthal, PhD, is the provost and vice president for academic affairs and John E. Andrus Professor of Sociology at Wesleyan University. He was a founding member of the Santa Barbara Homeless Coalition from 1983 to 1987, and has written extensively on homelessness and activism. He is the author of *Homeless in Paradise* (Temple University Press, 1994), a contributor to *Homelessness in America* (Oryx Press, 1996), and co-author of *Playing for Change* (Paradigm, 2012). He continues to be active in housing and homelessness struggles in Middletown, Connecticut.

Michael Rowe, PhD, a medical sociologist, is an associate professor of psychiatry at the Yale School of Medicine, and co-director of the Yale Program for Recovery and Community Health. His work on the encounters and transactions that take place between people who are homeless and outreach workers is characterized by a sociological perspective that highlights the institutional, professional, and societal contexts within which those encounters and transactions take place. He is the author of books on outreach to people who are homeless, critical illness and high technology medicine, and recovery-oriented practices, and is the lead editor of a volume of classic documents of community psychiatry since the 1950s.

Lynn A. Staeheli, PhD, is a professor of human geography in the department of geography, Durham University (UK). She has published extensively on citizenship, public space, and community activism. She is co-author with Don Mitchell of *The People's Property? Power, Politics, and the Public* (Routledge, 2007).

Trenna Valado, PhD, is an applied anthropologist who currently works with a consulting company that aims to improve the lives of children and families through interdisciplinary research and evaluation of social service programs. She has conducted research in the areas of homelessness, education, dropout prevention, mental health, substance abuse, co-occurring disorders, criminal justice, and systems integration. Her dissertation research, which was funded by the U.S. Department of Housing and Urban Development, examined the effects of restrictive legal and social policies on people living outside in Tucson, Arizona.

Talmadge Wright, PhD, is an associate professor of sociology at Loyola University in Chicago. For over twenty years he has written on housing, homelessness, urban gentrification, and redevelopment. In addition, he also teaches critical social theory, social inequality, mass media, and the power of play in modern digital culture. His current interests are centered on the social relationships that are developed between players in virtual games, as well as their utopian possibilities and dystopian dreads.

CPSIA information can be obtained at www.ICGtesting.com
Printed in the USA
BVOW032307270612

293835BV00002B/1/P